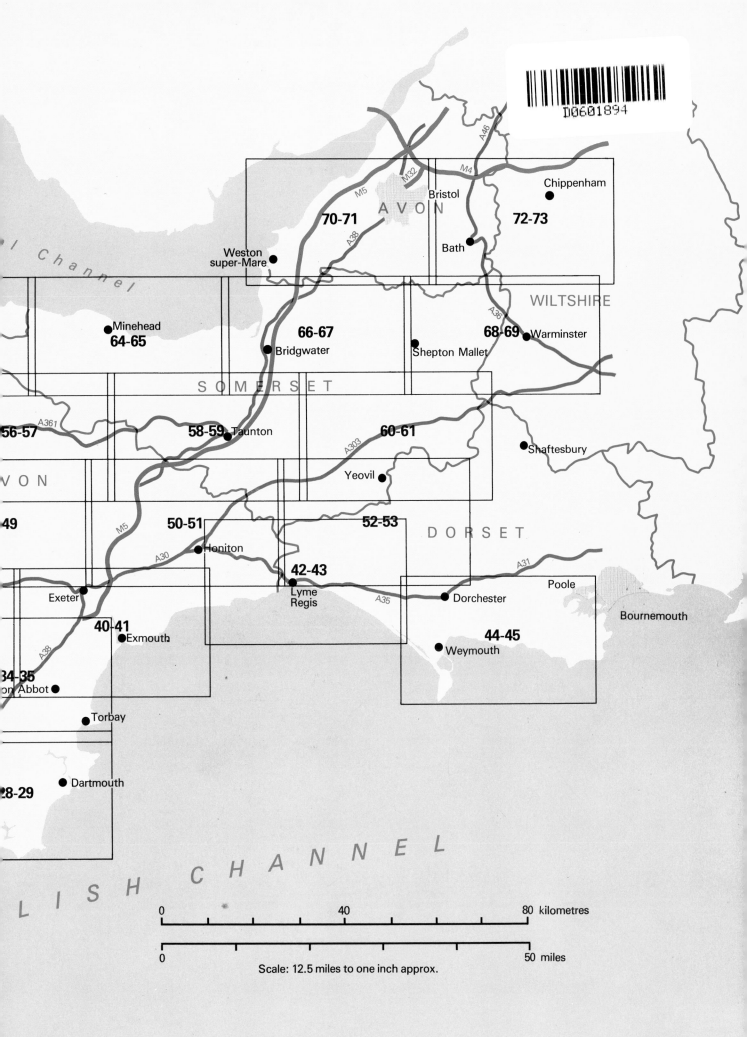

Channel

70-71

A V O N

Bristol

M32

M5

M4

A46

Chippenham

72-73

A38

Bath

Weston
super-Mare

WILTSHIRE

Minehead

64-65

66-67

Bridgwater

A36

Shepton Mallet

68-69 Warminster

S O M E R S E T

A361

56-57

58-59 Taunton

A303

60-61

Shaftesbury

V O N

Yeovil

49

M5

50-51

D O R S E T

A30

Honiton

52-53

A31

42-43

Lyme
Regis

A35

Poole

Dorchester

Bournemouth

40-41

Exeter

A38

Exmouth

44-45

Weymouth

34-35

on Abbot

Torbay

28-29

Dartmouth

L I S H   C H A N N E L

0   40   80 kilometres

0   50 miles

Scale: 12.5 miles to one inch approx.

Hamlyn
LEISURE ATLAS

West Country

Hamlyn
London · New York · Sydney · Toronto

Compiled and edited by Colin Wilson

The publishers would like to thank the English Tourist Board for
their help in the compilation of this book.

The publishers are grateful to the following individuals and
organisations for the illustrations in this book: British Tourist
Authority; Peter Crump; England Scene Colour Picture Library;
Kim Ludlow; Ian Muggeridge; Spectrum Colour Library.

First published 1981

Published by
The Hamlyn Publishing Group Limited
London • New York • Sydney • Toronto
Astronaut House, Feltham, Middlesex

Printed in Scotland by
John Bartholomew & Son Limited
Duncan Street, Edinburgh EH9 1TA

ISBN 0 600 34957 8

The representation in this atlas of any road or track, or the marking
of any object, is not an indication of the existence of a public right of
way. The contents of this atlas are believed correct at the time of
publication; while every effort has been made to ensure that the
information is accurate, no liability can be accepted by the publishers
for the consequences of any error. The latest position can be
checked with the appropriate Tourist Board.

Contents

How to use The Leisure Atlas

The Hamlyn Leisure Atlas of The West Country has been designed to be both comprehensive and flexible - there are a great many ways of using it.

First and foremost, it offers a superb atlas of The West Country, on an ideal scale of about 1·6 miles to the inch. The maps are detailed enough to show almost every tarmac road, however narrow, and a great many lesser tracks as well. With this atlas, there is no excuse for sitting in a main road traffic jam when attractive country lanes offer a more enjoyable and much less frustrating alternative.

Bartholomew's unique colour-coded height presentation provides a graphic picture of the geography of the region, while the maps show both natural and man-made features in remarkable detail. Careful interpretation of the maps themselves will do much to enhance any visit to The West Country.

Superimposed on these outstanding maps, however, are over 2000 symbols covering a range of 27 leisure activities and facilities, details of which can be found in the gazetteer section after the maps. The information represented by these symbols can also be used in many ways.

There are two basic ways of undertaking any holiday trip: you can plan every detail in advance, or you can simply turn up and find out what is available on arrival. This atlas works equally well in both cases.

For those who prefer to plan their holidays in advance, a brief perusal of the maps will quickly reveal those areas most richly endowed with one's favourite activities. Or one can browse through the gazetteer pages dealing with a particular pastime and thereby identify the map pages on which that pastime is best catered for.

The Atlas works just as well, of course, for the many people who prefer to take pot luck: after helping one reach the chosen destination, the appropriate map will reveal the full range of leisure activities available in that area.

Finding the Information

Each map page is divided into six squares, marked with red grid lines. Each of these squares is identified throughout this Atlas by its page number and a letter between a and i: the key to these letters appears at the top of each page.

To find out about any chosen symbol, therefore, one must first work out the map reference of that symbol. The reference of the Castle in the example shown here is 25c and details about it can be found in the section on Castles which can be found on pages 88 and 89.

In addition to its map reference, each symbol is usually identified in the gazetteer by a name in bold type corresponding to the name found at or near the symbol on the map. This is particularly helpful when several identical symbols appear in one map square.

Wherever possible, each symbol appear exactly on its actual location. In some cases, such as in towns, this has proved impossible and the address or some other description of the actual location has therefore been included in the gazetteer.

There are also some locations with so many activities that it proved impossible to fix all the symbols onto the site. In such cases, the symbols have been grouped together in a box. Each box has the name of the town printed above it; or it is placed adjacent to the town's name printed on the map; or the box is linked by a short line to the actual location.

Where maps overlap, the extent of the duplication can be seen on the small diagrams at the top of each page. Where maps do overlap, some symbols will obviously appear on more than one map: when this occurs, the later entry is cross-referenced to the earlier one.

Finally, don't forget that events which occur only occasionally are not marked on the map, but appear (with their map references) in the Calendar of Events.

Using the Gazetteer

Each entry usually includes details of its opening hours and of other facilities available at the same site: these are shown by symbols after each entry, indicating that further information can be obtained in the relevant section of the gazetteer, except for ➣ which means that refreshments are available (although not necessarily throughout the stated opening period) and ⌓ which simply indicates a picnic site, for which no details are given.

Where opening times are given, they apply throughout the specified period unless otherwise stated. If no dates are given, the site is open all year; however, it has been assumed that all sites will be closed on days such as Christmas and New Year's Day and anyone planning a visit at such a time should telephone first.

Telephone numbers have been supplied wherever possible, together with the appropriate STD codes: where the exchange name differs from the location given for the activity, the name of the exchange is also given, so that local calls can be made.

Many sites, particularly such non-commercial ones as prehistoric earthworks, scenic walks, nature trails, etc., will be free of charge even when this is not specified in the gazetteer. *Free* is only included when we have definite information to that effect and users must be prepared to pay for any activity not marked as *Free*.

Castles

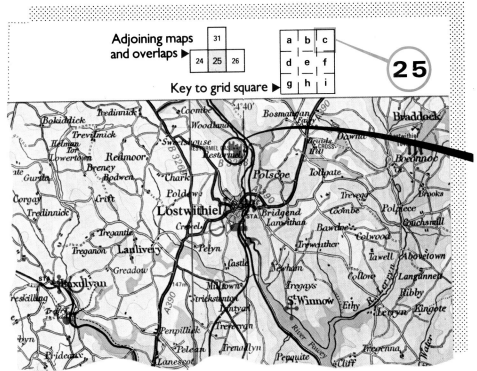

feared the Spanish might seize the Scilly Isles as a naval base. Built in the shape of an 8-pointed star with 96 loopholes and a moat.

25c Restormel Castle. The site was first fortified in wood just after the Norman Conquest, but a stone gatehouse was added about 1100. In 1264 the castle was surrendered to Simon de Montfort, after which much of the existing stonework was installed. Despite being in poor condition at the time, it was garrisoned by the Roundheads in 1644, but fell to the Royalists. The site then became overgrown but has since been thoroughly cleared to reveal ruins in surprisingly good condition. Almost perfectly circular, the castle stands on an artificially-raised hill surrounded by a 60 ft wide moat. *Daily from 0930 (winter Sundays from 1400).*

25g Caerhays Castle. Striking 'mock' castle restored by John Nash in Gothic style in 1802. Privately owned, but visible from the road. *Not open.*

How to get there

Communications to the West Country have improved immeasurably over the last 20 years. A network of motorways and dual carriageways has pushed futher westwards, by-passing major bottle-necks. These improved roads have, in their turn, encouraged better rail services and high-speed inter-city trains now make the going easier than it ever was.

M4/A30 is the principle artery of the West Country and it is often convenient to motor along this until close to one's destination. Since the cost of travel continues to increase, however, it is always worth considering a more interesting route to take advantage of the many quiet byways in the region. If bound for Cornwall, for example, you could leave M4 at Bridgwater then take A39 around the Quantocks, over Exmoor to Barnstaple then on through Bideford and Stratton, detouring from time to time to interesting spots on the coast. Better still, use the maps in this book to follow minor roads and lanes to hidden villages and forgotten combes. Following these deep, ferny byways is an experience to savour and it gives you a feeling for the area that no motorway can.

If your journey to the West Country seems unacceptably long, remember that it is easy to hire a car at any one of the major towns or cities, or you can put your own car on Motorail and have it taken down by train - details from British Rail Travel Centres or from your local station.

For those who want to fly there are domestic services from many parts of Britain to the airports at Bristol, Exeter, Plymouth and Newquay. Details of scheduled air services can be obtained from the West Country Tourist Board in Exeter.

Accommodation

There is an ample stock of all types of visitor accommodation in the West Country; and whether you seek a luxury hotel, a farmhouse holiday, bed and breakfast, a cottage or chalet to rent or a camping or caravan site you will be able to find it without too much difficulty. Popular places are, naturally, heavily booked during the height of the season, so if you are travelling in a peak period, remember to book well ahead.

If you want a touring holiday, accommodation can normally be easily found provided you do not leave it too late in the day. All tourist information centres hold details of local accommodation and most will make provisional bookings locally for personal callers. Some centres offer a "Book a Bed Ahead" service and can find accommodation the same night or following night outside their own locality.

Useful Telephone Numbers

Motoring Information

Recorded summaries cover road information within 50 miles of Bristol (taking in most of Somerset and Wiltshire, plus north Dorset)
.... 0272 8021

Weather

Recorded forecasts for the following areas:

Bristol and Weston-Super-Mare 0272 8091
Devon and Cornwall 0752 8091

Lynmouth Gorge (map 63e).

Tourist Information

There are over 60 tourist information centres in the West Country run by local authorities in accordance with standards laid down by the regional and national tourist boards. The staff at these centres can give advice on a wide range of subjects, from accommodation and travel to local events and attractions. All these offices, together with a number of centres run by other organisations (National Parks, the National Trust, etc.) are listed on page 122.

Information on the West Country as a whole can be obtained from the West Country Tourist Board, Trinity Court, 37 Southernhay East, Exeter EX1 1QS; information on eastern Dorset (parts of which are covered by this atlas) can be obtained from the Southern Tourist Board, Old Town Hall, Leigh Road, Eastleigh SO5 4DE. These organisations produce annual brochures, plus detailed information on specialist holidays of every kind.

Many tourist information offices will also provisionally book local accommodation for you: centres offering this service display the Tourist Accommodation Service sign shown on this page.

History and Legend

The West Country peninsula thrusting its long, enchanted finger out into the Atlantic is a land both mysterious and friendly, fertile and spare, warm and wild. Much of its attraction lies in its paradoxes, in the tensions between rock and sky, sea and land, man and nature and it is resolution of these opposites that gives it such a deep sense of harmony.

The structure, the bare bones as it were of the West Country has ensured that the region retains its thrusting shape. The rocks at the extremities of the great peninsula are hard - granite, quartz, serpentine - rocks that can resist centuries of pounding by Atlantic breakers. They give us the dramatic cliffs and smugglers coves, the beaches of brown, red and white sand and the wide uplands of Bodmin Moor and Dartmoor. Then, as the land swells and spreads eastwards of this natural breakwater, the softer sandstones and limestone blend into a mellow landscape of pasture and thatch where cattle drink from a multitude of small streams and rivers that meander through still water meadows.

With its immense variety, fertile soil and benign climate, it is not surprising that people have always wanted to live in the south-west. From the Stone Age cave dweller to the present day cottager retired from a city career, the West Country has exercised its magnetism. The earliest men arrived before the last Ice Age and some may have been able to survive in an Eskimo-like way when the rest of Britain was buried under a large glacier. As the world grew warmer the population increased and archaeologists know from the remains found in such places as Kent's Cavern, Cheddar Gorge and Wookey Hole that man was active here during his long centuries as a hunter-gatherer. The caves themselves are the best place to experience some kind of rapport with this ancient time, but most of the larger museums have examples of the skillfully knapped stone arrowheads and handaxes that these people seemed to make in such vast quantity.

The relics of the first major cultures to become established in the west are, in a way, more tantalising than the slight remains of the early hunter-gatherers. During the centuries known to archaeologists as the Late Stone, Bronze and Iron Ages, people from the Mediterranean area entered Britain in several waves and many of them became established in the west. These peoples had fairly substantial and complicated civilizations: they had an immense feeling for stone and much of western Europe is littered with their alignments, circles, monoliths, cromlechs and dolmens. Techniques for manipulating these often enormously heavy blocks would have been complex, but not only did they contrive to heave them about, sometimes over long distances, they were also singularly adept at getting them up in the right place. The 'right place' was very often something to do with astronomy, and there is little doubt that many of these monuments were carefully designed to mark particular phases of the sun, moor or stars. Precisely why these early people should have been so concerned about the movements of heavenly bodies is not known; some say it was to do with agricultural practice, that the alignments or circles were simply rather cumbersome farmer's almanacs, while others see religious significance . Modern opinion confuses the issue even more by suggesting that, in order to align the stones accurately in the first place, the builders would have needed the kind of astronomical skills which would have made these king-sized observatories unecessary: whatever they were for, therefore, it was not for predicting eclipses and equinoxes; they would have been able to do that anyway.

Cornwall and, to a lesser extent, Devon are the two western counties where the megalith builders were most active. On Dartmoor there are many sites of Iron Age villages normally marked on the map as 'hut circles'. In those distant days the climate was warmer and dryer and Dartmoor would have been a more hospitable place of open pasture or thin woodland while the valleys would have been an almost impenetrable swampy forest. The further west one goes the more interesting and complex the megalithic remains become. Cornwall is full of menhirs, quoits, fogous and other strange objects and, at Chysauster, a full scale Iron Age village from Romano-British times has been unearthed. Further on still, in the Isles of Scilly, ancient stones become bewilderingly thick on the ground - indeed there are more stone relics on these small islands than in the rest of England and Wales put together! One theory is that the islands were used by the ancients of the mainland as a burial ground and memorial to the dead and their spirits. Putting a substantial stretch of water between oneself and the departed may, in their view, have provided a precautionary fire-break against other-worldly interference.

So often are the ancient stones of the west associated with Druids and Celtic mythology that one can easily forget that they were the work of a pre-Celtic people. It is understandable that the Celts, when they started arriving in Britain during the Bronze Age, created all sorts of legends about monuments they did not understand. Many of our modern commentators are equally adept at seeking fanciful and magical explanations for the relics of the past. The many Cornish tale of giants stalking the land, for example, derive simply from vivid attempts to explain how stones weighing many tons were lifted into place.

The best Celtic monument in the West Country is the Cornish culture itself, with the place names reflecting a language (closely related to Breton and Welsh) now sadly extinct - the last native speaker died at Sennen near Land's End in 1777. The Tamar river, county boundary between Cornwall and Devon, was a very effective moat dividing the Celtic west from the Anglo-Saxon east: a glance at any map will show a wealth of clearly Celtic place names in Cornwall, but very few in Devon, a very different situation from that prevailing in the Welsh Marches where the linguistic boundary is far less precise. Immediately before the Roman conquest the whole of southern Britain was Celtic, and this is reflected in many of the more dramatic archaeological sites in the west. The great hill fort of Maiden Castle in Dorset, for example, was extended and elaborated by the Celtic Veneti who had been routed in Brittany by Julius Caeser some years earlier. This intricately fortified fall-back position did them little good, however, as they were defeated there by the Roman legions in 45 AD.

Another magnificent and evocative hill-fort is Cadbury Castle in Somerset. Excavations have shown that the site was occupied and extended during a 4000-year period from the New Stone Age. Its greatest claim to fame, however, is an association with King Arthur; while it is almost certainly not Camelot (as some have claimed it to be), it seems fairly clear that it was used by Arthur during his famous campaign against the Saxons.

Glastonbury is another site where a sense of the past is strong. It is associated in legend with Joseph of Arimathea (who is said to have planted his staff here, giving rise to the Glastonbury Thorn, a variety of Hawthorn that flowers very early in the year, close to the time that Christmas would have fallen in the old calendar); Glastonbury has been home to many different people over the centuries: in the Somerset Levels spreading away from Glastonbury Tor, the remarkable remains of Celtic lake villages built on artificial islands were found.

Roman remains in the West Country are less abundant than in many other parts of Britain although they had their cities and towns like Isca Dumnoniorum (now Exeter) and Durnovaria (now Dorchester). Mining was an important activity for the Romans: both they and the Phoenicians had long traded with the Scillies - called in Latin the Cassiterides - for tin and copper and very shortly after the Roman conquest lead mines were being worked in the Mendips.

The highlight of the Roman west is undoubtedly Bath, the wealthy Roman spa town of Aquae Sulis. Sulis was a god, probably Celtic, and the warm spring which was the key attraction of the place was dedicated to him. The Roman Bath, still in a remarkably good state of preservation, is an archaeological site of international importance. To stand up to one's neck in the warm, brown water of the Roman pool conducting civilised discourse with friends is a remarkable experience and one that gives a marvellous insight into the rich and sensuous culture created by these remarkable people from the Mediterranean.

After the Roman withdrawal Celt and Saxon were left to fight it out with each other. A reminder of the struggle between these two peoples is found in the Wansdyke which runs 50 miles from Hampshire to the coast to the west of Bristol. At Stantonbury (near Bristol) there is a fine stretch of this great earthwork that was used as a defensive line by the Roman-Celtic general Ambrosius against Hengist, the Saxon chieftain.

King Arthur

The real King Arthur was, undoubtedly, a genuine historic figure but a stream of legend and literature about him has made it impossible to disentangle fact from fiction. It seems certain that he was a Romano-British commander, probably a general, who fought valiantly against the colonisation of England by Germanic peoples after the last of the legions had departed for Rome. Perhaps his constant re-appearance in literature is because he was an outstanding figure during a period of great upheaval when two vigorous cultures, the Celtic and Teutonic, interlocked in one of their first great fusions. As the opposing sides struggled to get the measure of one another, so people moved constantly from place to place and a body of myth would have been encouraged. Larger than life figures would also have been provided some sense of security in such an uncertain world.

Places in the West Country with which the real King Arthur was probably familiar include the Wansdyke, Glastonbury and Cadbury Castle (sometimes, probably wrongly, identified as Camelot). Other places like Tintagel and Dozmary Pool are linked with him only in legend.

Dramatic Tintagel Head on the North Cornish coast was supposedly the site of King Arthur's Castle. The castle that stands there now was, in fact, built in the 12th century (some 600 years after Arthur's time) by Reginald, Earl of Cornwall although some earlier Celtic remains, of monastic origin, have been found on the site. Dozmary Pool on Bodmin Moor has been put forward as the bottomless lake from which the hand holding the magic sword Excalibur emerged but, rather unromantically, this evocative stretch of water has been known to dry up in long, hot summers.

According to some of the legends King Arthur's home was the land of Lyonesse which lay somewhere between Land's End and the Scillies and has now disappeared beneath the waves. There does seem to be evidence of substantial areas of sinkage between the islands of the Scilly archipelago during historic times and it could be that folk memories of this have somehow become confused with the tangled skein of Arthurian romance over the centuries.

The literary side of the Arthurian story is truly remarkable and there can be few figures who have inspired so many authors, poets and other creative people. The Welsh were the first to write about Arthur, but the basic outlines of many of the traditions with which we are so familiar were set down by Geoffrey of Monmouth in his "History of the Kings of Britain" written in the 12th century. It is here that figures like Merlin, Sir Gawain and Uther Pendragon appear. The French poet Chrétien de Troyes elaborated the story of Sir Lancelot, transmuting the Arthurian tradition into that of Mediaeval courtly love and the great 14th century English poem "Sir Gawain and the Green Knight" added still more to the story. In the next century Mallroy's prose classic "Le Morte d'Arthur" enlarged on the Holy Grail theme and the romance of Tristan and Iseult. The 16th century brought Spenser's "Faerie Queen", the 19th Tennyson's "Idylls of the King" and our own century "The Once and Future King" by T.H. White. After nearly 1500 years the power of Arthur to move the artistic imagination remains as strong as ever.

Maiden Castle (map 44b; see page 81).

King Alfred

Although generally peaceable, the West Country has had its share of troubled times. Back in the 9th century one of England's most brilliant kings, Alfred the Great, waged a complex and successful campaign against the Danes largely in the west. Alfred was a West Saxon who became King of Wessex during the period when England was under constant attack from the Scandinavians. In 876AD he organised what is generally regarded as the first navy in Britain as part of a land and sea campaign centred on Devon and Dorset. The Danes caught him unawares two years later, forcing him to flee to a camp on the marsh island of Athelney in Somerset. It was during this time, according to tradition, that he neglected to take the cakes from the oven in the house of a peasant woman who was sheltering him.

While at Athelney, Alfred planned his counter strike against the Danes and, following a successful sea battle in the Severn Estuary, he was able to push the Danes back to London and beyond. As well as having great skill as a military and naval strategist, Alfred was a learned and enlightened ruler. Having defeated his enemies he treated them with justice and compassion: to his own people, the English, he brought a creative and forward looking civilization. He deserved the accolade of being the first great example of a northern European under the influence of 'Christianity' and it is surely a pity that he has become most strongly connected with that probably apocryphal story of the burning of the cakes.

In the eleventh century the Normans moved into Britain, including the West Country, leaving many fine castles and abbeys in their wake. In Devon the castles at Launceston, Lydford, Exeter and Okehampton are symptomatic of the problems they were having with the independent minded people in the area. To the east, in more settled country, the Normans founded splendid abbeys like Forde and Cleeve, or Muchelney, built in superb, honey-coloured stone on earlier Anglo-Saxon foundations on an islet in the Somerset marshes.

The stability brought by the Normans allowed the West Country as we know it today to develop. Most of the original forest cover was cleared and a rich agriculture replaced it, bequeathing us the cream teas and cider, daffodil fields and market gardens, cheese and wool. The typical village with its thatch and cottage gardens, so beloved by packagers of chocolates, clustered round the churches that rural wealth and suitable stone provided, whilst at places like Wells mighty cathedrals sprang from the mediaeval imagination.

Sedgemoor and the Bloody Assize

During the period that James II was attempting to restore Catholicism to Britain, Protestant feeling ran high and came to a head at Bridgwater in Somerset where, in July 1685, the

Protestant Duke of Monmouth, an illegitimate son of Charles II was declared King. The followers of Monmouth encountered the forces of James II at Sedgemoor on the Somerset Levels to the south of Bridgwater. In the ensuing battle, the last on British soil, the Protestants were soundly beaten. The Duke of Monmouth was captured and subsequently beheaded. Many of his followers were condemned to death at the notorious "Bloody Assize" conducted by Judge Jeffreys and four other justices in Taunton Castle. Jeffreys, who became Lord Chief Justice at the age of 38, was undoubtedly a highly intelligent man but his bad temper and cruelty led to the judicial intemperance for which his name has become a byword.

In the 18th century towns like Bath, Weymouth and Lyme Regis became fashionable centres for the pleasure seeking society of the day and again we have a legacy of elegant art and architecture from those times: the curving, colonnaded streets of Georgian Bath in pale biscuit limestone have no equal anywhere in the world and the weakest imagination can catch the spirit of Beau Nash or Jane Austen relishing their society where niceties of behaviour were as fashionable as farthingales.

With the arrival of the railway in the 19th century the West Country's era as a holiday destination began, although it had been customary for naval officers and their families to await postings to their ships at Torquay, thereby giving it the atmosphere of a holiday town even earlier. Today the magnificent coastline has everything from the major international centre to the fishing village; it is truly a region to suit all tastes and is still the most popular holiday destination in the British Isles.

Adventurers

The earliest West Country adventurer of whom we have any detailed record is St. Boniface who is thought to have been born in Crediton in 680 AD. This man, who must have possessed remarkable courage and faith, set out to convert the wild Teutonic tribes of Germany to Christianity - decidedly not a task for the faint-hearted. Later in life he became Archbishop of Mainz and crowned Pepin, Charlemagne's father, as King of the Franks.

At the close of the Middle Ages there arose in Western Europe a powerful urge to explore fuelled largely be the desire for gold and spices. In England the centre of this ferment of activity was the city of Bristol. In May 1498 a Genoese, John Cabot, sailed from the city with his son Sebastian, in two tiny vessels with the hope of finding a westward sea route to the Indies. later in the year he reached eastern North America and returned to England. It was Cabot's discoveries that formed the basis of England's later claim to the whole North American continent.

As colonization of the newly discovered West Indies proceeded, the demand for slaves from West Africa increased. One of Britain's most able seafarers, Sir John Hawkins, from Plymouth in Devon, gained the initial impetus for his career through being involved in this appalling human traffic. The underhand, and often savage, tactics that were commonplace in those red-blooded times led him into frequent conflict with the Portuguese and Spanish and, after his defeat by the latter off the Mexican coast in 1567, he nursed a deep-seated desire for revenge which was brought to fruition by the destruction of the Spanish Armada in 1588. In the years leading up to this, Hawkins revolutionised the English navy and its ships and perhaps it is to him, more than to any other man, that we owe the early development of colonialism and the supremacy of the British at sea which, in its turn, led to our reputation as a trading nation and the rise of our industry through the need to process raw materials brought from the four quarters of the globe.

Hawkins' most famous protegé was the dashing young sea-rover Francis Drake. Born at Tavistock, Drake was regarded by the Spanish as the Devil incarnate and was the first Englishman to circumnavigate the globe. This epic voyage in *Golden Hind*, part discovery, part military adventure and part simply for

The full-size replica of Drake's *Golden Hind*, here seen at Brixham.

plunder, culminated in his being knighted by Queen Elizabeth I. Shortly after this he baited the Spanish navy in the harbour at Cadiz, destroying many ships and in 1588 he played a major role in the defeat of the Armada as vice-admiral of the English fleet. The bowls game which he was enjoying on Plymouth Hoe when news of the Armada was first brought to him, and which he insisted on completing before taking action, is the classic example of the daring insouciance of this great Elizabethan adventurer. Buckland Abbey, near Yelverton, originally a Cistercian monastery and now owned by the National Trust, was once the home of Sir Francis Drake.

If the genius of Hawkins made conditions right for colonisation, it was another Devon man, Sir Walter Raleigh, who ensured that theory was put into practice. Born in the middle of the 16th century, Raleigh was the archetypal Elizabethan polymath; a remarkable combination of explorer, soldier, courtier, poet and visionary.

Raleigh's dream was to see the English way of life established in different parts of the world, particularly in America, and he set out with considerable single-mindedness to establish colonies there at a time when England had no territorial claims on the continent whatsoever. His one successful colony was Virginia, now permanently associated with tobacco, the use of which was established in Europe by Raleigh. From South America he introduced the potato and was one of the first in a long line of seekers after El Dorado, the fabled land of gold.

It was through the work of men like Raleigh that North America became the prime destination of settlers escaping the political and religious intolerance of Europe and it is perhaps fitting that the first such enterprise, that of the Pilgrim Fathers, should have finally left Europe for the New World from Plymouth, a port Raleigh would have known well, in 1620.

The spirit of adventure and love of the sea shown by the people of the West Country is seen at its most heroic in the action of Devon-born Sir Richard Grenville. In 1591 his famous man-o'war *Revenge* was trapped off the Azores by 53 Spanish ships; rather than take flight Grenville decided to fight it out. Having inflicted great damage on the Spanish, *Revenge*, her masts gone, her upper deck torn away and half her crew dead was finally forced to surrender. Grenville, twice wounded, was treated with great respect by the Spanish and died on the deck of their flagship with the words that he had done no more than his duty.

Land of Contrast

The Coastline

The glory of the West Country is its coast line, unrivalled for its diversity and drama. Along the Bristol Channel opposite Wales, resorts shelter under grey stone headlands of Mendip limestone. A good example of this, south of Weston-super-Mare, is the whaleback projection of Brean Down which points across the north of Bridgwater Bay to the island nature reserve of Steepholm. The bay itself runs in a great, sandy sweep to Watchet, where the Quantocks reach the sea in multicoloured cliffs. From Minehead to Combe Martin the coast, running along under the north of Exmoor, is spectacularly beautiful with great woods reaching down to the sea and heathery valleys ending in hanging waterfalls that plunge over cliffs. The mouth of the river Taw has, in Braunton Burrows, one of the most extensive sand dune systems in Britain - in contrast to the wild coast from Clovelly to Bude with its remote, storm-swept beauty.

The great cliffs of North Cornwall are justly renowned and their savage heights can be enjoyed to the full between Perranporth and Bude, or around the Penwith Peninsula. Long, foam-crested waves from the open Atlantic thunder across the beaches at resorts like Newquay making the area a Mecca for surfers.

South Cornwall is softer, its colour-washed fishermen's cottages and palm-trees having earnt for it the title of 'riviera'. Mount's Bay, stretched between Land's End and Lizard Point as between finger and thumb, is noted for its quaint fishing villages like Mousehole and Mullion and for St. Michael's Mount off Marazion. Smuggling and shark fishing are traditionally associated with South Cornwall, the former activity epitomised by villages like Polperro and Mevagissey, while the twin towns of East and West Looe are modern centres for shark fishing.

South Devon with wide estuaries (technically drowned valleys) and long beaches has a well-deserved reputation as a holiday destination. Even so there are many remote and quiet stretches of coast with red sandstone or limestone cliffs, while Britain's most westerly outcrop of chalk lies between Beer and Sidmouth.

Dorset has an extraordinarily intricate geology. East of Lyme Regis the belt of oolite that runs diagonally across England from

---

South-West Peninsula Coast Path. Stretching 515 miles from Poole Harbour (45c) in Dorset, around Land's End (19g), to Minehead (64f) in Somerset, this is the longest long-distance footpath in Britain. It divides naturally into four sections:

Dorset. Renowned for its varied and unusual coastline which includes the limestone cliffs around Lyme Regis (42f), unequalled for their abundance of fossils, the unique geological formation of Chesil Beach (44d) and the beauty of the grassy downlands of the Isle of Purbeck (maps 44/45).

South Devon. A geologically complex coast with estuaries, sandy flats, impressive promontories of chalk or red sandstone and remote bays set off by lush vegetation and a profusion of wild flowers.

Cornwall. Magnificent cliffs and headlands, spotless beaches, quaint harbours, bustling little seaports and places of historic interest, and a wide range of wildlife including an abundance of seabirds.

Somerset and North Devon. Probably the least demanding of the four sections, it is no less rewarding in its variety, ranging from wide, high cliffs with panoramic views of the Exmoor National Park to the sandy flats and pebble beaches around Braunton (55a).

Although this whole walk is now officially open there are still some sections where the right of way is being contested. However, access is good and many parts of the path can be walked in small sections. Access is only really restricted at Lulworth Firing Ranges on the Dorset coast when those ranges are in use (indicated by red flags and/or lights).

Clothing and shoes should be suitable for an overgrown, muddy terrain with some hill walking. The route is marked with wooden signposts; it is also clearly marked on the maps of this atlas with a red hatched line.

National Parks

The national parks of Britain are large areas of country, usually wild and sparsely populated, where special care is taken to conserve the natural landscape. However, most of the land is not nationally owned and even the open moorland usually belongs to someone, so that rights of access may be limited. National parks are run by local planning committees and the Countryside Commission. They receive government aid for a range of activities: control of design and development of buildings; conservation measures such as the removal of eyesores, tree planting and laying out footpaths; and the provision of facilities like car parks, camp sites, information centres and country parks. The boundaries of all national parks are clearly marked on our maps with heavy green lines.

Dartmoor The largest area of open moorland remaining in southern England, it is characterized by massive tors, fast-flowing streams, rivers running through steep-sided valleys overhung by oak woods, by wild Dartmoor ponies which roam the moors freely, and by a variety of historic monuments which mark man's 4000-year occupation of the land. Along with the ancient cairns, hill forts and stone circles are an abundance of charming villages and churches, many dating from Plantagenet times, when Dartmoor was a royal forest.

Exmoor. The 265 square miles of Somerset and North Devon that make up the National Park of Exmoor offer a strong contrast in scenery: it varies from the upland cultivated country of the east — with its stone farmsteads, hedged fields and conifer forests — to the desolate, open moorland of the central plateau, once a royal forest. Exmoor is bounded in the north by a magnificent coastline with dramatic cliffs and panoramic views. The whole area is dotted with rivers and streams offering some of the best salmon and trout fishing in the country, the best of which is described in the Fishing section on pages 111-115.

The best way to see both Dartmoor and Exmoor is on foot or on horseback. The section on the Countryside (page 74) describes some of the best footpaths and nature trails in the area. Remember when walking on open moorland that it is essential to wear good shoes and weatherproof clothing, as you can walk all day without crossing a single road, fence or wall. For those who prefer travelling on horseback, pages 116-118 give a detailed list of the riding establishments in both areas.

The National Parks of the West Country, together with the South-West Peninsula Coast Path. The numbers show the map pages on which each section falls.

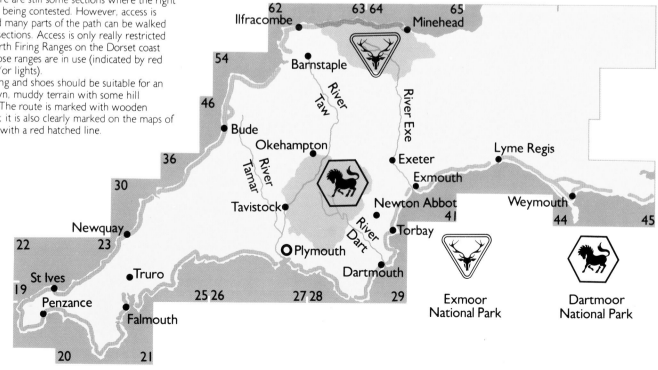

The engine house of the old Levant tin mine (map 19d; see page 103).

Yorkshire (forming the Cotswolds as it does so) reaches the sea. The area is rich in fossils as are the limestones of the Isle of Portland and Purbeck further east. Portland, famed for stone that was used to build St. Paul's Cathedral and many other notable public buidings, is connected to the mainland by Chesil Beach, an 18 mile long shingle bank whose pebbles are carefully graded by the tides. Purbeck has some delightful coastal scenery at places like Lulworth Cove and Durdle Door as well as boasting a small oil field with 'nodding donkeys' pumping out the black gold.

Hills and Vales

Inland, the West Country has hills and vales, wide moorlands and fen-like levels where dykes meander among pollarded willows, windblown downs and rocky gorges. This richness of scenery and mood is the perfect foil to the pleasures of the coast.

The greatest altitudes in the south-west are on the moors, 2038ft being the maximum at High Willhays on Dartmoor. The Moor itself is the wildest stretch of Devon with a trackless tangle of bogs at its centre. Exmoor is gentler, with a sweeping brown and purple beauty of its own, while Bodmin Moor in eastern Cornwall has a unique sense of remote mystery.

Exmoor runs from Devon into Somerset where its eastward extension is known as the Brendon Hills. Beyond these again lie the brackeny Quantocks and the long, low ridge of the Polden Hills offering magnificent views over the Somerset Levels and the distant line of the Mendips with their grey carboniferous limestone cut into great gorges at Cheddar and Ebbor. Another magnificent gorge, still largely clothed in its natural vegetation, is the one that carries the River Avon its last few miles from Bristol to the sea.

East of Bristol the Cotswolds swing down like a gigantic flattened S through Bath and Sherbourne to the Dorset coast. The building stone won from these gentle hills ranges from palest buff to rich gold at Ham Hill where the quarries provide the material for superb country houses like Montacute. Much of eastern Dorset is a contrast between wide, windswept chalk down and the low lying heaths that Thomas Hardy loved, but limestone again dominates the Isle of Purbeck with its pretty villages and grey houses huddled together like doves.

Climate

Thanks to the Gulf Stream and its south-westerly, maritime situation, the West Country is the mildest part of Britain. This softness of climate reaches its maximum in Cornwall and Devon, while there are substantial differences in the quality of the air in different parts of the region. The northern coasts are generally bracing and the southern very relaxing: indeed many people newly arrived in South Devon experience an overpowering desire for little else than sleep during the first day or two. In common with the rest of western Britain, the region has a relatively high rainfall although again this varies from place to place: central Dartmoor, for instance, gets more rain each year than places only a few miles away on the coast. Statistics can often be confusing, especially when they are coupled with the claims of holiday advertisers who all want to present their district in the best light: on Dartmoor, for instance, it may simply be raining harder rather than more often, and the more significant measure is the number of rain-days per annum. Generally speaking May, June and September are the driest months in the region. This being the case, people sometimes wonder why July and August have become so popular as holiday months; the reason seems to be that the days are still reasonably long and the sea approaches its maximum temperature.

The fact that sub-tropical plants flourish in many resorts is often used to imply that they have a sub-tropical climate. Lovely as these plants are, the truth is climatically less dramatic: the factor that prevents these plants surving inland, or further north, is frost rather than lack of summer sun. Sheltered parts of the south-west are virtually frost-free in winter and it is this that allows plants from warmer climes to survive outdoors from year to year.

This benign climate has indeed allowed some wonderful gardens to be created in the West Country. The most exotic is almost certainly at Tresco Abbey in the Isles of Scilly, where budgerigars live freely outdoors among many unusual plants. Other fine gardens include Knightshayes Court in Devon, with its wonderful displays of spring bulbs, and Lanhydrock, famed for its fine collection of trees and shrubs.

The Industrial Past

Although not in any sense an industrial area, the West Country has many reminders of the workaday world of the past. Rich in minerals, Cornwall is liberally sprinkled with mines, now mostly abandoned, where tin, copper, silver and lead were once won. The Mendips also have lead mines worked since pre-Roman times and coal mines only recently abandoned. Rarer minerals have also been found; arsenic in the Tamar Valley and strontium (the metal that produces the crimson element in fireworks) near Bristol.

In Cornwall the characteristic, gaunt remains of abandoned mine engine-houses still add a poignant accent to bare moors and along lonely cliffs. A number of museums in the Duchy have displays covering mining and at the Tolgus Tin Mine near Redruth there is an active tin-streaming mill. Other Cornish minerals include slate, the quarrying of which can be seen at Delabole, and china clay. This latter has been excavated in large quantity in the St. Austell area creating a moonscape of pits and spoil heaps. The open-air Wheal Martyn Museum gives a good idea of the china clay industry as it was in the last century.

As miners drove their shafts deeper they increasingly met the problem of flooding and much effort was expended in trying to devise mine pumps. The first satisfactory answer was provided by a Dartmouth man, Thomas Newcomen, who invented a steam powered pump. Examples of his massive engines can be seen in Royal Avenue Gardens in his home town.

If it was the railway that made the West Country popular as a holiday destination, it was that great engineer Isambard Kingdom Brunel who made sure, through his efforts on behalf of the Great Western Railway, that the region had an excellent railway system, The section of line between Bath and Bristol remains a classic example of railway engineering, as does the truss bridge of two 455ft spans which crosses the Tamar at Saltash. Bristol has two other remarkable memorials to this great man: the Clifton Suspension Bridge, slung so elegantly over the Avon Gorge and, further upstream, the SS Great Britain, the first screw-driven steamer to cross the Atlantic.

Reminders of more recent scientific achievements include the Marconi Memorial at Mullion in Cornwall, from where the first morse signal was sent across the Atlantic; and the communications centre only a stone's throw away at Goonhilly Downs, famed for its reception of satellite broadcasts.

Wildlife

With its favoured climate, varied geology (giving a wide range of soils and habitats) and geographical situation on the western seaboard of Europe, the West Country is rich in wildlife despite human pressure on the environment for many hundreds of years. The region as a whole is of great ecological interest as the native flora and fauna originate from three different zones. Most of England is populated by species that crossed from Europe before the Channel was formed after the last Ice Age and many of these have reached the south-west as they have reached Scotland and Ireland.

Because of its warmth, the West Country has a smaller group of species termed 'Mediterranean'. Their route to the south-west is not known for certain and the fact that they seem able to penetrate no further into Britain indicates that they are on the very edge of their range. Example of these Mediterranean species are Hare's Ear and Slender Marsh Bedstraw.

The third group has been called the Lusitanian by ecologists and comprises species confined to the western edge of Europe and North Africa. One theory that accounts for this strange distribution of a handful of plants and animals is that, when sea-levels fell as a result of water being converted to ice during the Ice Ages, the Lusitanian species found refuge in warmer areas to the south and west. These lands are now, once more, under the Atlantic but, as the ice retreated, the Lusitanian survivors returned. Their confinement to the edge of Europe indicates, perhaps, that they could not compete very satisfactorily with the colonisers from the Continent. Examples of this Lusitanian element are Dorset Heath and Cornish Moneywort.

Apart from the alpine and the arctic, virtually every type of habitat found in Britain is represented in the West Country: the coast with its beaches and cliffs, saltmarshes and sand dunes; the moors, heaths, bogs and marshes; limestone, chalk and granite hills; ancient woods and modern forests - and a handful of islands, each with a fascinatingly unqiue wildlife.

The glory of the coastline is unquestionably its bird life and the ornothologist can spend many happy hours in summer or winter watching the activities of waders, gulls, terns and other seabirds. The Cornish estuaries of the Fal and Hayle are good spots for seeing waders in winter, but of outstanding quality in this respect is the National Nature Reserve of Bridgwater Bay at the mouth of the River Parret. Immense flocks of wildfowl gather here (especially during the spring and autumn migrations) and the bay is renowned for its White-fronted Geese and Shellduck.

The numerous cliffs in the region have seabirds like Puffin, Guillemot and Kittiwake as well as species usually associated with inland sites such as Buzzard and Raven. Some of the lakes near the sea, like Slapton Ley or Radipole Lake at Weymouth, are noteworthy - the former for its Reed and Sedge Warblers, the latter for migrants and Bearded Reedlings. At Abbotsbury, the lagoon formed by the western end of Chesil Beach has been used as a swannery for hundreds of years.

A considerable amount of ornithological research is done in the West Country at places like the island of Annet in the Scillies, where Storm Petrel and Manx Shearwater number among the nesting birds; at the Portland Bill observatory where many migrants are ringed each year; and at the gull research station on Steepholm.

As well as birds the coast has a large population of Common and Grey Seals and much of botanical interest. Cliff plants include the Sea Stock, Small Restharrow, Wild Leek and Samphire. Shore Dock and Purple Spurge are confined to the south-west, while the Warren Crocus grows only on one small area of sand-dune. Perhaps the finest spot for coastal wildlife is the undercliff near Lyme Regis, this immense landslip (made famous in John Fowles's

This idealised cliff shows the wide variety of species which can be seen in such locations throughout the region. The birds shown are: **A** Puffin, which prefer the grassy slopes above the cliffs, but will also nest in crevices near the top; **B** Fulmar, which favour the broad ledges near the summit; **C** Kittiwake, which prefer steep cliffs; **D** Guillemot, which nest close together along exposed sections of cliff face; **E** Cormorant, which nest among the rocks at the cliff base; **F** Black Guillemot, which use caves and/or crevices along the cliff base near the sea; **G** Razorbill, which favour rock crevices at the corners of cliff.

novel "The French Lieutenant's Woman") offering everything from enormous fossils to mature ashwoods.

The heaths and moors of the West Country have all the interest of northern moors plus a number of local specialities. Dartmoor has Buzzard, Raven, Dipper and many other birds, its own breed of pony and the remarkable Wistmans Wood, one of the very few remnants of Britain's original forest cover which has here remained intact because the tangle of boulders around it has prevented sheep and cattle from penetrating and destroying seedling trees. Composed primarily of gnarled and contorted oaks, it is easy in its mossy depths to conjure up visions of the Enchanted Wood of Arthurian legend.

Exmoor is not dissimilar to Dartmoor but has the additional attraction of Red Deer. The ponies of the moor are particularly interesting as they are the British breed closest to the original wild horse.

Of the drier, lower-lying heathlands, the two most interesting areas are at opposite ends of the region. In the east, the Dorset heaths, immortalised by Thomas Hardy, are the home of such rarities as the Dartford Warbler, Smooth Snake and our most flamboyant heather, the crimson-purple Dorset Heath. In the west, the heathland on Predannack Downs near the Lizard has a complex ecology deriving from the different types of soil there. The great speciality is the local, lilac-flowered Cornish Heath.

The calcareous content of the soil overlying ranges of chalk and limestone hills give rise to groups of species that are virtually confined to these particular habitats. Wherever the ancient, sheep-cropped turf has been conserved one can expect to find cowslips, Stemless Thistles and a range of wild orchids. In summer, black and scarlet Burnet moths bumble through the grass and Marbled White butterflies sip nectar from Greater Knapweed flowers. Highlights of the limestone are found in the great gorges of the Avon at Bristol, and Cheddar and Ebbor in the Mendips. The Avon Gorge has two plants named after the city: Bristol Rock-cress and Bristol Whitebeam while Cheddar has the Cheddar Pink, so ruthlessly collected in the past that it now grows only on inaccessible rock ledges. Other benefits to wildlife afforded by limestone are its value to snails in helping them to make their shells and the fact that the solubility of the rock allows caves to form. The first attribute has ensured that edible Roman Snails flourish in the Mendips, while the second has provided the West Country strongholds of Greater Horseshoe Bats. Some people do not care for bats, but they are considerably less formidable than the hyenas that used to drag animals into their cave at Wookey Hole some thousands of years ago.

Other good limestone areas include Brean Down, one of the few British stations for the White Rockrose, and the area of Dorset coast around Lulworth, home of the Lulworth Skipper. This small, brown butterfly has a very restricted range in Britain but is widespread across the Continent.

As well as Wistmans Wood on Dartmoor, there are many fine woodlands in the region. Leigh Woods (south of Avon Gorge) are noted for their bird life with Nightingales, Hawfinches and other characteristic species. In the Forestry Commission plantations of fir and pine, Roe Deer are spreading, while the remaining deciduous woods in Devon are one of the best habitats for that fine butterlfy the Silver-washed Fritillary. At Dunsford and Meadhaydown Woods, also in Devon, there are extensive colonies of wild daffodils that put on a show each spring that would delight the heart of the most ardent Wordsworthian soul.

As well as woods, the West Country has a number of unique wild trees. The Bristol Whitebeam has already been mentioned, but there is a closely related species almost confined to Devon and locally known as French Ales, *Sorbus devoniensis* ('Ales' derives from the French word *alies* meaning a Wild Service Tree). The brown berries were formerly sold as a desert fruit in local markets. Other rare Whitebeams occur at Cheddar, along the North Devon and Somerset coast and in one or two places. In hedges near Plymouth a few examples of the Plymouth Pear survive, while Cornwall's special tree is the neatly upright Cornish Elm.

Because of their relative inaccessibility, small islands everywhere are ready-made nature reserves and the West Country is no exception. Steepholm, now owned and run as a reserve by the Kenneth Allsop trust, is famed as the only British home of the Wild Paeony, originally introduced by monks for medicinal purposes. Also on Steepholm is a unique variety of Sea Plantain and the introduced Muntjac Deer, tiny creatures with a dog-like barking call.

Lundy has its own ponies and a herd of wild goats, both introduced by man, and a wild cabbage found nowhere else in the world but on the island cliffs. But that is not the end of it: the leaves of this Lundy Cabbage are devoured by a beetle that also occurs nowhere else.

The Isles of Scilly have a rich flora and fauna. There are several unique sub-species of butterfly, some superb areas for bird-watching and the tiny Scilly Shrew which can sometimes be observed foraging around the high tide mark on beaches. The Scillies have many rare plants, some like the minute Early Adder's Tongue Fern growing in natural habitats such as the short grass near cliff edges, while others are found in the bulbfields as weeds of cultivation. Some of these 'weeds' like Whistling Jacks (*Gladiolus byzantinus*) and Rosy Garlic (*Allium roseum*), are very attractive.

To single out the wildlife highlights of the south-west overlooks the fact that there are many relatively abundant things found throughout the area and which make a major contribution to the landscape. The deep, West Country lanes starred with sweet smelling Primroses each spring and hung with the deep green, glossy fronds of Hart's Tongue Fern are justly famous. Because of the smoke-free air coming straight from the Atlantic, trees and bushes in the west are still festooned with mosses and lichens, while Mistletoe is abundant and particularly noticable on leefless winter trees. There are commons bright with almond-scented Gorse, a plant we do not respect enough - the Russians grow it in greenhouses they think so highly of it - and streams banked with violets where nimble Brown Trout flicker among the water shadows.

Pressure on wildlife in the West Country is great. Many of the most important sites are close to busy holiday areas and people can, often quite unwittingly, do a great deal of damage by trampling or making a noise.

To get the best from the region's riches it makes very good sense to consult a local naturalists' trust or reserve warden. They are normally pleased to help and will advise on how disturbance can be kept to a minimum. If every visitor shows reasonable respect for the countryside, the work of conservationists will be much easier and the area will retain its high wildlife interest for future generations to enjoy. Details of nature trails, naturalists trusts and much else relating to wildlife can be found at any Tourist Information Office (see page 122).

Country Code

Throughout the West Country, especially in the national parks, efforts are being made to maintain a balance between the interests of those who work and those who play within their boundaries. Visitors must remember that much of the land, the mountains and the hills also provide farmers' livelihoods. So whenever and wherever you are out walking, please follow these simple rules:

* Guard against risk of fire
* Close all gates behind you, especially those at cattle grids, etc.
* Keep dogs under control
* Keep to paths across farmland - you have no right of way over surrounding land
* Avoid damaging fences, hedges and walls
* Leave no litter - take it away with you
* Safeguard water supplies
* Protect wildlife, plants and trees - do not pick flowers, leave them for others to enjoy
* Drive carefully on country roads
* Respect the life of the countryside - and you will be welcomed.

Angling

More people practise angling than any other sport in Britain. There are three main forms of angling, of which the most popular is coarse or freshwater fishing. This is followed by sea fishing, with holiday makers each year adding to the number of regular sea anglers. The third category is game fishing, traditionally with flies, but increasingly with spinners or bait, for game fish such as salmon and trout. Although a more specialised form of angling, this has rapidly become more popular in recent years. With new reservoirs being stocked with rainbow and brown trout, trout fishing is no longer the privilege of those with access to a small number of jealously guarded waters.

Coarse fishing

Angling for coarse fish is very varied, with numerous techniques. Freshwater is either flowing, as in rivers and streams, or still, as in natural lakes or man made waters such as gravel pits. A typical river might have a number of different zones, each with distinct characteristics and containing different species. A river with its source in mountains or hills will begin with a fast runnning stretch in which might be found trout. This will merge into a lower zone where in summer the water might reach 15°C, and where the beautiful grayling might be found, along with dace and gudgeon. As the river widens and runs more smoothly, the barbel zone will be reached, where chub, roach and perch will also have their territories. In the last zone in which the water remains fresh, the river is likely to meander more slowly over a wider valley and the species become more numerous: bream, tench, carp, perch, roach, rudd and the predatory pike and zander can be caught. The last distinct zone is where the water is brackish as fresh and seawater meet. Here will be found migratory fish, such as eel and flounder, and strictly sea fish such as mullet, bass and shad.

Still waters can also be roughly categorised by their height above sea level. High natural lakes are likely to contain trout, carp, pike and perch; lower, warmer waters will contain the same fish as the slow, meandering rivers mentioned above.

A fisherman buying line, hooks and floats for the first time would do well to seek advice from the local tackle shop. There are numerous techniques, the most popular being float fishing. In fast water, however, legering can be profitable: the bait is offered on the bottom, with a single large lead weight used to hold the line down. On a strange water it is good practice to watch the methods and baits the regulars are using.

Sea fishing

Many readers of this section will be coarse anglers planning to do some sea fishing on their holidays. Plenty of fishing is available, as generally speaking wherever you are allowed access to a coastline, you can fish without a permit. The variety is wide, as piers, estuaries, beaches and rocks provide differing conditions and catches; and there are opportunities for boat fishing.

The rod required will vary with the type of fishing. It will usually be of glass fibre for lightness and flexibility, but where a rod of 8ft might be suitable for boat fishing, one of around 12ft is better for long casting from the shore - a rod of about 8-10ft will enable a fisherman to try all forms of sea fishing.

Pier fishing: fishing from a pier is a good introduction to sea fishing. No great casting skill is necessary and there are usually plenty of fellow anglers around to learn from. Mullet are often caught from piers, as they feed on the algae around old pier supports. Bass, pollack and, from September onwards, whiting can also be caught. Ragworm, sand-eels or slivers of small fish caught on the spot can be used as bait. A drop net is needed for bringing up the catch.

Estuaries, beaches and rocks: food is moved around on the tide in estuaries; bait natural to the estuary, such as lugworm, ragworm, mussels and small crabs, will catch mullet, bass and flounder.

Beaches provide opportunities to practise long casting - a cast of 100 yards or more will be necessary to achieve any success. Remember, though, that commercial fishing has severely reduced fish stocks and even experienced anglers suffer many fishless days. When casting, the tackle should hang about 2ft from the tip. With (for right-handed casters) the left shoulder facing the sea and the feet apart, swing smoothly forward and overhead, releasing the line as the rod reaches the vertical. Bass are a popular species to seek from beaches, particularly after dark.

Boat fishing falls into categories of its own: fishing in harbours and tidal rivers, inshore boat fishing (i.e. within 3 miles of the shore), fishing on deep water reefs and wreck fishing. The techniques, baits and range of species to be caught are so numerous that it is impossible to deal with them all here. Most people will go out first with experienced friends, or with a skipper plying for hire, and should discuss in advance what equipment it will be necessary to bring. When booking a place on a boat with a professional skipper, check the terms of the charter. Many skippers operate a rule that the angler may keep two fish only; this often causes disappointment to anglers who catch a boatful and have not checked the terms in advance.

Game fishing

Fishing for salmon and trout is a specialised form of angling. There are three methods of catching the fish: with fly, spinners or bait. Rods vary with the method and with the depth and width of the water. Generally a fly rod is longer and more flexible than a spinning rod. The method used is not always the choice of the angler: on some rivers spinning is not allowed or is restricted to certain times of the year, forcing the angler to employ the more difficult fly fishing. There are two methods: sunk line and floating line. With the sunk line, the fly is allowed to sink slowly towards the bottom. Floating line fishing is usually used for salmon, when the water warms up and the fish are likely to be in shallow water. The flies used are dry flies, which are almost weightless and float on the surface film of the water. When casting a dry fly, the weight of the line is used to carry the fly out. Spinning is a method of catching game fish using lures, such as the ever-popular Devon Minnow, which resembles a small fish and spins through the water. These are the normal methods of fishing, but game fish are occasionally caught with natural bait such as sprats, prawns or worms.

Another difficulty, especially with salmon fishing, is its expense: the best waters are private. However, reservoirs and lakes all over England and Wales now provide excellent trout fishing, many such waters being listed on pages 111-115. It is always advisable to plan fishing visits in advance and to make enquiries about availabilty and permits in good time rather than to arrive in the hope of some immediate fishing.

These fish typify the zones of a river as described above.

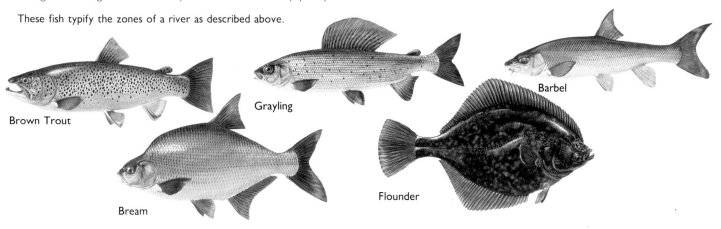

Brown Trout

Grayling

Barbel

Bream

Flounder

Sailing

On all but the wildest sections of coast, there are extensive facilities both for those with their own boats and for those who wish to hire. Slipways offering access to the public are also shown on the maps.

However experienced you are, the seas in this region can be treacherous and there are a number of safety precautions which must always be taken. Before setting out, always obtain a weather forecast - the local coastguard station is the best source for this; they are marked CG on the maps, or you can obtain the telephone number from the nearest Tourist Information Office (see page 122). Whenever a gale of Force 8 or above is expected within 6 hours, warning flags are hoisted at coastguard stations and at harbours and piers.

Always leave details of your trip with someone, or leave a note on the car windscreen, so that people know when you are missing and can instigate a search. The information needed is: a description of your boat (length, colour, name, type); the number of people on board; a list of any safety equipment carried; when you set sail and when you expect to return.

Carry extra clothing (especially waterproofs) even in summer, as you could be stranded or becalmed and it can become very cold at sea at any time of year. Always wear an approved design of life jacket.

If you fall overboard, remove your shoes and any heavy clothing immediately, but retain the rest of your garments, as these will help keep you warm. Tread water as slowly as possible to preserve energy, although a proper life jacket will keep you afloat with no effort on your part. Recognised distress signals include: standing up with arms apart, raising and lowering them as if imitating a bird; waving a flag or any item of clothing; flying the Red Ensign (normally flown from the stern) high in the rigging or upside down. If you see any of these from the shore, dial 999 and ask for the coastguard.

Although the general rule is that steam gives way to sail, you must bear in mind that modern supertankers and the like simply cannot manoeuvre with any speed at all - it can take them a couple of miles to stop, for example! - and that in narrow or crowded sea lanes large vessels may have no choice but to maintain their course. Standard horn signals are: 1 blast "am turning to starboard", 2 blasts " am turning to port", 3 blasts "am reversing".

Racing

With over 400 different types of sailing dinghy and roughly the same number of sailing clubs, you can always be sure of seeing some racing somewhere. For the uninitiated, yacht races often appear to be little more than confusing melees of milling boats, with a great deal of manoeuvring before the actual start. It may help the spectator to know the procedure, which is as follows: ten minutes before the start, a cannon or maroon is fired and the flag of the yacht class involved is broken from the club flagstaff; five minutes before the off, there is another bang and a Blue Peter flag appears alongside the other; the actual start is signalled by a third report and by the lowering of both flags. When yachts are actually racing, they usually fly a small, square racing flag from the masthead (rather than the usual burgee).

Whenever a gale of Force 8 or above is expected, flags are flown from each Coastguard station indicating the wind direction.

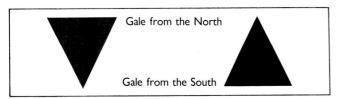

Gale from the North

Gale from the South

Moor and Mountain

Although there is no mountaineering in the Alpine sense anywhere in the region, the uplands offer a surprising diversity of activities: hill walking, scrambling, orienteering, rock climbing, and even some skiing in winter - all of which are detailed in the gazetteer.

On a fine summer's day, the high peaks look very inviting, their seemingly gentle slopes apparently quite benign. You should not be taken in: the weather can change with alarming speed and the combination of height, wind and rain can be (and often is) a killer. The effect of wind speed on temperature can be seen in the accompanying chart; but the temperature also falls by about 1°F for every 300ft you climb. This combination of height and wind is a powerful one: if the temperature at sea level is 50°F (typical of a spring day), a gentle 10mph breeze at the rather modest height of 1, 000ft will produce a temperature only just above freezing point!

Nor are the slopes as gentle as they appear from the comfort of your car: it can take far longer than you think to reach your destination on foot - expect to average no more than 2mph, and allow one hour extra for each 1, 500ft above sea level.

These rather alarming figures should not deter you from enjoying the spectacular scenery available; they are intended to force home the need to take elementary precautions. Always plan your route first - this atlas is ideal for that. Remember that mist and fog can descend very quickly, especially from autumn to late spring, so you must know where you are at all times. Travel in company and stick to waymarked or well established paths where possible. Wear the right clothes: woollens, stout footwear and windcheaters (ideally in a bright colour, just in case someone has to look for you). Take with you a compass, a watch, a whistle, a torch, some chocolate, a small first-aid kit and coins for emergency telephone calls.

If you do get into trouble, remember that six of anything is the recognised emergency signal: 6 flashes of the torch, 6 blasts on a whistle or just 6 yells.

Rock climbers, in addition to all the above, should wear safety helmets, tough boots and should always climb roped together with good quality nylon rope. Leave the heroics to the experts, many of whom you can enjoy watching at the more severe locations described in the gazetteer section on Climbing.

Wind Chill
Shows the effect of wind speed (expressed on the Beaufort Scale, details of which are shown on page 109) on temperature (in degrees Fahrenheit). The temperatures listed on the top row are those which would be shown on a thermometer protected from any wind; those below are the equivalents at the various wind speeds. The area coloured blue represents the danger zone, in which there is risk of exposed flesh suffering frostbite. Remember that freezing point is +32°F.

Wind Force	Temperature							
	+50	+40	+30	+20	+10	0	−10	−20
2	+48	+37	+27	+16	+ 6	− 5	−15	−26
3	+40	+28	+16	+ 4	− 9	−21	−33	−46
4	+36	+22	+ 9	− 5	−18	−36	−45	−58
5	+32	+18	+ 4	−10	−25	−39	−53	−67
6	+29	+15	− 1	−17	−31	−46	−61	−77
7	+27	+11	− 4	−20	−35	−49	−67	−82
8+	+26	+10	− 6	−21	−37	−53	−69	−85

Food and Drink

The western counties offer a rich variety of food and drink; not only is the land good for market gardening and orchard farming, it also provides good pasture for dairy herds. Sheep and pigs give a good supply of meat and the coastal areas provide a good choice of fish and seafood. It is hardly surprising, therefore, that specialities in fish, meat, dairy and fruit dishes have all been established over the years.

Mackerel, pilchards and eels are traditionally caught about the West Country coastline, so many dishes make use of these. In Cornwall the meat pasty may reign supreme, but other fish pastry dishes have become famous: star-gazer dishes, notably star-gazy pie, which has the heads of herrings sticking out of the pastry, are a long-standing tradition. The nutritious juices from the heads run into the pie during cooking - the heads are broken off for serving. Other fish specialities include mackerel with gooseberry sauce, pilchard hot pot, Severn elvers, elvers with bacon, Cornish crab soup and mussels with saffron.

Pork and dairy farming and the large herds of sheep on Exmoor have produced such delicious favourites as Wiltshire porkies, jellied pork brawn, pork with apples and sage, Exeter stew (a beef-based dish) and squab pie. This last is, misleadingly, not mainly pigeon, but lamb with the addition of some pigeon breast meat.

Cornish pasties, of course, are world famous; the fishermen used to have their initials baked on to one end of their pasty so that, if the fish should bite while they were eating, they could return to their own initialled lunch later.

Throughout the south-west, yeast-baking is preferred to the griddle-cookery so popular in northern and midland regions. Some of the most common dishes are Devonshire splits, Sally Lunn cakes and revel cakes. Revels were held in the West Country in much the same way as wakes in the north or goose fairs in the shires, and revel cakes, rich with clotted cream and saffron were baked for the ocasion. Other baked specialities include crunchy spice biscuits called fairings, Dorset apple cake and a rich currant pastry called figgy hobbin.

Creamy puddings are at their best made from the rich local milk; Bath offers a ground rice pudding and Cornwall uses its dairy produce to make burnt cream pudding and Granny Dart's junket.

The dairy farms of the West Country are responsible for some of the most famous of British cheeses - Cheddar and Double Gloucester. Both these hard cheeses are used in cooking and are eaten on their own or in that most simple and satisfying of meals, the ploughman's lunch, where it is served with a pickled onion or pickle, a big hunk of fresh bread and plenty of butter. Cheddar was originally made from May to September, while the cattle were grazing on the rich summer grass, but demand has meant that the larger creameries now make Cheddar all the year round. The process of 'Cheddaring', that is chopping the curd very finely and removing the moisture in a press, has been copied in many countries, so imported Cheddars are quite common. The cheese needs at least six months to mature after pressing, making good Cheddar rather expensive, so that much of the output is now sadly debased by factory production methods.

Real Cheddar is at least relatively easy to find, however, which is more than can be said for one cheese boasted by Dorset: Blue Vinney. This is as elusive as the Holy Grail, the search being complicated by a confusion between two quite distinct types of cheese: the Blue Vinney and the Dorset Blue. Blue Vinney was a rock hard substance made from skimmed milk and is no longer produced for sale (one or two people can remember how to make it and occasionally do so to settle gastronomic arguments): Dorset Blue is a delicious, full cream, soft blue cheese which, at its best, resembles a good Gorgonzola. Although widely available in Dorset and elsewhere (often wrongly labelled Blue Vinney) people are secretive about where it is actually made - it takes several pints of local ale or cider to discover the reason.

Other West Country specialities of interest to the gourmet include Roman snails from the Mendips, saffron cakes in Cornwall, Bath Oliver biscuits and elvers from Severnside. The latter are baby eels that appear in vast numbers most Aprils on their way from the Sargasso Sea. Elver catching is centred on one or two pubs north of Bristol and the traditional way of serving them is to scramble them quickly with some egg.

The West Country is, of course, cider country, with the main centre of production being the Taunton area, although Norton Fitzwarren and many other parts of Somerset also have long associations with the trade. The fruit's sweet juice and acid pulp combine to make a strong drink, containing up to 8% alcohol, which is available in a variety of local brands. The connoisseur, however, will want to try the farmhouse version, known as 'scrumpy'. Although the alcohol content of this drink is actually no higher than that of strong ale, it has a ferocious reputation: orchard pigs, snouting among the fermenting windfalls, have been known to stagger and pass out from the effects of the alcoholic apples. The real reason for the reputation, however, is probably that scrumpy contains substances other than alcohol which tend to generate king-sized hangovers. If you want to show off, try it hot with ginger, still a popular custom among a few old-timers in the Bristol area.

Although cider is thought of as the principal drink in the south-west, the 'real ale' buff will find several independent breweries. Dorset is particularly rich with Hall and Woodhouse in Blandford Forum, Devenish at Weymouth, Palmer at Bridport and Eldridge Pope of Dorchester. The latter produce, on occasions, a special brew called Thomas Hardy Ale, Britain's strongest beer.

Some very passable white wine is now produced on a small scale in the West Country, while somewhere between the wine market and the cider market lies babycham, a champagne-perry from Shepton Mallet in the Mendips. Bristol, with its long history of trade remains an important centre for sherry and madeira while two curious regional cordials, shrub and lovage, were originally introduced to disguise the flavour of rum and brandy that had deteriorated during its inward voyage.

Also produced in Devon and Cornwall is mead, a sweet, honeyed drink with a varying alcoholic content. At least nine different types are made in Cornwall and after being the commonest alcoholic drink until the 14th century, when ale and wine superseded it, mead is making a comeback.

Traditional West Country cream tea

Calendar of Events

Events are listed by map reference, making it easy to discover what other attractions are available in any area at the same time. Remember that dates and times may vary from year to year and that you should always obtain more information before travelling by telephoning either the number suppied or the nearest Tourist Information Office (see page 122).

February

24c St Columb Major: Hurling. Although almost extinct elsewhere, this ancient Cornish game, using an applewood ball encased in silver, is here played annually by hundreds of townsfolk. *Shrove Tuesday from 0430.*

March

19f Penzance: West Cornwall Spring Horticultural Show, St John's Hall, Alverton Street. *3rd Tuesday and Friday.*

April

31d St Endellion: Easter Festival of Music, Collegiate Church of St Endelienta. *Easter Sunday for 1. week.*
35i Torre Abbey: Devon Art Society Picture Exhibition. *Last 3 weeks.*
35i Torquay: Gastronomic Festival, Imperial Hotel, Park Hill Road. *2nd week: Thursday to Sunday 1000 - 2000.*
44e Weymouth: Easter Hockey Festivals. Ladies' events at the Weymouth Athletics Centre, Knightsdale Road; men's at Redlands Sports Ground, Dorchester Road. *Easter weekend.*
71 Bristol: Distribution of the 'Tuppeny Starvers' - sugared buns with currants. This ancient custom takes place at the church of St Michael on the Mount Without, St Michael's Hill (see town plan). *21st at 1030.*

May

20f Helston: Cornish Flurry (floral) Dance. Developed from an ancient pagan festival, this now consists of several processions which weave their way through shop and houses; also folk dancing, etc. No cars are allowed into the town centre during the day. Programme: schoolchildren at 0700 and 1015; main procession at 1200, led by the mayor and band; general procession at 1700, in which the public can join. *8th.*
22b St Mary's: Crowning of the May Queen, The Park. *1st at 1400.*
24b Newquay: Carnival Week, with events throughout the town. *Last Week.*
30f Padstow: 'Obby 'Oss Festival. Ancient processional ceremony to mark the end of winter - represented by the hobby horse (a man dressed in a fearsome mask) - which parades through the streets followed by locals and willing visitors. Dancing around the maypole in the Market Square. *May Day from midnight.*
37d Trewint: Wesley Day at Wesley Cottage. *24th.*
40c Whipton: Devon County Show at Exeter Showground. Mainly agricultural, but including arena events such as showjumping. *3rd week: Thursday to Saturday 0900 - 1900.*
47c Great Torrington: May Fair. Procession, beauty queen, maypole dancing and other traditional events. *1st week.*
55c Barnstaple: Folk Festival, Queen's Hall, Boutport Street. *Last weekend from 1030.*
64f Minehead: Sailors' Hobby Horse. Ancient ceremony in which the brightly-coloured 'hobby horse' dances through the streets to the music of drum and accordion. *May Day AM.*
67e Glastonbury Tor: Beltane. The coming of spring is celebrated by the Order of British Druids.
67e Glastonbury Abbey: Roman Catholic Pilgrimage.
67f Wells: May Fair, Market Place. *1st Saturday.*
Folk Festival, Market Place. *1st Monday 1000 - 1600.*
Bath Festival. Events in Wells Cathedral. *Last week (or 1st week in June).* See 72e Bath.
71e Ashton Court: North Somerset Agricultural Show. *Last Monday 0900 - 1900.*
72e Bath: Bath Festival. Started by Yehudi Menuhin in 1959, it now attracts international performers for a fortnight of concerts at

various venues, including the Guildhall, Abbey, Assembly Rooms and at Wells Cathedral (67f). *Last week and 1st week of June.*
73a Chippenham: Lacock and Chippenham Folk Festival at various venues in both towns. *4th weekend: Friday to Monday.*

June

22b Hugh Town: Gig Racing. Six-oared rowing boats, originally designed to carry pilots out to ships entering the English Channel. Some of the boats are over 100 years old. *Friday evenings.*
23i St Day: St Day Feast, through the streets of the town. *29th at 1400.*
27c Plymouth: Music Week at various venues. *2nd week.*
Devonport Field Gun Public Runs at HMS Drake, part of the Royal Navy base at Devonport. *Last 3 weeks.*
Naval Base Fair, HMS Drake. *2nd Saturday.*
29b Dartmouth: Carnival Week. *Last week.*
31d Wadebridge: Royal Cornwall Agricultural Show. *2nd week: Thursday to Saturday 0830 - 2030.*
31h Bodmin: Children's Folk Dance Festival, Priory Park. *Last Saturday.*
35c Powderham Castle (tel. 062 689 243): Historic Vehicle Gathering. *1st Sunday.*
35i Torquay: Hotels Fiesta Week at various venues. *3rd week.*
Babbacombe & St Marychurch Annual Charity Carnival Fayre, Babbacombe Downs. *3rd Wednesday 1000 - 1900.*
Babbacombe Regatta, Oddicombe Beach. *Last weekend: from 1400.*
37e Newport: Water Fair. *1st Saturday.*
41c Farway Countryside Park (tel. 040 487 224): Guide Dogs for the Blind show. *Last Sunday.*
55e Bideford: Foot Race. Contestants try to cross the mediaeval town bridge in less than the 22 seconds it takes the parish church clock to chime eight times. *Early in month.*
60d South Petherton: Folk and Craft Festival, Town and Market Squares. *3rd weekend: Friday to Sunday from 1030.*
63b Lynton: Annual Festival, including Morris Dancing. *1st week.*
67b Draycott: Strawberry Fayre, Recreation Ground, Wells Road. *2nd Friday/Saturday.*
67e Glastonbury: Church of England Pilgrimage. *Last Saturday.*
68d Shepton Mallet: Royal Bath and West Show, at the showground south-east of town. Agricultural, but with arena events. (showjumping, etc.). *1st week: Wednesday to Friday 0900 - 1900; Saturday 0900 - 1800.*
69d Longleat: Great Stationary Engine Rally. *3rd weekend 1000 -1800.*
70g Weston-Super-Mare: Annual Open Bowling Tournament for Men, Clarence Park. *Last full week: 0900 - 2100.*
71e Ashton Park: Bristol Horse Show. *2nd weekend from 0900.*
Classic and Historic Motor Club's Motoring Montage. *3rd Saturday from 1000.*
72e Bath: Bath Festival. *1st week (and last week of May).* See May.
73a Chippenham: Carnival Week. *Last full week.*

July

19i Mousehole: Carnival, with procession through the streets of Mousehole and Newlyn, ending in Penzance. *Last Saturday 1800 - 2000.*
22b Hugh Town: Gig Racing. *Friday evenings.* See June.
26b Bray Farm: Morval Vintage and Steam Rally. *Last weekend from 1100.*
28d Yealmpton: Agricultural Show, The Showground. *Last Wednesday from 0830.*
29b Dartmouth: Town Week, with events at Royal Avenue Gardens, Coronation Park, Guildhall, North Embankment and Victoria Road. *Last weekend: 1000 - 2100.*
32c Launceston: Agricultural Show. *3rd Thursday.*
32h Liskeard: Agricultural Show, Addington. *2nd Saturday 0900 - 1800.*
33e Tavistock: Carnival at various venue in the town. *3rd week.*
35c Powderham Castle (tel. 062 689 243): 17th Century Fair and mock Mediaeval Battle. *Last weekend.*
35f Teignmouth: Carnival and Procession through the town centre. *4th Thursday from 1900.*
35h Berry Pomeroy: Totnes and District Agricultural Show. *Last Thursday from 1000.*

45c Poole: Pram Prix, Poole Park. *3rd Sunday.*

46i Furze Farm Park (tel. Bridgerule 028 881 342): Threshing Demonstration and Harvest Lunches. *Wednesdays and Sundays: 1300 - 1630.*

50a Tiverton: Carnival. *2nd Saturday.*

51g Honiton: Annual Fair, first held in 1257.

58b Wiveliscombe: Taunton Deane Festival Week. *Last week.*

59d Taunton: Siege of Taunton, part of the Taunton Deane Festival. *3rd weekend.*

64f Minehead: National Morris Ring Meeting. *1st weekend.*
Minehead and Exmoor Festival. Two weeks of arts, music, folk dancing, drama, crafts and exhibitions, held at various venues in Minehead and in Dunster, Crowcombe and Exeter. *3rd week.*

69d Longleat: Fiesta. *2nd weekend: 1000 - 1800.*
More Wheels display. *Last weekend: 1000 - 1800.*

70g Weston-Super-Mare:Summer Carnival at venues throughout the town. *3rd Saturday.*
Great Weston Air Day, Sea Front. *Last Thursday.*

71 Bristol: Clifton Festival. *Last 3 weeks.*

August

19i Mousehole: Furry Dance. *2nd Friday.*

21b Falmouth: Port of Falmouth Sailing Association Regatta Week. *2nd full week.*

22b Hugh Town: Gig Racing. *Friday evenings.* See June.
St Mary's carnival. *Last weekend.*

25f Fowey: Royal Regatta and Carnival Week, at venues in the town and on the river Fowey. *3rd week.*

27c Plymouth: Navy Days, Royal Navy base, Devonport. *Last weekend.*

28i Salcombe: Regatta.

29a Totnes: Carnival Week, with events at various venues in the town. *2nd week.*

29c Paignton: Regatta, Sea Front.*2nd week.*

29g Dartmouth: Port of Dartmouth Royal Regatta. *Last Thursday to Saturday: 0800 - 2345.*

30h RAF St Mawgam: International Air Day. *2nd Wednesday.*

33e Tavistock: Festival, with events at various venues. *Last full week.*

35c Dawlish: Carnival Week, The Lawn. *3rd week.*

35f Teignmouth: Regatta, Sea Front and Den Green. *1st full week.*

35h Cockington: Cockington Fayre. *1st Wednesday from 1000.*

35i Torre Abbey: Devon Art Society Summer Picture Exhibition. *Middle 2 weeks: daily 1000 - 1300, 1400 - 1730.*

40f Cockwood Harbour: The Revels. *2nd Sunday from 1900.*

41b Sidmouth: International Folklore Festival. One week of concerts and dance displays sponsored by the English Folk Dance and Song Society, with performers from Britain, Europe and occasionally further afield. *1st week.*

42f Lyme Regis: Regatta and Carnival Week at venues throughout the town. *1st week: daily 1030 - 0200.*

43d Bridport: Carnival Procession through the town centre. *4th Saturday from 1900.*

44e Weymouth: Grand Carnival. Includes an impressive procession of floats.

46e Bude: Blessing of the Sea. Service in St Michael & All Angels' Church, followed by the actual blessing from the breakwater. *Thursdays at 1930 (subject to tide).*
Revel and Cuckoo Fair, Poughill. *1st Thursday from 1430.*

46h Marhamchurch: Marhamchurch Revel, Revel Field, Village Square. *3rd Monday from 1430.*

46i Furze Farm Park. See July.

47e Alscott Farm Museum: Heavy Horse Working Display. *3rd Sunday.*

49i Thorverton: Country Fair, Netherexe. *1st Sunday 1000 - 1800.*

56e South Molton: Sheep Fair. *Last Wednesday.*

59d Taunton: Mediaeval Fair, Castle Green Car Park. *1st Saturday.*
Mediaeval Banquet, Vivary Park. *1st Saturday.*

62e Ilfracombe: Boat and Shore Fishing Festival, The Pier. *Last week.*

62f Combe Martin: Annual Carnival.

63f Brendon: Annual Brendon Show.

64f Dunster: Horse and Agricultural Show, Dunster Lawns. *3rd Friday from 1000.*

67b Priddy: Sheep Fair, Priddy Green. *3rd Wednesday from 1100.*

67i Baltonsborough: Annual Show, Village Playing Field. *Last Monday from 1200.*

68d Shepton Mallet: Mid-Somerset Agricultural Show (Saturday) and Sports Festival (Sunday) at the showground south-east of town. *3rd weekend.*

70g Weston-Super-Mare: Annual Open Bowling Tounament for Ladies, Clarence Park. *Last week: Monday to Saturday 0900 - 1900.*

71e Ashton Court: Bristol Steam Rally. *Last weekend.*

September

19c St Ives: September Festival. Two weeks of folk and classical music, concerts, films, poetry, bands, choirs, etc. *Mid-month.*

24c Summercourt: Summercourt Fair. *Last Friday.*

27c Plymouth: Annual *Mayflower* Celebrations.

28f Borough Farm: Kingsbridge Agricultural and Horticultural Show. *1st Saturday from 1000.*

34f Widecombe-in-the-Moor: Widecombe Fair. Made famous by the ''Uncle Tom Cobbleigh'' song, this annual event now attracts thousands of visitors. *2nd Tuesday.*

44b Came Park: Dorchester Agricultural Show. *1st Saturday from 0900.*

49i Thorverton: River Exe Struggle and Fair, on the River Exe between Thorverton and Tiverton. *1st Sunday from 1000.*

55c Barnstaple: Annual Fair. Three days of traditional events, including a parade of civic dignitaries, a banquet, cattle and horse fairs, a carnival and a fun fair. *Starts on the Wednesday preceeding the 20th.*

58f Wellington: Charity River Race. Floating beds, bathtubs and other makeshift 'boats' make their way to Taunton; the route includes 'shooting the rapids' over 8ft weirs. *3rd Sunday from 1000.*

66h Bridgwater: St Matthew's Fair.

67e Glastonbury: Tor Fair. *2nd Monday.*

68c Frome: Carnival, including procession through the streets. *3rd Saturday from 1900.*
Cheese Show, The Showfield. *4th Wednesday from 0900.*

71e Ashton Court: Bristol International Balloon Fiesta. *1st weekend: flying at 0730 and 1730 Friday and Saturday; 0730 and 1600 Sunday.*

October

33d Callington: Honey Fair. *1st Wednesday 1000 - 2200.*

33e Tavistock: Goose Fair. Traditional combination of cattle mart and fairground amusements which has been held for centuries. Various venues are used, including Bedford Square and car park and Plymouth Road. *2nd Wednesday.*

35c Powderham Castle (tel. 062 689 243): Horse Trials. *1st Saturday.*

38c Okehampton: Carnival, using all main streets. *3rd Saturday 1500 - 1900.*

49h Crediton: Carnival, with procession via Mill Street, Charlotte Street, Union Road and High Street. *1st Saturday from 1900.*

57f Bampton: Pony Fair. Celebrates the annual round-up of wild Exmoor Ponies. *Last Thursday.*

59d Taunton: Annual Carnival and Cider Barrel Race. *3rd Saturday.*

63f Brendon: Sale of Exmoor Ponies, in the yard of the Stag Hunters' Inn. Follows the annual round-up. *3rd week.*

November

25d St Austell: Music Festival, St John's Methodist Church, Bodmin Road. *Last weekend and 1st week of December: daily (except Sunday).*

32c Launceston: Annual Carnival. *1st Saturday.*

49i Cowley: The Exe Descent. Canoe race over the 18 miles down river to Exeter (40b), usually attracting over 100 competitors. At Cowley are the famous 'steps', where divers are stationed to rescue the inevitable casualties. *Mid-month.*

52i Ottery St Mary: Guy Fawkes Night. Celebrated here in fine style, including the rolling through the streets of blazing tar barrels. *5th.*

59b North Petherton: Guy Fawkes Carnival. *Saturday nearest 5th.*

59d Taunton: Taunton and Somerset Music and Drama Festival at various venues. *3 weeks mid-month.*

66e Highbridge: Highbridge and Burnham-on-Sea Guy Fawkes Carnival. *Monday after the 5th.*

The West Country - Key to map pages

Motorways	**M5**	National Parks		Battlefields	⚔
M'ways under const. & proposed		Forest Parks		Lighthouses	⊤
Motorway Junction Numbers	**23** **24** Restricted Access	Woods & Forests		Lightships	⚓
Motorway Service Areas	EXETER	Car Ferries		Summits	△ 672m
Dual Carriageways		Passenger Ferries		Spot Heights	. 223m
Dual C'ways under construction		Railways	STA L.C. (Level Crossing) Tunnel	Waterfalls	～
Main Roads		Mineral Railways	+++++++++++++	Marshes	⊥ ⊥ ⊥
Secondary Roads		Disused Railways	- - - - - - -	Caves	⌒
Other Good Roads		Canals		Churches	+
Minor Roads & Tracks		Long Distance Footpaths	— — — —	Coast Guard Stations	CG
Route Classification Numbers	A69 B631	Footpaths & Bridle Paths	- - - - - -	Lifeboat Stations	LB
National Boundaries		Youth Hostels	▲ Y H	Sandy Beaches	～
County Boundaries		Airfields	⊕	Rocky Foreshore	～
Military Danger Zones	/////////	Windmills	⚹	Low Water Line	～
National Trust Property	NT ● ▱	Antiquities	∴	Cliffs	～

HEIGHT OF LAND IN METRES AND FEET

	0	165	330	490	655	985	1310	1640	1970	2295	2625	2950	3280	3610	Feet
Land below sea level															
	0	50	100	150	200	300	400	500	600	700	800	900	1000	1100	Metres

Activities covered in the gazetteer (with page numbers)

Where appropriate, these may be overprinted on the relevant black symbol above

Countryside 74 - 76

Picnic Sites 74

Gardens and Arboreta 77 - 79

Historical Sites 79 - 83

Museums and Art Galleries 84 - 87

Castles 88 - 89

Historic Buildings 90 - 94

Religious Places 95 - 99

Bird Watching 100 - 101

Wildlife in Captivity 101 - 102

Industry Past and Present 103 - 105

Tourist Railways 106

Cruising by Boat 107

Water Sports 108

Surfing Beaches 108

Sailing and Boating 109 - 110

Launching Slipways 109

Fishing 111 - 115

Riding and Pony Trekking 116 - 118

Skiing 119

Climbing 119

Aviation 121

Motor Sport 121

Activities of Special Interest 119 - 121

Golf Courses, with number of holes 121

Towns Having Extensive Tourist Facilities 121

Tourist Information Offices 122

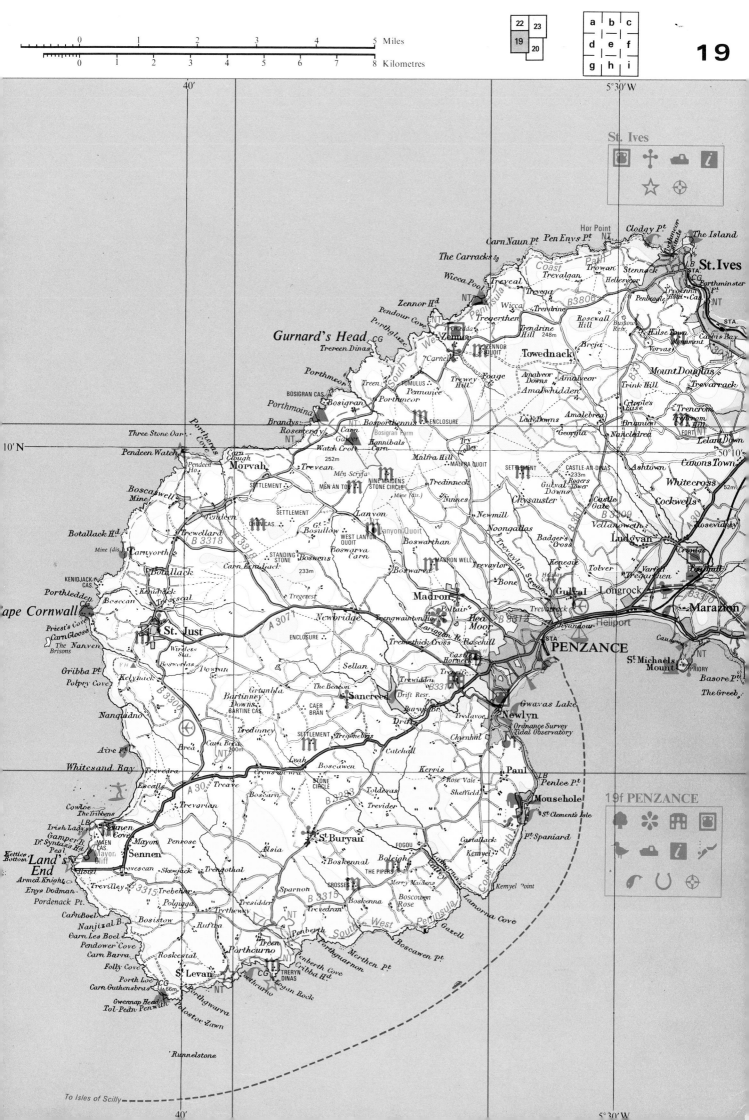

22

a	b	c
d	e	f
g	h	i

22	23
19	

0 1 2 3 4 5 Miles

0 1 2 3 4 5 6 7 8 Kilometres

25'   6°20'   15'

ISLES OF SCILLY
(28 miles south-west of Land's End)
on the same scale

Round Island
Lion R^k
White Island
Men-a-vaur
Golden Ball
St. Helens
Gt. Merrick Ledge
St. Martin's
Shipman H^d
Piper's Hole
Kettle
Northwethel
St Martins Bay
St Martins H^d
Old Man
Teän
Middle Town
St Martins
Hard Lewis Rocks
Hell Bay
Bryher
Oldgrimsby
Tresco
Higher Town
Chimney R^{ks}
Hanjague
Scilly R^{ks}
Harb
New Grimsby
Lizard P^t
Cruthers
Nornour
Irishman's Ledge
Gweal I.
Pentle Bay
Guthers I.
Eastern
Great Ganilly
Black R^{ks}
ABBEY
G^t Ganinick
Isles
G^t Innisvouls
Maiden Bower
Castle Bryher
Skirt I.
Lit Ganilly
Ragged
Menawethan
Seal R^k
Tresco Flats
Landing Place
Crow P^t
Lit. Ganinick
G^t Arthur
Illiswilgig
Puffin I.
Crow
Sound
Minvarlo
Samson
Bar P^t
Innisidgen
Biggal
White I.
Stony I.
Trenoweth
Watermill Bay
Green I.
Carn Morval P^t
Tolls Island
G^t Minalto
CG
A3110
Pelistry Bay
St. Mary's
Taylor's I.
Holy Vale
Deep P^t
The Road
Star Castle
Pier
LB
Hugh Town
Porth Hellick P^t
49°55' N   49°55'
The Garrison
Porth Cressa
Old Town
Giant's Cas.
Woolpack P^t
Nature Trail
Inner H^d
Peninnis H^d
To Penzance
St. Mary's Sound
Gunners
Gt. Smith
Kittern Rock
St. Mary's Sound
Crim Rocks
Annet H^d
Gugh
Haycocks
Burnt I.
St. Agnes
Dropnose P^t
Annet
(Disused)
Hoe P^t
Broad Sound
Hellweathers
Horse P^t
St Smith's Sound

22b **Hugh Town**

G^t Crebawethan
Melledgan
Bishop Rock
Western Rocks
Rosevear
Crebinicks
Roseveanı
Gorregan
Retarrier Reefs
Gilstone
Pednathise H^d

25'
6°20' W
5°40' W   15'
30'

North West Channel

St. Ives

Hor Point
Clodgy P^t
The Island
Carn Naun Pt
Pen Enys Pt
St
NT
The Carracks
St. Ives
Wicca Pool
Treveal
STA.
Coast Path
Trowan
Stennack
CG
Porthmin
Zennor H^d
Trevalgan
Trevega
Helesveor
Pendour Cove
Trendrine
NT
Rosewall Hill
Porthglaze
Wicca
Tregerthen
B3806
Busvary
STA.
Gurnard's Head
CG
Zennor
248m
Trendrine Hill
Breja
Halse Town
West Penwith Peninsula
ZENNOR QUOIT
Trewey
Foage
Trink Hill
Vorvas
Treen Dinas
Towednack
Trewey
Analveor Downs
Amalveor
Mount Douglas
Porthmeor

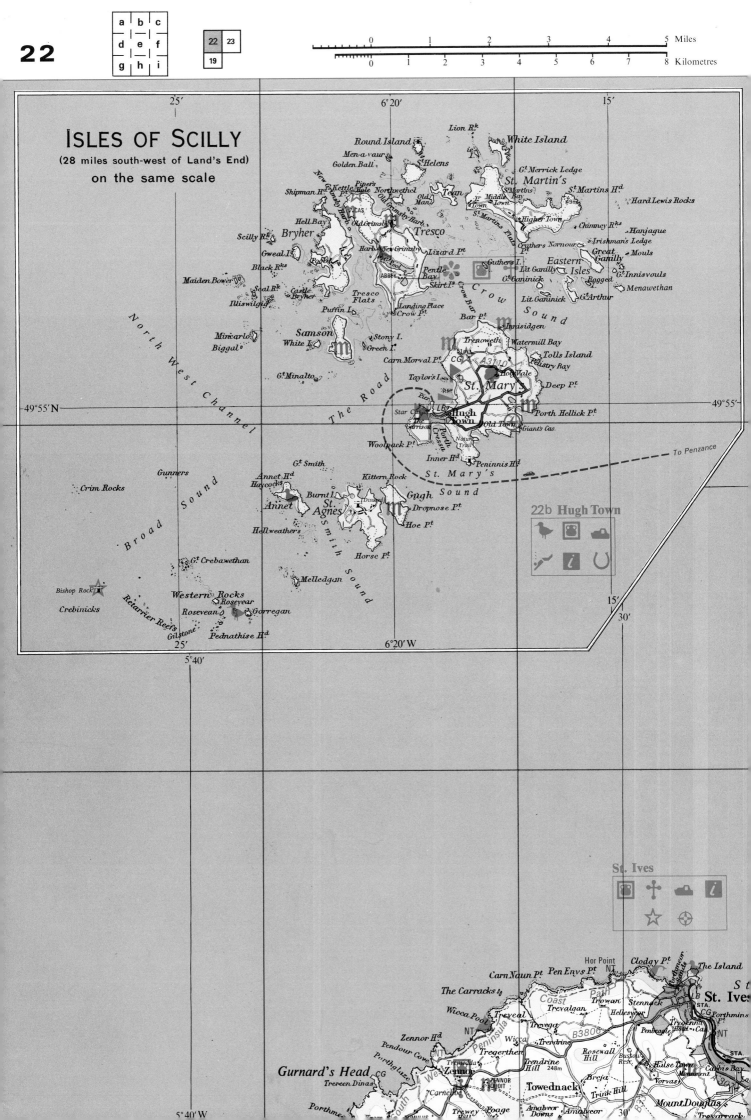

a b c
d e f
g h i

22 | 23 | 24
20 | 21

23

20'
5°10'

Carter's or
Gull Rks.
Penhale Pt.

Hoblyn's Cove
Ligger Pt.

Ligger
or
Perran
Bay

23f Perranporth

Chapel Rock
Droskyn Pt.
Shag Rk.
Perranporth

Cligga Hd.
Hanover Cove
Perran 50°20'N
Coombe

Bowden Rks. or
Man & his Man

Green I.
Trevellas Porth
Trevaunance Cove
Cross
Coombe
Trevellas

Newdowns Hd.

Crams
CG
St Agnes Head
Wheal
Kitty
Backla
Shop
Mithian

Tubby's Hd.
NT
St Agnes
Beacon
△191m
NT
St. Agnes
Penwartha

Chapel Porth
Goonvrea
Chapel
Coombe
Coombe
Mine
(dis.)

Mine
(dis.)
Towan Cross
Mingoose
Silverwell

Porthtowan
Trevarnhayle
Mount Hawke
B 3277

Tobban Horse
Mine
(dis.)
Banns
Three Barrows
148m

Gullyn Rk.
Porthtowan
Menagissey
Skinner's
Bottom

Diamond
Nancekuke Common
Mawla
Two Barrows
Blackwater

23h CAMBORNE

Nancekuke

Wheal
Busy
Wheal Rose
Chacewater

Gull Rk.
Portreath
B 3300

Carvannel
Downs
NT
ROUND
Bridge
Illogan
North Country
Scorrier
Hilliveth

Samphire I.
NT
Scorrier Ho.

Crane Is.
18
Paynters
Lane End
Highway
Trefullon
Mine (dis.)

Godrevy I.
Navax Pt.
Fishing Cove
Hell's Mouth
Deadman's
Cove
CRANE
CAS
Tehidy Ho.
89m
Wheal
North Country
St Day
Crofthandy

Godrevy Pt.
NT
Reskajeage
Down
NT
Menwinnion
Park Bottom
REDRUTH
STA
Gwennap Pt.
Carharrack
Mine (dis.)

Godrevy
Towans
NT
Coombe
25m
Illogan
Highway
Mount Ambrose

Bessack Rk.
Strap
Rocks
Greealavellan
Red R.
Beskudinnick
Busveggill
Mine
Carn Brea
MON FORT
Carn
Marth
Trevince
Tanner
Gwennap

Ceres Rk.
Gwithian
Towans
Gwithian
Nancemellin
Kehelland
CAMBORNE
Treswithian
88m
Brea
Carnkie
Piece
Selligan
Buller Hs.
Trevarth Ho.

es Bay
Upton
Towans
Trevarnon
Newmill
Roseworthy
Polstrong
ROSKEAR
Pengegon
Troon
Bolenowe
Lancarrow
Penhalurick
Penhalvean
Hendra

Black
Cliff
The Towans
R. Hayle
Angarrack
Connor
Downs
Barripper
Pendarves
Mine
Four Lanes
Penhalurick
Trembroath
Gilly

Phillack
Power Sta
WHARF
Copperhouse
Hayle
Gwinear
Carnhell
Green
Holgarrack
Trevoole
Grill
B 3297
Suthians
5°10'
20'

27b PLYMOUTH

35
28 29
a b c
d e f
g h i

29c Paignton

29b Dartmouth

29c Brixham

Paignton

Goodrington
Saltern Cove
Broad
Sands
Fishcombe Pt
C.G.
Shoalstone Pt
Berry Hd
Cod Rock
Durl Hd
St Mary's
Bay
Sharkham Pt
Southdown
Cliff
Man Sands
Crabrock Pt
Cod Rocks
Long
Sands
Scabbacombe Sands
Scabbacombe Hd

Totnes
Bridgetown
Weston
Bramemore
Follaton Ho
Pier
Car
The Mount
385
76m
Longcombe
Blagdon
Barton
Collaton
St Mary
Primley
Ho
Zoo & Gdns
Windmill Hill
Clump
104m
Lo.
40'
Br.
Belsford
Tristford
Ho
Peak Cross
Gerston
Bowden
Ho
Stancombe
Sharpham
Barton
Luscombe
Cross
Sharpham Ho
Aish
Whitehill
Yalberton
Crabbs Park
Clennonhill
A 379
Goodrington
Sands
Harberton
Leigh
E. Leigh
Dundridge
Ho
Luscombe
Ashprington
Painsford
Bow Creek
Duncannon
Port Bridge
ENCLOSURE
Stoke Gabriel
South Downs
Waddeton
Galmpton
Warborough
Hookhills
A 22
Broad
Sands
Elberry
Em.
Elberry Cove
18
C.G.
LB.
Churston
Court
Cove
Quarry
Park
Harburton Ford
Bow
Yeatson
Muckenhay
Cornworthy
Lr. Washbourne
Barton
Washbourne
Bowden
E. Cornworthy
135m
17m
Court
RIVER DART
Sandridge
Park
Galmpton Creek
Galmpton
Ferrers
Churston
Alston
Lupton Ho
Higher
Brixham
Upton Manor
Brixham
47m
STA
A 3022
B 3205
Holiday Camp
Ashwell
Holster
Poulston
Bernaford
R. Wash
Bickleigh
Newhouse
Lower
Tideford
Upper Tideford
Allaleigh
Woolcombe
Rowden
Dittisham
Kingston
Bozomzeal
Cross
Bozomzeal
Ferry
Greenway
Ho
Greenway
Anchor
Stone
Lr. Greenway
Higher
Greenway
Hillhead
FORT
Guzzle
Down
148m
Southdown
Raddicombe
Southdown
Cliff
Man Sands
207m
reston
A 381
Halwell
CAMP
196m
Collaton
Stanborough Ho.
188m
B 3207
West
Hartley
Dreyton
East
Hartley
Oldstone
191m
Capton
Downton
Halwell
Bruckton
Chapton
Hemborough
Hole
FORT
Dartmouth Ry.
Parland
Croftland
Hoodown
A 379
Nethway Ho.
Boohay
Woodhuish
Crabrock Pt
Cod Rocks
Long
Sands
Moreleigh
anborough
Brake
CAMP
Ritson
Bowden
Grimpstone
Seawardstone
Wood
Fm.
B 3207
Chilley
Cliston
Woodford
Blackawton
Oldstone
B 3207
Lr. Wadstray
Bugford Fm.
CAMP
Royal
Naval Coll.
Old Mill
Old Mill Creek
Dartmouth
Norton
147m
CAMP
150m
Kingston
Dartmouth
B 3205
Scabbacombe Sands
Scabbacombe Hd
Ivy Cove
Brownstone
Pudcombe Cove
Hutcherleigh
Pasture
Fm.
Pool
Fm.
Fallapit
E. Allington
Millcombe
Shepleigh
Court
Abbotsleigh
176m
Combe
Dallacombe
Eastdown
Sweetstone
Ash
Broomhill
Cotton
Wheatland
Worden
Bowden
Riversbridge
Stoke
Fleming
150m
Poundhouse
Warfleet
Kingswear
159m
Coleton
Brookhill
Down End
Kiln Cove
Warren
Newfoundland
Harbour
Kelly's Cove
Outer
Froward Pt
Eastern Black Rock
Inner Froward Pt
Mew Stone
GALLANTS
BOWER
NT
MILDO
Meg Rocks
Combe Pt.
C.G.
Redlap
Ho.
Redlap Cove
Leonards Cove
50° 20'
Higher
Heathfield
Norton
Dittiscombe
Coles Cross
Flear Fm.
Kimpston
Fursdon
Harleston
Higher
Coltscombe
117m
Slapton
Manor Ho.
Start
Field Studies
Centre
Blackpool
Matthews Pt
Streta
Sea Cliff
Asherne
Pilchard Cove
Scarswell
Buckland
Southwood
Fuge
Lowerty
Merrifield
START BAY
Sherford
113m
Frittiscombe
Coleridge Ho.
Keynedon
Barton
Stokenham
Frogmore
Chillington
A 379
Damacombe
Sherford
Down
Ranscombe
Malston
scombe
Slapton Ley
South West
Coast Path
Slapton Sands
FORT
Winslade
Widewell
North Pool
Kernborough
Widdicombe Ho.
N.T.
Sunnydale
Beeson
Torcross
South Pool
Ford
Dunstone
Cousins
Cross
116m
Beesands
Middlecombe
Tinsey Hd
Kellaton
Muckwell
Bickerton
S. Allington
Hallsands
Goodshelter
Chivelstone
emouth
Holset
Borough
West Prawle
139m
Woodcombe
C.G.
Lannacombe Mill
Start
Start's
Start Pt.
Black Stone
Peartree Pt
E. Prawle
Ballsaddle Rock
Sharpers Hd
Langerstone Pt
Black Cove
C.G.
N.T.
Gammon Hd
Prawle Pt.
40'
30'

a	b	c
d	e	f
g	h	i

30	31
24	

0   1   2   3   4   5 Miles

0   1   2   3   4   5   6   7   8 Kilometres

10'

5°W

30f Padstow

The Mouls

Newland 39m   Rumps Pt   CLIFF CAS.

Co

Pentire Point   Pentire   Carnweather Point   Portquin

NT   Com Hd

P a d s t o w   Peninglaze Forte

B a y   Hayle Bay   Trenant

Gullard Rock   Beacon   Stepper Pt   **Polzeath**

Pepper Hole   Trebetherick

Butter Hole   ST. ENODOC'S CH.   Trevang

Gunver Hd   Lellissick   The   Brae Hill   Pityme

Trevose   Porthmissen   Crugmeer   JESUS WELL   Splatt

Head CG   Bridge   Porthmissen   **Rock**   Penm

74m   LB   Trevone B   Trethillick   Stoptide

Dinas Hd   Prideaux   Porthilly

Trevose   Trevone   Place   **Padstow**   Treve

Booby's Bay   Harlyn   St Cadoc   Treator   Cant

18   9   B 3276   Dinas   Hill

Constantine Bay   ST. CONSTANTINE'S CH.   Trelowsa   A 389   River

Hr Harlyn   Trencarne   Track of   Ca

Treyarnon Beach   Towan   **St Merryn**   Treravel   Railway

Constantine   Shop   Tregellt   Tregonce   Penu

Bay YH   Treyarnon   Trevorrick   Buddlick

Pepper Cove   Trethias   Tregonborne   Trevorgus   Trevisker   Burgois   Penrose

Fox Cove   Rosken   Tregonna   Trevance   Car

Carnivas   Trevoyan   Treburrick   Lit   **St Issey**

Porthcothan Beach   NT   Trevorrick   Tregolds   **Petherick**   A 389

Porthmear   Trevethan   Porthcothan   Tregolds   Trenance   Trevear

Park Hd   Treginegar   Treleigh   EARTHWORK

Penrose   Blable

50°30'N

Penrir   Trevemedar   Penrose   Treravel   **Trevillador**   No M

NT   Treburrick   **St Ervan**   Tredinnick   Canalidgey   Lan

Diggory's I   Tregona   Trerair   Rumford   Trevibban

Queen Bess   Engollan   Trembleath   Trevengenow   Trelow

Bedruthan   Townhill   Trevisker

Pendarves I   Steps   Carnewas

Pendarves Pt   Carnewas   **Trelow**

Carnewas I   NT   Eddystone   **Downs**

Trerathick Pt   B 3276   Bears Downs   161m

Trenance Pt   Trevilledor   Lit Penmattlies   NINE MAIDENS

Trennee   Denzell   B 3274

Hotel   **Downs**

Mawgan Porth   Trevillador

Berryl's Pt   Ford   Gluvian   Denzell   Winnards Perch   Borlasevath   Ro

Beacon Cove   Vale of Lanherne   Rosedinnick   Retallick

CLIFF CAS.   Ford   Lanvean   Whitewater   Killegar

B 3276   Trevarrian   **St Mawgan**   Talskiddy   Trevornick   Trewan

W a t e r g a t e   H. Tolcarne   Tremayne

Trenurrum   Gurlyn   Trehowel   Trewan   Tregamere   Tregonet

B a y   Carlogas   Nanskeval   Gluvian   Reverth

Carnanton   Halvepr

Horse R   **St. Columb Major**

Zacry's I   Bosworgey   Trenatillian

Trebelzue   Roserrane   Castle

Trevithick   Tregaswith   Higher   **Downs**

Trevelgue Head   Trekenning   29.4m   CAST

Towan Head   Tregenna   Trevithick   Trekenning Ho.

Gazzle   Porth   Trebarber   Tregoose   Quoit

Newquay   Porth Res.

Fistral   **Bay**   St Colum   Halton   The Fir   Trebudannon   Nankelly

Bay   Minor   Hill   EARTHWORK 5°W   Providen

18   **Newquay**   Ennisworge

30h Newquay

10'

36
30 31 32
25

a b c
d e f
g h i

31

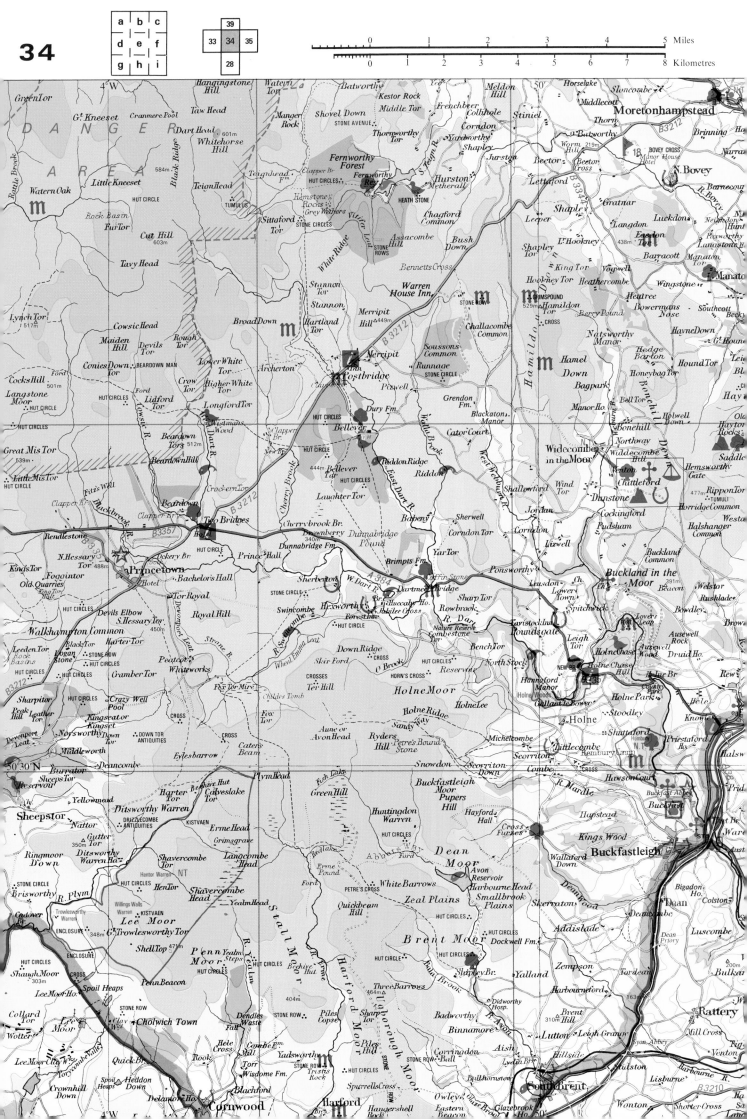

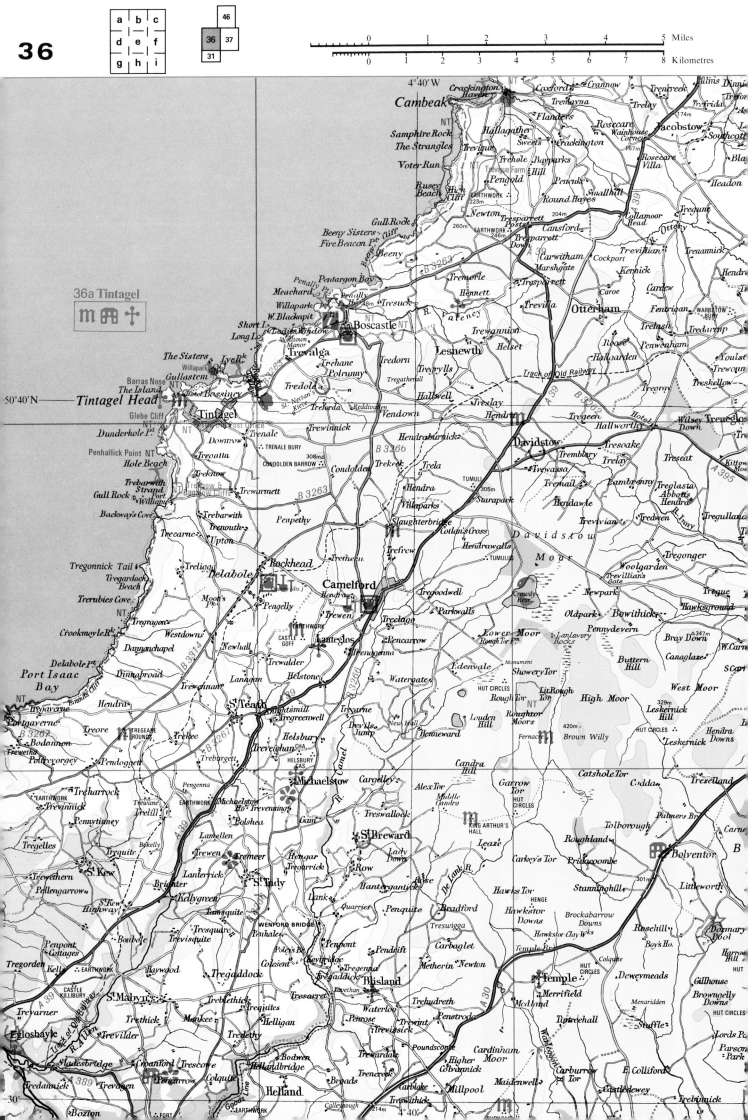

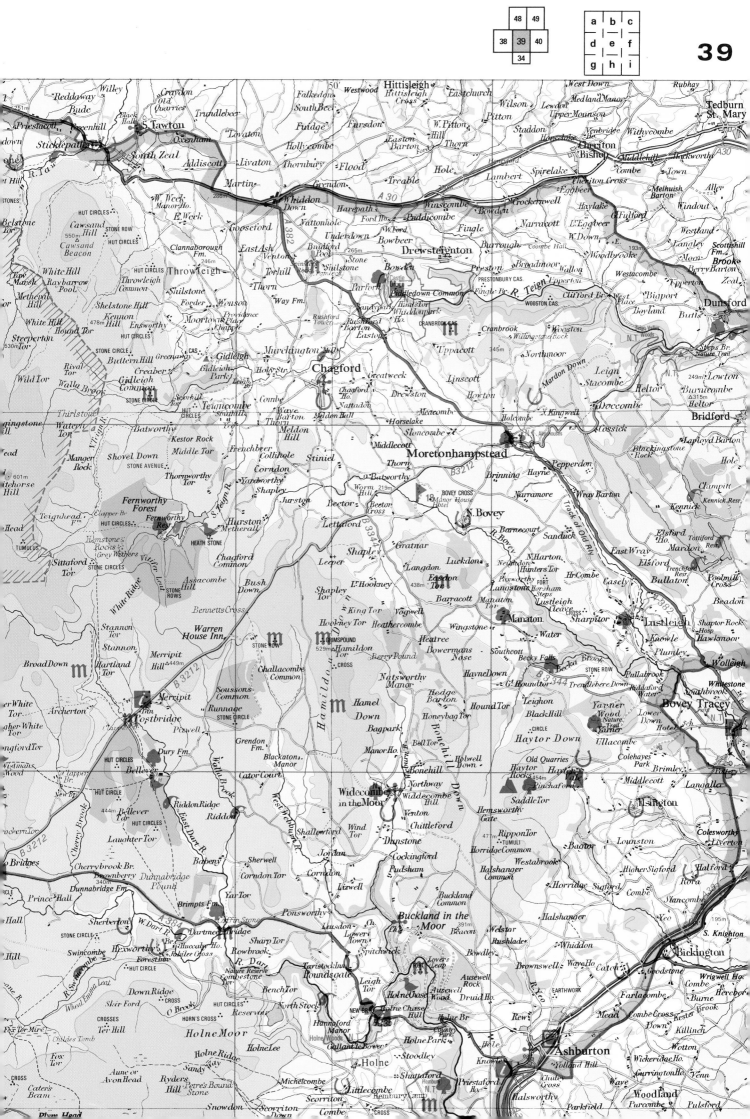

LYME BAY

41d EXMOUTH

40f Dawlish

40b EXETER

EXETER

Clapton
Seaborough
Mosterton
Drimpton
Netherhay
Childhay
East Swilletts Fm.
Littlewindsor
New Ho. Whetley Cross
Chapel Marsh
Dibberford
Burstock
Hursey
Broadwindsor
Clanden Hill
Stoke Knap
BURSTOCK GRANGE
Pilsdon Pen FORT
277m
Newesdon Hill NT
Craig's Hill
Stoke Abbott
Four Ashes
PARNHAM
Pilsdon
Blackney
Strode Manor
Monkwood
S. Bowood
L° Strode
Whitecross
Netherbury
SLAPE MANOR
Melplash
MELPLASH CO.
Shave Cross
Char
Filford
Kingsland
Waytown
Oxbridge
Broadoak
Salwayash
Lambrook
Camesworth
Atrim
W. Milton
Moorbath
Dottery
Mangerton
Whitchurch canonicorum
Ryall
N. Chideock
Pymore
Bradpole
Loders
Yondover
Manor Ho.
Symondsbury
Allington
Langdon Hill
Chideock
Bridport
Golden Cap NT
Sea Cliffs
Seatown
Thorncombe Beacon NT
Eype NT
Watton
Bothenhampton
Hyde
Walditch
Eype Mouth
North Hill
West Bay

S. Perrott
A 356
Crook Hill NT
Weston
Court
Chedington
Winyard's Gap NT
251m
Chapel Court
R. Axe
Mosterton
Buckham
Beaminster Down
Tunnel
Horn Park Fm.
Newtown
MEERHAY
White Sheet Hill
Beaminster
B 3163
Toller Down Gate
Toller Down
Toller Whelme
Hackthorn Hill
Coombe
Mapperton
Mythe Hill
N. Poorton
Loscombe
S. Poorton
Nettlecombe
Mappercombe
Powerstock
MOTTE & BAILEY
Whetley
Eggardon Hill 252m
Eggardon Fms.
TUMULI
BURIAL CHAMBER
EARTHWORKS
West Compton
EARTHWORK
Matravers Spyway
Uploders
Vinney Cross
Askerswell
Askerswell Down
Shipton Hill
Shipton Gorge
Hammiton Hill
Chilcombe
H° Coombe
L° Coombe
FORT
STANDING STONE
ROMAN ROAD
Kingston Russell
Martins Down
Litton Cheney
YH
R. Bride
Long Bredy
LONG BARROW
Kingston Russell Ho.
Graston Ho.
B 3157
18
Burton Bradstock
Berwick
Burton Cliff
NT
Bind Barrow
South West
Burton Mere
Swyre
Looke Fm.
Bexington
The Knoll
NT Lime Kiln NT
West Hill
B 3157
Ashley
Littlebredy
ENCLOSURE
Bridehead
Long Barrow
Sheep Down
STONE CIRCLE
ENCLOSURE
Gorwell Fm.
The Grey Mare & her Colts
West Bexington
Labour in Vain Fm.
East Bexington Fm.
FORT
White Hill
Abbotsbury
St. Peter's Abbey
ST. CATHERINE'S CHAPEL
Abbotsbury Swannery
Linton Hill
Elworth
75m
Chester's Hill
New Barn
Bridge Lane
West Fleet
Chesil Beach
Peninsula Coast Path

Stockwood
Hell Corner
Melbury Sampford
Melbury Park
Melbury Bubb
Redford Beach
A 37
E. Chelborough
Corscombe
W. Chelborough
Evershot
223m
Holywell
Benville Lane
Knapp Fm.
Uphall
Fortune's Wood Fm.
Rampisham
CHANTMARLE
Frome St. Quintin
R. Frome
Hr. Chalmington
Chalmington
H° Wraxall
209m
L° Wraxall
Sandhills
EARTHWORK
Cattistock
HOOKE CO.
Hooke
R. Hooke
H° Kingcombe
L° Kingcombe
Chilfrome
Whitesheet Hill
Clift
Toller Porcorum
A 356
Combe Bottom
Maiden Newton
STA.
Track of Old Railway
Wynford Eagle
Cruxton
Shatcombe Fm.
Wynford Ho.
Compton Valence

Bridport

Manor Ho.
30m
Hosp.
124m
Grove Ho.
124m

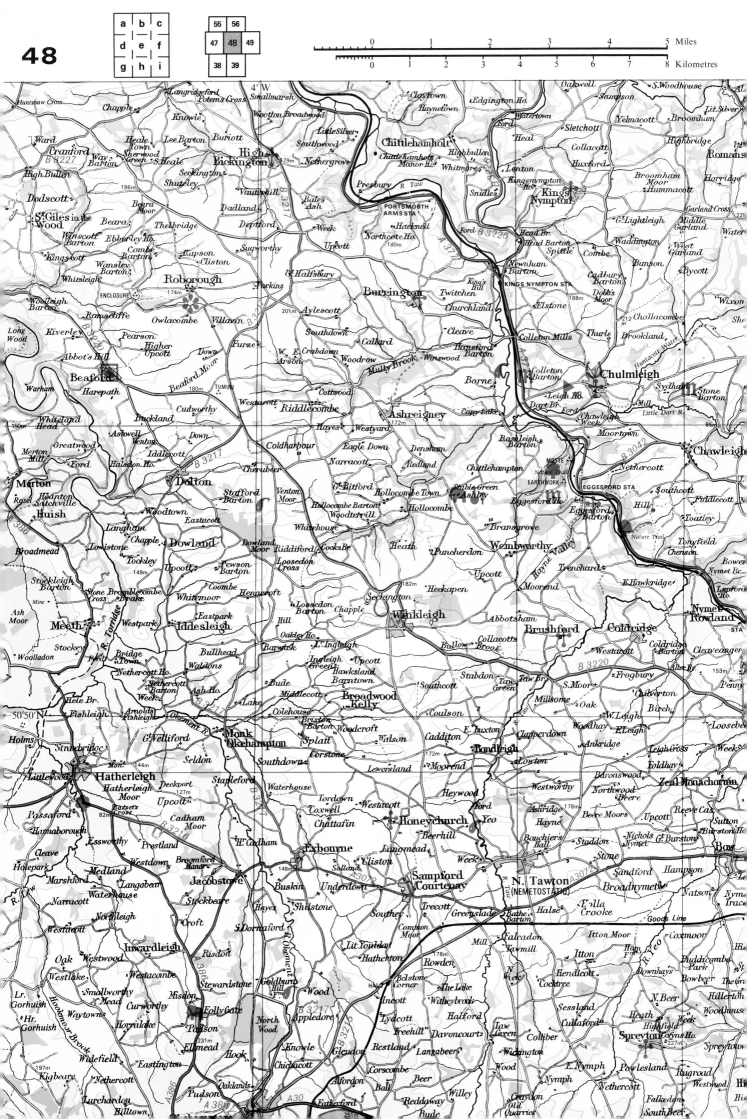

62
54 55 56
47 48

a b c
d e f
g h i

55

LE

BAY

Braunton
Burrows

Braunton
Marsh

Saunton Sands

Toll
Line Closed
4°10'W
A 361

Heanton Punchardon
Wrafton
Horridge
Tutshill
Upcott
Ashford
FORT Brightlycott
Coxleigh Barton
Raleigh Ho.

Bradiford Water
R. Yeo
A 39

Barnstaple Bar

DANGER ZONE

19m

Horsey I.

Chivenor

RIVER TAW

Penhill Pt.

Bradiford
Bradiford

Pilton

Stoneyard

Barnstaple

NT
Derby
Gorwell Ho.
Lilly

South Gut

Nature Trail

(Disused)

The Neck
The Crow
Rock

East Yelland
Power Station

(Goods)
Yelland

Fremington
A 39

Penhill

6m

Bickington

Hele
Horton

STA
JUN

Newport
Portmore
Runsam
A 377

Chestwood
Whitemoor

Appledore

Northam
Burrows

LB

Instow
Worlington
Y.H.

Rickleton
Manor Ho.

Collacott

Harracott

Barnstaple

Rookabear
Rowden
Lookout

Brynsworthy
Tawstock

Bishops
Tawton

Westward Ho!
CG

Holiday Camp
B 3236

Diddywell

Bloody
Corner

Northam

RIVER TORRIDGE

Huish

Tapeley

Treyhill

Holmacott

Pyewell
Litchardon

Voscombe
Rushcott

Nottiston
St. Johns
Chapel
Eastcombe

Colden Hill
192m

Rock Nose
Mermaids Pool
NT

Buckleigh

Halwill

Westleigh

Westleigh

Eastleigh

Horwood
16m

Loveacott

Collabear
Linscott
Upcott

Overton
Heaton
Fisherton

Cornborough

Puschill
Pushill

CAS

5m

Bradavin

Southcott

Weach Barton

Newton
Tracey

Pristacott
Hiscott

Lower
Rollstone
Harracott
Bridgetown

Hall

Chapelton
STA

Greencliff Rk.

Abbotsham
Court
Rickards
Down

Combe
Walter

11m

Bideford

Moreton

East the Water

Woodtown

Webbery
Bulworthy

Alverdiscott
Alverdiscott
Barton
Woodland

Kennacott

Ensis
Langham Lake

Heriner

Birbrook

Hollick
Langley Barton

51
Fishley
Barton

Greencliff Rk.

Abbotsham

Coxington

Bibbacombe

Ford

Portledge
104m

Highpark

Caddsdown
Jennets Resr.

A 39

Ashridge
Hallsannery

Pillmouth

The Barton

Gammaton
Gammaton
Resrs.

Oldiscleave
Gammaton
Cross
151m

Garnacott

Guscott
Garnacott
Nethercott
Delley

Higher Ho.

Northchurch
B 3217

Chiddlecombe
Gilscott

Winscott
Fairy Cross

Yeo Vale
41m

Littleham
Court

6m
Landcross

Huxwill

Lt. Netherdowns
Southcott
Park

Huntshaw

Darracott

Wiggadon

Southdown

Cogworthy

Debworthy

Yarnscombe

Eastacombe
Langridge
B 3217

Langridgeford
Poterns
Cross

oldworthy

Alwington
Rollston

Ballard

Littleham

Orleigh
Court
R. Duns
Upcott

R. Yeo

Armery Ho.

Salterns
Cottage

The Hill
Huntshaw Cross
206m
Huntshaw
Cross
Ward

Chapple

Knowle

Lee Barton

am

Tuckingmill
Howley
Halsbury

Stone

Burrow

Petticombe

Wear
Giffard
Furze
20m

Darracott

Darracott Moor Resr.
Cranford
B 3227
High Bullen

Heale
Town
Way
Barton
Sherwood
Green
S. Heale
Seck
Shuteley

ocombe
am

Cabbacott

Buckland
Brewer
EARTHWORK

Downes

Beam Mansion
Furzebeam
Hill

Moortown
Pidgham Barton

Dodscott
Beara
Moor

Bableigh

Bearah
Gorwood

Monkleigh

18

Culleigh
111m

Stevenstone Ho.

St. Giles in the
Wood

Winscott
Barton

Beara

Thelbridge

Melbury
Hill

L.
Twitchen

Goutsland
nnmills

N. Hele

Craneham

Frithelstock
PRIORY

Frithelstock

Frithelstock Stone

Ash

Preston

Cleave

Castle Hill

New
Br.

Great
Torrington

Taddiport
23m

Rosemoor

Ley

N. Healand

Kingscott

Ebberley Ho.
Combe
Barton

Rapson
Cliston

Melbury Resr.

Bilsford

HEMBURY CASTLE

Smithacott

Priestacott
Stretchacott

Eckworthy

Tythecott

Ashbury

Knoworthy

Bowden
Watergate Br.
126m

Hill

S. Healand

Whitsleigh

Roborough
174m

6m

Collingsdown

Milford

Vielstone

Hollamoor

Southcott

Little Torrington
Beaslake

Smytham

Woodland
EARTHWORK

Castle
Hill
Monkleigh
Barton

ENCLOSURE

Ramscliffe

Owlacombe
Villavin

Galsworthy

195m

Cholash

Bibbear
Buda

Langtree Week

Hollam
Homer

Long
Wood

Kiverley
B 3230

Pearson
Higher
Upcott

Down

Mamhury

Thorn
Moor

Holwell

Withacott

Langtree

Collacott

Bagbear

Hunshaw

Abbot's Hill

Stowford

Eastacott

Bower

Stibb Cross
A 388

Burstone

Berry Cross
Yard

Gt. Potheridge
Speccott
Barton

Warham

Beaford

Harepath

Beaford Moor
180m
TUMULI

Bulkworthy

Downmoor
Venn

Binworthy

Browns

Rivaton
176m

Suddon

Lit. Potheridge
Dunsbear

Whiteland
Head

Buckland

Ashwell

Iddlecott
B 3217

Bickington

Eastbridge

Darpley
DURPLEY
CASTLE

Badworthy

Stapleton

Woollaton
Week

Willeswill

Dunsbear Halt
Moorhill
150m

Merton
Mill

Greatwood

Venton

Halscott Ho.

Down

Dolton

Woodford Br.

L. Combe

Mineral Line

Merton

Ford

Langham

Chapple
Eastacott

Forestreet
Shop
Whitebear

Newton St. Petrock
Holwill

Rowden

Ladford
169m

Paddon

Alscott
Galmington

Awsland

Stone

Allisland

Lit. Marland

Heaton
Barton

Rosehill
Burymoor Bry.
Burstone

Huish

Woodtown

Lowistone

Milton Damerel

Gratton

Vaddicott

Caute

Pennicknold

Grascott

110m

Brightmans
Hayes
170m

Bury

Broadmead

Dowland

R. Torridge

Bagbeare

Oxenpark

Chapel Gidcott

Bramblecombe
Brake
Whitemoor

Eastpark

Crawley

Berry
Pidbridge

Ruxhill

College

Buckland
Filleigh
Ho.

West
Heanton

North Town

Petrockstow

Stone
Stockleigh
Barton

149m

Upcott

Bagbear

Henscott

Shebbear

Dumpinghall

4°10'W

Hartleigh

Halwood

Ash
Moor

Mine

Meeth

Iddesleigh

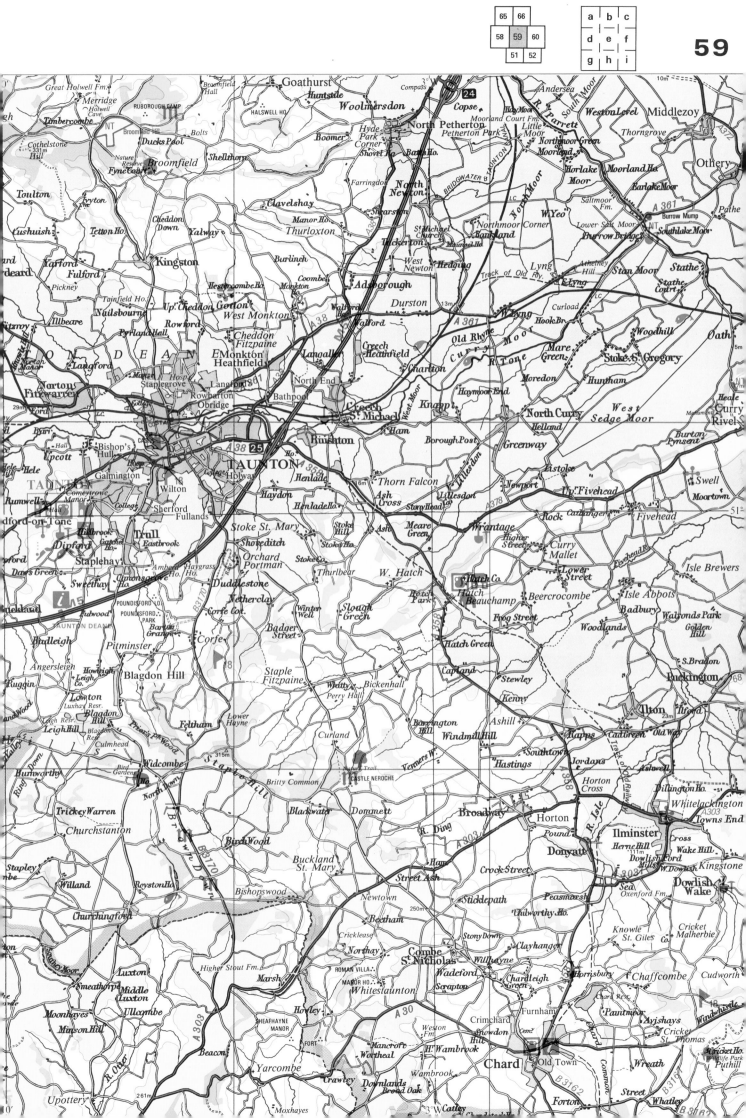

a	b	c
d	e	f
g	h	i

62	63
55	56

0 1 2 3 4 5 Miles

0 1 2 3 4 5 6 7 8 Kilometres

10'

LUNDY (*To Devon*)

Hen & Chickens
Seals'R.ᵏ
North West Pt.
North East Pt.
North End
Gannets' Bay
Mousehole & Trap
St. James's Stone
Knoll Pins
Tibbetts' Pt.
Gull R.ᵏ
45°
Jenny's Cove
Needle R.ᵏ
Beacon Hill Lundy
(Disused)
Half Tide R.ᵏ
Goat I.
Shutter Pt.
Lundy Roads
Quay
Lt. Shutter R.ᵏ
Rat I.
to Ilfracombe
The Race
Black R.ᵏ

19 miles west of Morte Point

B R I S T O L

Watermouth

Ilfracombe

to Lundy Island

Samson's Bay
Billage Point CG
Widmouth Hd.
Burrow Nose
Hangman Pt.
Rawns Rocks
Beacon Pt. Hele Bay
Watermouth Cave
Combe Martin
Little Hangman
Watermouth Castle
Bay
Wild Pear Beach
Capstone Pt.
Hillsborough
18 Lydford
Sandy Bay
Comb
LB
Ilfracombe
A 399
Widmouth Hill
Brandy Cove Pt.
Hele
Home Barton
Flat Pt.
Beera
Shag Pt.
Torrs
Cairn Top
Hagginton
Berrynarbor
Lee Bay
Lee
Clorridge Hill 147m
Bull Pt.
Lee
Pludd
Lincombe
Slade
Winsham Score
Warmscombe
Sterridge
Ruggaton
Hodges
Rockham Bay
NT
Hl. Warcombe
159m
Windcutter Hill
Shaftsborough
Slade Resrs
Oakridge
Cockhill
Woolscott Barton
Bodstone Barton
Henstridge
Morte Stone
N. Morte
135m
G. Shelfin
Bowden
Morte Pt.
Mortehoe
Two Pots
Ettiford
Hempster
Thornland
Twitchen
Mullacott Cross
B 3343
Grunta Pool
Twitchen
262m
Brinscott
Barricane Beach
NT
Seymour Villas
B 3343
Berry Down
Berry Down Cross
Dudland Hol
Woolacombe Hotel
Trimstone
Cleglinch
Yelloways
B 3230
Ossaborough
W. Stowford Barton
Narracott
E. Stowford Barton
Willingcott
Wigmoor
Morte Bay
200m
Blakwell
W. Down
Hobwell
Shortac
Roadway
Buttercombe
Lower Aylescott
Upcott
Collacott
Spreacombe
Dean
Bittadon
Reeds
262m
Fullabrook
237m
Bowden Corner
Hartnoll Barton
Bowden
Wheeler's Stone
Pickwell
Oxford Cross
N. Buckland
R. Caen
NT
Metcombe
Whitefield Barton
Okxewill
Baggy Pt.
Croyde Hoe
74m
Putsborough
Georgeham
Nethercott
Winsham Down Ho.
Halsinger Down
Patsford
Milltown
Viveham
Witchel
Middleborough Hill
CG
Croyde
Darracott
Halsinger
Rooklear
EARTHWORK
Upcott
Croyde Bay
B 3231
South Hole
Winsham
Bees Charter
117m
Middle Marwood
Higher Muddiford
Muddiford
141m
Youlston
Saunton Down
139m
N. Lobb
THE CASTLE
Knowle
Boode
Westcott Barton
Marwood
Stoley Barton
North Hill
TERRACES
Lobb
Buckland
Ash Barton
Whitehall
Guineaford
Broomhill
167m
Saunton Court
St. Brannocks
Boode
Lee Ho.
Kingsheanton
Saunton Sands
Hotel B 3231
Pippacott
Prixford
Varley
Blakewell
Hartpiece
Brightlycott
18
Braunton
Luscott Barton
Mainstone
Tutshill
FORT
Coxleigh Barton
Braunton
Knowl Water
Horridge
Upcott
Raleigh Ho.
Heanton Punchardon
Ashford
Bradford Hl.
A 39
R. Yeo
Braunton Burrows
Wrafton
A 361
Bradford
Bradiford Water
NT
Pilton
Nature Trail
Line Closed
Chivenor
Penhill Pt.
Stoneyard
Braunton Marsh
Toll
Penhill
Barnstaple
Gorwell
Lilly

Barnstaple Bar

Saunton Sands

DANGER ZONE

Nature Trail
19m
Horsey I.
Fremington
Yelland
Bickington
Newport
Hele
Portmore
South Gut
The Neck
The Crow
(Disused)
East Yelland Power Station
R I V E R T A W
(Goods)
JUN
STA
Derby
10'

51°10'N

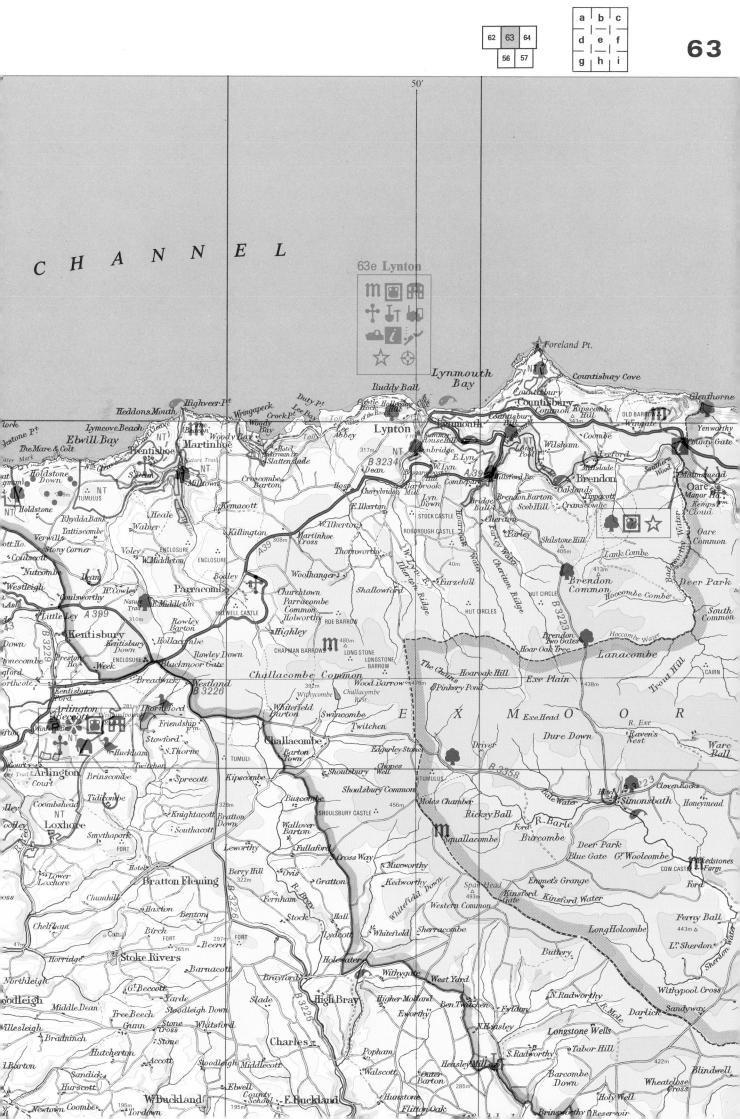

BRIDGWATER BAY

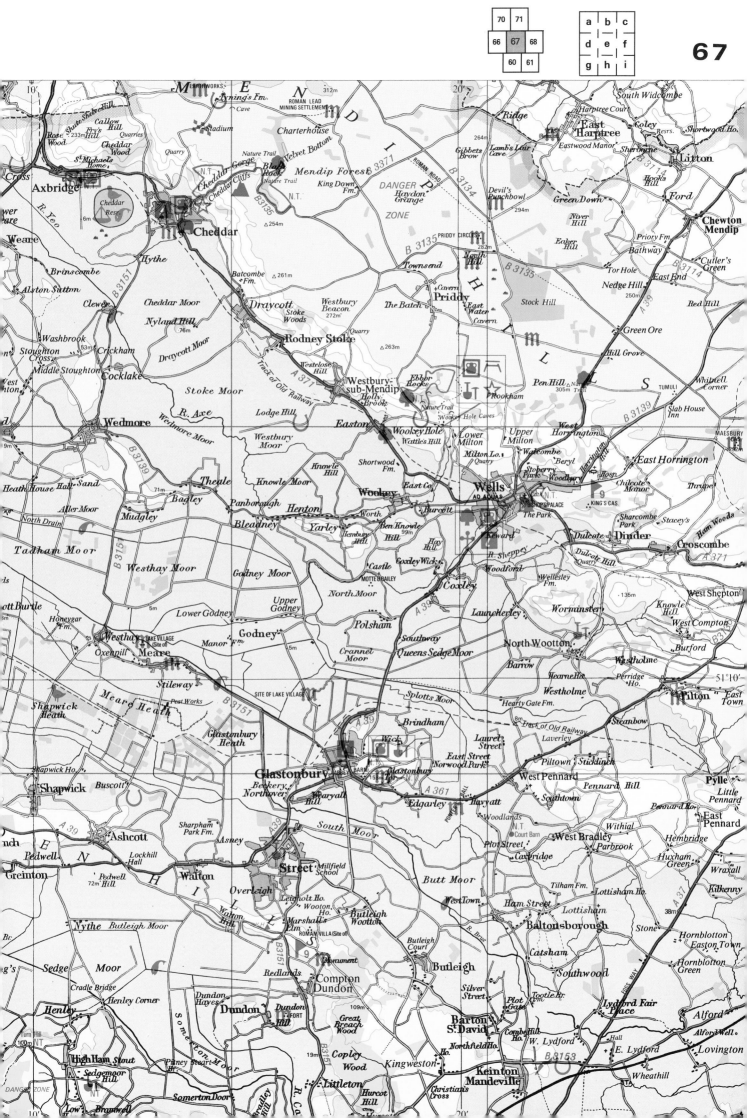

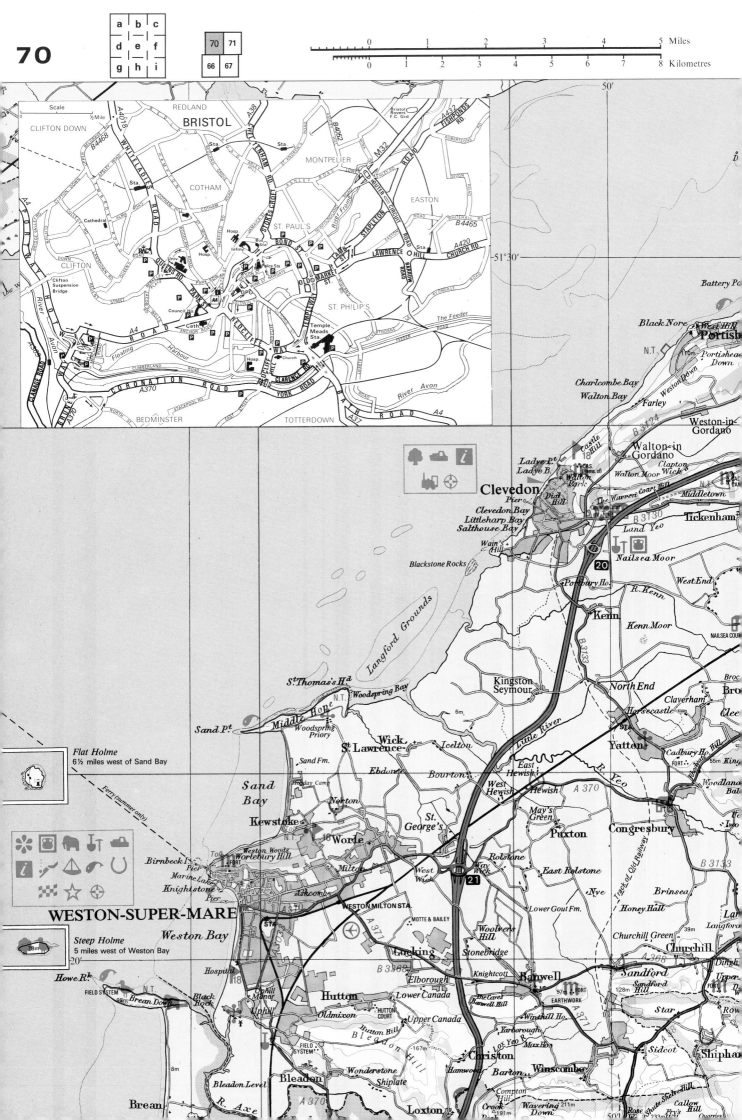

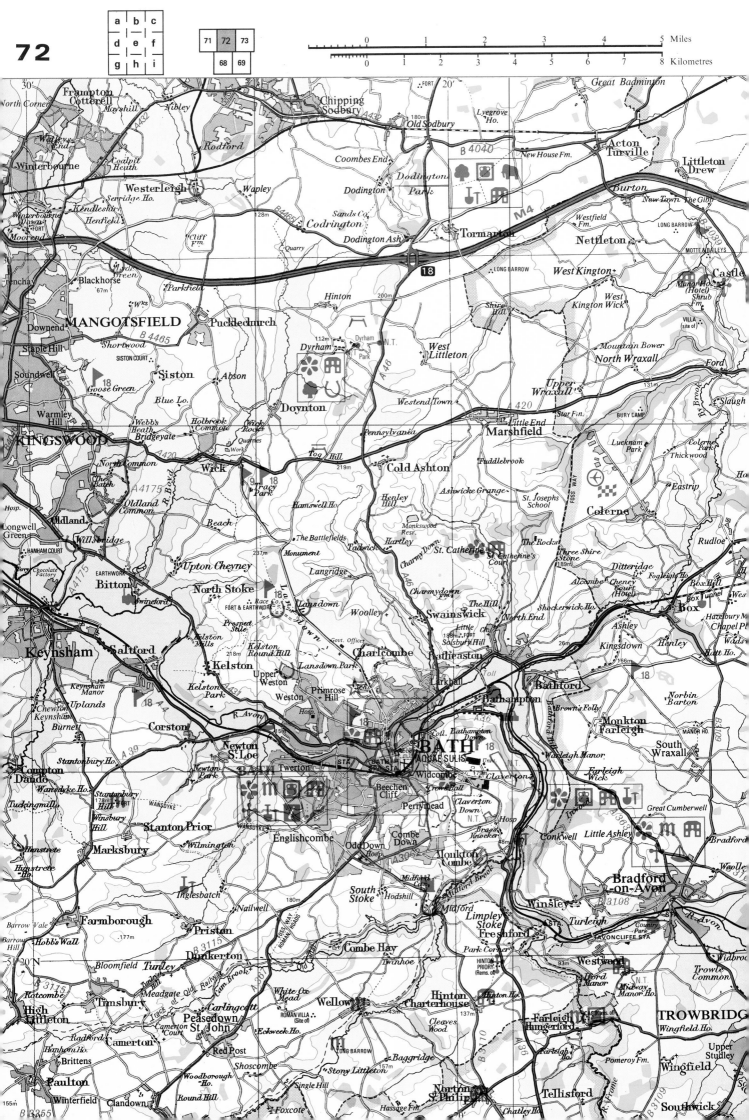

Countryside

Nature trails, scenic walks, country parks, field and nature study centres and areas of outstanding natural beauty, including woods, waterfalls, moors, coastline and interesting natural features. See page 10 for details of long distance walks and National Parks.

19d Cape Cornwall. Enjoyable coastal walk to Lands End, taking in interesting caves at Polpry Cove.

19f Penzance: Penlee Memorial Park. 15 acres of lovely parkland with sports facilities.

20e The Loe. Footpaths, from the car park behind the lake, provide beautiful walks around this peaceful, unspoilt area of cliffs, shingle beach, sea and freshwater, with woodland and farmland beyond.

20i Poltesco: Cadgwith Nature Trail. Circular 3 mile walk through wooded valley past caves and cliffs with interesting rock formations.

20i Frying Pan Caves. Footpath from Church Cove leads to an enormous crater caused by the collapse of a cavern roof.

20i Kynance Cove. Well known beauty spot with a series of caves and curiously named rocks (Asparagus Island, Devil's Bellows etc) which can be explored, but beware of being cut off by the rising tide. *Low tide only.*

22b Holy Vale. Higher Moors Trail covers 1 mile through wooded valley and marsh to the seashore, past a lake with notable aquatic plants and ferns. Lower Moors Trail offers a ½ mile walk through marshland and withy plantation along the bank of a drainage dyke.

23g Navax Point. Splendid cliff walk with many flowers and ferns, including the royal fern and sea spleenwort. Good place to watch seals, which breed in the caverns to the east of the point.

24a Holywell Bay. Unspoilt beach, backed by high dunes, with a cave visited by pilgrims for the healing properties of the water contained in its natural rock basins.

24b Newquay: Yonder Towan Field Centre (tel. 063 73 2756). Holidays arranged covering all aspects of the local history and countryside. Equipment supplied. Minimum age 14. *March to June; August to November.*

24h Trelissick. Nature trail through superb park, planted in 1820s; also woodland with views over the Fal estuary. *March to October: daily 1100-1800.* ➤ ✿

25f Hall Walk. Charming walk along the north and south banks of Pont Pill, through the restored hamlet of Pont with its delightful quays and footbridge.

26a Woodlay: Deerpark Woods. Forest trail through 130 acres of mixed conifer and broad-leaved woods. Natural habitat supports a wide variety of animals, including red deer.

27a Anthony House, Torpoint (tel. Plymouth 0752 812191). Extensive grounds with fine lawns and woods, filled with flowering shrubs. *1 April to 30 October: Tuesday to Thursday and Bank Holiday Mondays; 1400-1730.* ✿ ⊞

27b Mount Edgcumbe Country Park. Estate of wooded avenues, a deer park and fine lawns which sweep down to and give good views of Plymouth Sound. *Daily. Free.* ➤ ✿ ⊞

27c Saltram House Park (tel. Plymouth 0752 336546). Fine expanse of landscaped park and woodland. *April to end October daily: 1100-1800. November to end March daily: dawn to dusk.* ➤ ✿ ⊞

29d Slapton Ley: Nature Trail covers 1½ miles along the inner shore of a 460 acre nature reserve, starting from Slapton Bridge. Shingle Walk is a 3

mile footpath along Slapton Sands, with views of rare plants and seabirds.

29e Slapton Field Study Centre (tel. Kingsbridge 0548 580466). Residential courses available on all aspects of the surrounding countryside, including the study of wild flowers. Unaccompanied children over 16 accepted. ➤

30h Newquay. See 24b.

31h Lanhydrock House (tel. Bodmin 0208 3320). Nature trail through woods and particularly beautiful country park, which falls to the valley of the River Fowey. *Daily: dawn to dusk.* ➤ ✿ ⊞

31i Cardinham Woods. Forest trails through woods which form part of Kernow Forest. In addition there are splendid panoramic walks with views of the valley.

32d Cannaframe: Halvana Plantation. Forest trail of 1½ miles through conifer woods of Norway and Sitka spruce.

32e Cheesewring. An extraordinary pile of granite stones, in which the largest are held up by the smaller ones, sitting atop 1250 ft high Cheesewring Hill. Well worth a visit.

33c Lydford Gorge (tel. 082 282 320). 1½ mile long gorge, scooped out by the River Lyd into a succession of potholes—like the Devil's Cauldron—emerging into a steep-sided wooded valley; an enchanting riverside walk leads to the graceful 90 ft White Lady waterfall. Access from Lydford village or from Manor Farm. *April to end October: daily 0900 to dusk. November to end March: daily from Manor Farm only.*

34b Fernworthy Reservoir. 6 mile circular walk through Fernworthy Forest, part of Dartmoor National Park.

34b Bellever Forest. Walk through a plantation of Norway and Sitka spruce and Contorta pine. Good views of the East Dart River. ➤

34c Moretonhampstead. Quiet, beautiful walk to the Giants Grave on Mardon Down (39c), along twisting lanes over open moorland.

34c Manaton. 4 mile ramble starting at the church, to Easdon Tor and Whooping Rock, supposed to

Picnic Sites

These are usually situated in areas of natural beauty, often with a nature trail or walk nearby. They generally consist of wooden tables, log seats, litter bins (please use) and, if near a road, parking spaces. Do not expect any conveniences or other facilities. Although mainly run by the Forestry Commission, others are maintained by local councils, National Parks, the National Trust and by private concerns.

Although the blue symbol above is used to indicate a picnic site on the maps, many locations are marked 'on the ground' with signs bearing the symbol shown here.

cure children of whooping cough. Marvellous panoramic views of Dartmoor. See also 35a Lustleigh.

34d Two Bridges. 4 mile walk to Wistman's Wood—an oakwood protected by a ring of enormous stones—and to Beardown Tors with its marvellous views.

34e Dartmeet Bridge. Waymarked walk of 3-6 miles via Yar Tor and Corndon Tor overlooking the beautiful valley of the East Dart River.

34f Widecombe in the Moor. 3 mile walk up Bonehill and north onto Honeybag Tor with breathtaking views.

34f Haytor Rocks. 2 walks (7 or 4 miles) to Hound Tor and Saddle Tor, via Becka Brook. Although not a dangerous walk, beware of mists—take a map, compass and waterproof clothing. ▲

34f New Bridge. 2 walks: a 4 mile loop north alongside the River Dart, through the beautiful woods of Holne Chase, then west to Poundsgate; and a 6/7 mile walk to Venford Reservoir through the delightful village of Holne.

34f Hembury Woods. 1½ mile circular walk through oak woods beside the River Dart.

34h Shipley Bridge. 1½ mile walk to the beautiful Avon Reservoir set amidst open moorland.

34i Cross Furzes. 5 mile circular walk to the Avon Reservoir (34h) partly following the Abbots Way—a post-road linking Buckfast Abbey with Buckland Abbey.

35a Lustleigh. 6 mile circular walk to Manaton (34c) via Hunters Tor (steep climb) and back through the valleys of the River Bovey and Becka Brook (see 35a Becky Falls).

35a Becky Falls (tel. Manaton 064 722 259). Beautiful and unspoilt waterfall set in 50 acres of natural woodland; riverside walks. *Easter to late Autumn. Free.* ➤

35a Yarner Wood: National Nature Reserve. 2 walks: The Dartmoor Trail of 1½ miles through woodland and heathland with trailside exhibits; and the Woodland Walk, a 3 mile extension of the trail which introduces woodland conservation and management techniques and the work of the Nature Conservancy Council.

35b Haldon Forest. Several waymarked walks, both north and south of the racecourse, can be found in this large forest, which is run by the Forestry Commission.

35b Hennock. 5 mile walk—tough and demanding—through Bovey Forest, past a recently restored Elizabethan mansion at Canonteign Barton, and alongside Beadon Brook.

35b Chudleigh. 3 mile circuit around the peaceful village and its surrounding countryside, including Ugbrooke Park. ⊞ ☆

35b Ugbrooke House (tel. Chudleigh 0626 852179). Park designed by Capability Brown; two lakes and magnificent scenery. *May Bank Holiday Sunday and Monday, then June to September Sunday to Thursday 1400-1730.* ⊞

35b Ideford. Series of walks around this picturesque rural village, all starting from the Royal Oak pub.

35c Kenton. 4 mile walk exploring the countryside around Powderham Castle and the rivers Exe and Kenn. ⌂ ⊞

35e Bradley Manor. Delightful 3 mile ramble through the grounds along the banks of the River

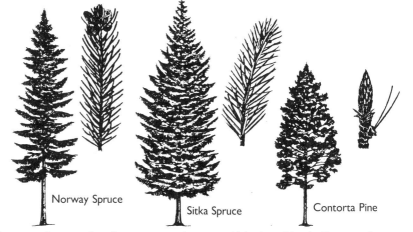

Norway Spruce Sitka Spruce Contorta Pine

Above are three species of trees among the most widely planted by the Forestry Commission.

Lemon. *Early April to end September. Wednesdays 1400-1700.* 🏛

35f Coombe Cellars. Attractive and unusual 4 mile walk along the south bank of the River Teign Estuary. Attention must be paid to tide tables and waterpoof clothing should be taken.

35f Teignmouth. 5 mile walk from the sea wall to Dawlish, including flat and hill walking on country roads and farm tracks.

36b Crackington Haven. Some of the most splendid cliff-walking in England; 500 acres of land stretch unbroken for 3 miles.

36b Rocky Valley. Footpath follows a pretty wooded vale east to the magnificent St Nectan's Kieve waterfall, a double cascade that plunges down mossy rocks. ☆

37g Cannaframe. See 32d.

37g Cheesewring. See 32e.

38e Lydford Gorge. See 33c.

38i Two Bridges. See 34d.

39b Bowden: The Teign Gorge. Excellent 5 mile walk both on the heights above and alongside the river. Also explores the pretty village of Drewsteignton and the magnificent Castle Drogo. 🏰

39c Steps Bridge. 2 mile nature trail through Dunsford Wood and alongside the River Teign.

39d Fernworthy Reservoir. See 34b.

39d Bellever Forest. See 34b.

39f Moretonhampstead. See 34c.

39f Manaton. See 34c.

39f Lustleigh. See 35a.

39f Becky Falls. See 35a.

39f Yarner Wood. See 35a.

39g Dartmeet Bridge. See 34e.

39h Widecombe in the Moor. See 34f.

39h New Bridge. See 34f.

39h Hembury Woods. See 34f.

39i Haytor Rocks. See 34f.

40a Steps Bridge. See 39c.

40d Hennock. See 35b.

40e Haldon Forest. See 35b.

40e Chudleigh. See 35b.

40e Ugbrooke House. See 35b.

40e Ideford. See 35b.

40f Kenton. See 35c.

40g Bradley Manor. See 35e.

40h Coombe Cellars. See 35f.

40i Teignmouth. See 35f.

41c Farway Country Park (tel. 040 487 224). 130 acres of natural countryside with nature trails and walks. *4 April to 30 September; Sunday to Friday and Bank Holiday Saturdays; 1000-1700.* 🐾 🗺

41d Budleigh Salterton. Walk on 500 ft high cliffs gives amazing views of the whole of Lyme Bay.

42e Dowlands Cliffs and Landslips Nature Reserve. A 5 mile coastal strip covering 800 acres, where a massive landslip occurred in 1839. 7 mile nature trail from Axmouth (42d) to Lyme Regis (42f) on which can be seen a large variety of wildlife, including badgers, lizards and over 400 species of wild flower.

42f Stonebarrow Hill. 3½ mile walk into the Golden Cap Estate, with open heathland, rolling hills and rugged cliffs from which there are magnificent views.

43d Golden Cap. Fine views from this 617 ft high cliff, the highest in southern England.

43i Chesil Beach. 18 mile natural breakwater made up of pebbles thrown up by tides and storms and

graded by the sea into sizes—from 3½ inches at Portland (44h) down to less than 1 inch at Abbotsbury.

44a Hardy Monument. 3½ mile walk, from the monument south to the village of Portersham, with impressive views of Weymouth, Portland, Chesil Beach and Abbotsbury.

44b Higher Bockhampton. 4 mile walk through the heart of Hardy Country, taking in Stinsford church, Hardy's cottage and Puddletown Heath. 🏛 ✝

44c Puddletown Forest. Nature trail of 3 miles through pleasant woodland, mainly composed of conifers. Also a mile of rhododendrons and abundant wildlife, including deer. 🦌

44d Chesil Beach. See 43i.

44d East Fleet. 3½ mile walk through this tiny village, made famous by J. M. Faulkner's novel "Moonfleet", and beyond to The Fleet, a salt-water lake behind Chesil Beach.

44f Ringstead. 3 mile walk from Osmington Mills to Burning Cliff where a peat fire, perhaps started by lightning, burnt for 6 years in the 18th century.

45b Northport Heath. 2½ mile nature trail through the pine trees of Wareham Forest; many deer and small mammals.

45c Arne Heath Nature Reserve. ¾ mile trail through a variety of trees and plants. 🦌

45d Dagger's Gate. 8 mile circular walk south to Durdle Door, then west to Swyre Head and White Nothe and back along Chaldon Down; magnificent views.

45d Lulworth Cove. 3 mile walk from one of the most famous beauty spots on the Dorset coast over Dungy Head to Durdle Door an impressive natural arch of Portland stone standing in the sea.

45e West Orchard Farm. 4½ mile walk to Corfe Castle (45f) across beautiful countryside typical of the Isle of Purbeck.

45f East Hill: The Purbeck Hills. 4½ mile walk east to Brenscombe Hill and Nine Barrow Down, part of a barrier of chalk hills; wonderful views.

45f Kingston. Magnificent 3½ mile walk south to the unspoilt area of Chapman's Pool and Hounstout Cliff.

45f Worth Matravers. 5 mile walk to Winspit and thence along the coast to St Adhelm's Head (45i). Tremendous views of the Purbeck coast.

46b Bursdon Moor: Summerwell Nature Trail. 1½ mile walk through Hartland Forest.

46e Coombe Valley. 1½ mile nature trail through a small oak wood and part of a Forestry Commission plantation. 🦌

46e Bude: Ebbingford Manor Park (tel. 0288 2808). Nature trail in the extensive grounds. *Early June to mid September; Tuesday to Thursday; also July to September Sundays; 1400-1730.* 🏛

46g Crackington Haven. See 36b.

47i Passaford. 3 mile walk through wooded country around the River Lew and Medland Brook.

48f Eggesford Barton. 2 walks, each of 1 mile, through Eggesford Forest, one of the first acquisitions of the Forestry Commission. 🗺

48g Passaford. See 47i.

49a Yard: Rose Ash Woods. Densely wooded combe beside a brook, crossed by the attractive Cuckoo Mill Bridge.

49f Bickleigh. 5 mile walk that follows the River Exe, between the road and Backs Wood, to Tiverton.

49i Stoke Wood. 1½ mile walk through mixed woodland, jointly sponsored by the Forestry Commission and Exeter City Council. 🗺

51b Castle Neroche. 2 mile nature trail through the broadleaf and conifer woodlands of Neroche Forest 🏰

51g Farway Country Park. See 41c.

52b Ham Hill Country Park. Historic hill-top site, formerly a quarry, with outstanding views. 🗺

53b Sherborne Park. Walk through the grounds of Sherborne Castle (53a) which were laid out by Capability Brown. Rather boggy walk; it is advisable to wear waterproof clothing. Watch out for deer. *Easter Saturday to last Sunday in September; Thursdays, weekends and Bank Holiday Mondays; 1400-1800.* 🐾 🏰 🏛

53h Cerne Abbas. 8 mile circular walk through the town to Giant Hill, where the Giant is carved out of the hill, and north to Up Cerne, a beautiful hamlet with a 17th century manor house. 🏰

53i Puddletown Forest. See 44c.

54e Bursdon Moor. See 46b.

54f Wood Rock. Footpath west towards Blackchurch Rock offers a delightful secluded walk along the cliffs.

54f The Hobby. A delightful 3 mile track through woodlands with the occasional extensive view of the sea. Access from the Clovelly to Bideford road; can be done on foot or by car.

54g Coombe Valley. See 46e.

55b Braunton Burrows Nature Reserve. 2 nature trails: Braunton Marsh offers 1½ miles through the dunes and marshy depressions where rare plants, including orchids, grow; The Neck is 1½ miles along the shore. The Army uses the central area as a firing range. *No access when red flags fly.*

56h Eggesford Barton. See 48f.

57a Withypool Common. 3 mile walk north west to Landacre Bridge (64g) returning along the banks of the beautiful River Barle.

57b Winsford. 5½ mile circular walk south west through Burrow Wood to Winsford Hill and returning alongside Winn Brook, from which Winsford gets its name.

57b Tarr Steps. A short walk south to Hawkridge (2½ miles)—a pretty village typical of Exmoor—can be extended (to 7½ miles) to Anstey. This covers almost the whole spectrum of Exmoor landscape: large and small river valleys, hardwood and conifer plantations, farmland and open moorland. 🏰

57b Venford. 3½ mile walk along Dane's Brook, a tributary of the Barle, through the surrounding woods to Castle Bridge. There is a good chance of seeing herds of red deer.

57b Dulverton. 3½ mile walk up the magnificent valley of the River Barle to Court Down; remarkable mixture of trees, including sweet chestnuts (rare in the area); also much wildlife.

57c Baronsdown: Louisa Gate. 5 mile walk (very steep in places) through the Pixton Estate, with oak woods and rhododendrons; thence east along the Lower Haddeo Valley to Hartford. Good chance of sighting red deer.

57d Yard. See 49a.

57i Beside A 396. See 49f Bickleigh.

58a Raleighs Cross. 6½ mile walk around Treborough Common and the old railway line of the iron ore mines. Starts at the viewpoint on B3190, with its remarkable view to North Exmoor and the coast. Walk involves steep climbs.

59a Fyne Court. Former pleasure grounds of the now demolished house of pioneer electrician Andrew Crosse; it is now a visitor centre for the Quantocks and headquarters of the Somerset Trust for Nature Conservation. *Daily 0900-1800 (dusk if earlier). Free.*

59e Castle Neroche. See 51b.

60e Ham Hill Country Park. See 52b.

61d Sherborne Park. See 53b.

62d Morte Bay. In the summer this is a stunning beach, one of the finest in North Devon; wild flowers and butterflies abound in the dunes; ideal picnic spots.

62g Baggy Point. National Trust headland with foreshore riddled with caves; seals can often be seen on rocks around the caves.

62h Braunton Burrows. See 55b.

63b Valley of the Rocks. 2½ mile walk in a covered valley with pillars of rock which have been eroded into strange shapes. The most impressive is the 800 ft high Castle Rock; others have names like Ragged Jack, The Devil's Cheesewring and White Lady. Wild goats can often be seen.

63c Countisbury. 2½ mile walk (with steep climbs) on the Foreland, 1000 ft above Lynmouth Bay; staggering views. Access from Barna Barrow car park. ☆

63c Glenthorne. 3 mile nature trail through the Glenthorne Estate to a beach of coloured pebbles. Footpath passes a derelict Victorian icehouse, where snow stored in winter did not melt until midsummer because the building was always in shade.

63d Holdstone Down. Wonderful views from 1000 ft cliff-edged moors; Sherrycombe Valley Waterfall drops 100 ft into the sea but is more visible from offshore (boat trips from Combe Martin, see page 107).

63d Milltown. Nature trail starts from Hunters Inn alongside the River Heddon, emerges from the woods into a deep ravine and ends at the small rock-bound cove of Heddon's Mouth.

63d Cowley Cleave Nature Trail. ¾ mile walk by a fast flowing stream into mixed woodland with a large viewing hide.

63d Arlington Court. (tel. Shirwell 027 182 296). Nature trail explores the park, woodlands and lake and takes approximately 1 hour. *Daily during daylight hours.* ☞ ✻ ▣ ⊞ ✝ 🐎 ↳

63e Lynbridge: Glen Lyn Gorge.   Spectacular water course where the West Lyn River has gouged a ½ mile ravine.

63e Driver (B3358). 4 mile walk north to Pinkery Pond on an old road built for the carriage of lime. Very wet area, the source of many Exmoor rivers.

63f Countisbury Hill: Watersmeet. Popular and beautiful walk (well signposted) in the wooded valley of East Lyn River, from the confluence of the East Lyn, Farley and Hoaroak Water, west to Lynmouth.

63f Hillsford Bridge. 4 mile walk following Hoaroak Water to Watersmeet and the East Lyn River to Rockford, both in densely wooded valleys.

63f Malmsmead. 3 mile walk in popular 'Doone Valley'; follows the Badgworthy Water and Oare Water via Oare Church ▣ ☆

63f Brendon Common. Start of a 7½ mile walk to the 'Doone Valley' where the famous fictional characters of R D Blackmore's "Lorna Doone" played out their life. Well signposted, it runs down the valley of Badgworthy Water to Cloud Farm and back over Malmsmead Hill. Not a tough walk.

63f Brendon Two Gates. 4½ mile walk to the head of the River Exe and Hoaroak Water over isolated, lonely moorland, with some bogs; stout walking shoes advisable.

63i Simonsbath. 6½ mile walk above and along the valley of the River Barle south east to Cow Castle, through conifer woods.

64a Glenthorne. See 63c.

64d Malmsmead. See 63f.

64d Oareford: Robbers Bridge. 4½ mile walk along Weir Water to Pitt Farm through a plantation of conifers. Peaceful and enjoyable area of Exmoor.

64d Hookway Hill. 3½ mile walk, from the car park at the start of the Porlock toll road, east to Porlock Common and Hawkcombe, a beautiful wooded valley. 🌲

64e Porlock Weir. 5 mile walk west through the mixed woodland and rhododendrons of Yearnor Woods to Culbone (64d) and its tiny chapel. ✝

64e Bossington Hill. 3 mile walk circling the hill, with another path going north west to Hurlstone Point (dangerous). Good access to an area full of superb viewpoints over the north east of Exmoor.

64e Horner Mill. 4 mile walk south along the delightful wooded valley of Horner Water and through Horner Wood itself, which is being preserved by the National Trust. ☞

64e Horner Hill. 2¾ mile walk on the National Trust's Holnicote Estate, exploring the Luccombe and Horner Plantations. Start from the symbol which marks the car park at Webber's Post, one of the most attractive places to park in all Exmoor. 🌲

64e Brockwell. Arduous 6 mile walk south west to Dunkery Beacon, rewarded when visibility is good by particularly fine views of north Exmoor.

64f Minehead: North Hill Nature Trail. 3¾ mile circular trail passing through woodland and heathland with abundant wildlife.

64f Dunster Park (tel. 064 382 314). 30 acres of woodland around Dunster Castle with 3¼ mile walk through an enclosed 18th century Deer Park with many fine trees. *Early April to end September: Sunday to Thursday 1100-1630. October: Tuesdays, Wednesdays and Sundays 1400-1530.* ✻ 🏚 ⊞ 🌲

64g Exford. 2 walks: 8½ mile walk south in and around the valley of the River Exe following the area's many bridleways; also a 5 mile footpath leading north to Exford Common and Dunkery

Beacon, the highest point of Exmoor (1075 ft), with spectacular views.

64g Waterhouse. See 57a Withypool Common.

64h Winsford. See 57b.

64h Tarr Steps. See 57b.

64i Brendon. 4 mile walk through forestry plantations and across pastures to Lype Hill, one of the highest points in the Brendons. 🌲

65g Nettlecombe Court: Leonard Wills Field Centre (tel. Washford 098 44 320). One week residential courses available on various topics connected with the countryside. *February to November.* ⊞ ↳

65g Raleighs Cross. See 58a.

65i Adscombe: Quantock Forest Trail. 3 miles through woodland on the edge of the Quantock Hills; abundant wildlife including deer. Start at the Seven Wells Bridge.

66g Fyne Court. See 59a.

67b Black Rock Nature Reserve. 1½ mile circular nature trail through plantation, woodland and downland grazing.

67b Ebbor Gorge Nature Trail. 2 walks through a gorge similar to Cheddar but enclosed in broadleaf woodlands and emerging on top of the Mendip Hills in magnificent scenery.

67c Pen Hill. 2½ mile nature trail offering geological interest as well as wildlife and plants.

67e Easton: The Moors Trail. 4 mile walk from the church south to Wookey through typical Somerset moorland.

67f Wells. 4 mile nature trail around the eastern side of the city through fields and woodland.

68i Stourhead (tel. Bourton 074 784 348). 1½ mile walk along a series of footpaths to a lake, Grotto, Pantheon and stone rotunda. *April, September and October: Mondays, Wednesdays, Saturdays and Sundays; May to August: daily (closed Fridays); 1400-1730 (sunset if earlier).* ✻ ⊞

69a Hawkeridge: Phillips Country Park   (tel. Westbury 0373 822238). 88 acres of natural woodland with nature walks and a Forestry exhibition. *All year daily: 1000 to dusk.* ☞ ▣

70f Clevedon: Poets Walk. 1 mile nature trail circling the headland of carboniferous limestone formed by the twin hills known as Church Hill and Wain's Hill (south of town).

70g Steep Holme Nature Reserve with interesting plants such as the wild peony. Boats from Weston-super-Mare. ↳

71b Leigh Woods National Nature Reserve. Woods where 110 kinds of mosses and liverwort are recorded. Mixed conifers to broadleaf trees. 3 nature trails, starting from stone arch beside A369, explore these and a variety of wildlife, including badgers and foxes. ↳

71d Failand House Park. 363 acre National Trust estate with several farms and several attractive walks through extensive woods.

71e Ashton Court Nature Trail. 2 walks (1½ and 2⅓ miles) through park and woodland, with an abundance of deer.

72b Dyrham Park. 263 acre estate with 18th century deer park. *Daily 1200-1800 (sunset if earlier).* ☞ ✻ ⊞ 🌲

72b Dodington Park (tel. Chipping Sodbury 0454 318899). 700 acres of parkland laid out by 'Capability' Brown. *April to September: daily 1000-1700.* ☞ ▣ ⊞ 🐎 ⛲ ☆

72e Bathampton: Kennet and Avon Canal. 2 mile nature trail along the tow path to Widcombe, in the south-east suburbs of Bath.

72i Bradford-on-Avon: Barton Farm Country Park. Extensive grounds with walks down to the Avon and excellent views of the town.

Gardens and Arboreta

Cultivated, wild and herbal gardens, including privately owned ones which open at specific times of the year; formal arboreta; horticultural exhibitions; floral displays. For country parks see the section on the Countryside pages 74-76.

19e Trengwainton House. An outstanding collection of shrubs, including magnolias and rhododendrons, are displayed in the garden and surrounding park. The walled garden contains tender and sub-tropical plants not grown elsewhere in England. *March to October: Wednesday to Saturday and Bank Holidays; 1100-1800.*

19f Penzance: Morrab Gardens, Daniel Place. A profusion of sub-tropical plants grow in the mild climate, including palm-trees, camellia, myrtle, aloe and geranium.

21a Penjerrick Gardens (tel. Mawnan Smith 0326 659). Beautiful sub-tropical gardens with a fine display of spring-flowering shrubs. *1 March to end September: Wednesdays and Sundays, 1330-1630.*

21b Falmouth. The town's sub-tropical gardens are nationally famous and the exotic flowers, shrubs and trees lend a Mediterranean air to this seaside town. The Fox Rosehill and Gyllyngdune Gardens off Melvill Road and Kimbereley Park are well worth visiting.

21d Durgan: Glendurgan Gardens. Wide variety of fine trees and shrubs in a wooded valley. Walled and water gardens, laurel maze and a Giant's Stride. *March to end October: Mondays, Wednesdays and Fridays; 1030-1630.*

22b Tresco Abbey Gardens. Large collection of sub-tropical flora unique in the British Isles, including rare plants like the cabbage trees, Burmese honeysuckle and Himalayan ginger. *Weekdays 1000-1600.* 🔲 ✝

24b Newquay: Trenance Park, on A3075 (tel. 063 73 4385). 8 acres of landscaped grounds with a sheltered garden containing over 300 unusual varieties of shrubs and flowers. *Daily* 🍵 🔲 🐾 🔱 ✈

24f Probus: County Demonstration Garden and Arboretum (tel. Truro 0872 74282 ext 349). Demonstrates many aspects of garden layout, plant selection and the results of modern gardening techniques in a permanent display. *May to September: Monday to Wednesday and Fridays 1400-1700; Thursdays 1400-2000; Sundays 1400-1800. October to April: Thursdays 1400-1700.*

24f Trewithen Gardens (tel. St Austell 0726 882418). Outstanding landscaped garden of camellias, magnolias, rhododendrons and many rare plants of distinction. *March to September: Monday to Saturday and Bank Holidays 1400-1630. Nurseries open all year* ⊞

24h Truro: Boscawen Park. Large gardens with many sub-tropical plants.

24h Trelissick Garden. Large, well-planned garden with a fine collection of magnolias, rhododendrons and sub-tropical plants. *March to end October: daily 1100-1800 (sunset if earlier).* 🍵 🌸

25f Polruan: The Garden House. 2 acre garden with shrubs, roses, heathers, fuschias and many other colourful summer plants.

25g Caerhays Castle Gardens. Fine flowering shrubs with beautiful rhododendrons, azaleas, magnolias and camellias. *By permission only.* 🏰

27a Antony House Gardens (tel. Plymouth 0752 812191). Extensive grounds and gardens include lawns and woods filled with flowering shrubs and fine trees; some topiary. *April to September: Tuesday to Thursday and Bank Holiday Mondays 1400-1800.* 🌸 ⊞

27b Mount Edgcumbe Gardens. Especially fine and varied ornamental shrubberies; wide lawns

sweep down to the waters edge. *Higher gardens: 1 May to 30 September: Mondays and Tuesdays 1400-1800. Lower gardens and park: all year. Free.* 🍵 🌸 ⊞

27c Saltram House Gardens (tel. Plymouth 0752 336546). 300 acres of landscaped grounds with a shrub garden, 18th century octagonal summerhouse, an orangery built in 1775 and a small classical garden called Fanny's Bower. *November to end March: daily during daylight hours. April to end October: daily 1100-1730.* 🍵 🌸 ⊞

28i Sharpitor Gardens. 6 acre garden with rare plants and shrubs overlooking the Salcombe estuary. *1 April to 31 October: daily 1100-1800.* 🔲 ⊓

29b Paignton: Zoological and Botanical Gardens, Totnes Road (tel. 0803 557479). 100 acres of zoo and gardens with tropical plants and shrubs, a palm house and woodland. *Daily 1000-1930 (1730 in winter).* 🍵 🐾

29c Paignton: Oldway Mansion Gardens (tel. 0803 550711). Contain a large variety of sub-tropical plants, rock gardens, two lakes, a waterfall, an Italian garden and woodland. *Daily. Free.* 🍵 ⊞

30h Newquay. See 24b.

31e Michaelstow: Bearoak Gardens. 2 acre garden containing plants useful to man in basket-making, dyeing, etc. — plus vegetables, oil seeds, and Grannie's herb garden with herbs used in old fashioned remedies. *Easter to October daily.*

31e Tremeer Gardens. 6 acres with a wide variety of camellias, rhododendrons, trees and shrubs. *April and May: Sundays and Wednesdays. June to September: daily.*

31e Pencarrow Gardens (tel. St Mabyn 020 884 369). 35 acres of woodland gardens with a large granite rockery, bog garden, palm house and an Italian garden around a lake. Large rhododendrons, camellias and hydrangeas and a specimen conifer collection; plant shop. *15 March to end September: daily.* 🍵 ⊞ ⊓

31h Lanhydrock House (tel. Bodmin 0208 3320). Extensive grounds with formal garden laid out in 1857; shrub garden with rhododendrons, magnolias and fine view. *April to end October: daily 1100-1800; November to end March: daily, daylight hours.* 🍵 🌸 ⊞

33g Cotehele (tel. St Dominick 0579 50434). Terrace garden falling to sheltered valley with ponds, stream and unusual shrubs. *April to 23 December: daily 1100-1700.* 🍵 ⊞ 🔱⊤ 🍽

33h Buckland Monachorum: The Garden House (tel. Yelverton 082 285 2493). Trees, lawns and terraces in attractive landscape; collection of flowering shrubs; ornamental cherries. *Early April to Mid September: Wednesdays 1500-1900; also by appointment.*

33h Bickham House. Shrub garden with camellias, rhododendrons and azaleas; good views. *April to July: Sundays 1400-1800.* 🍵

35f Shaldon: Homeyards Botanical Gardens. Fine collection of plants; extensive views of the estuary.

35g Dartington Hall Gardens. (tel. Totnes 0803 864171). Large landscaped garden with ornamental trees and shrubs laid around 14th century Hall. Garden centre. *Daily.* 🔱⊤

35h 35i Paignton. See 29b, 29c.

35i Torre Abbey Mansion, The Kings Drive (tel. 0803 23593). Italian garden, water garden and palm house with a wealth of sub-tropical plants; extensive views. *April to October: daily 1000-1730.* 🔲 ⊞

36g Tremeer Gardens. See 31e.

36g Pencarrow Gardens. See 31e.

36h Michaelstow. See 31e.

40b Exeter University (see town plan). Set in 300 acres of beautiful grounds it has an arboretum containing 150 species of trees.

Northernhay Gardens. Laid out in 17th century beyond the city walls, it is believed to be the oldest public park in Britain.

40i Shaldon. See 35f.

41a Bicton Gardens (tel. Colaton Raleigh 0395 68465 or Budleigh Salterton 039 54 3881). Italian garden, designed by Andre le Nôtre in 1735; American garden, including rare Montezuma pine; Pinetum with an outstanding collection of conifers; also tropical and cacti houses. *March to May: daily 1400-1800. May to September: daily 1100-1800.* 🍵 🔲 ⊓ 🍽

41b Sidmouth: Connaught Gardens. Fine views of the sea from lawns laid out with attractive flower displays.

41d Leeford: Lee Ford Gardens. Georgian house in 40 acres of parkland, containing spring bulb planting, herbaceous borders and flowering shrubs. *By appointment only: Mr Lindsay-Finn, Lee Ford, Budleigh Salterton.*

42a Dalwood Hill: Burrow Farm Garden. 4 acre woodland garden with rhododendrons, azaleas; pond with waterside planting. *Mid-April to mid-July: daily 1400-1900.* 🍵

42c Forde Abbey (tel. South Chard 0460 20231). 30 acre garden with many fine shrubs and specimen trees. Herbaceous border, rock, water and kitchen gardens, arboretum. *Easter Sunday and Monday; then May to September Sundays, Wednesdays and Bank Holiday Mondays: 1400-1800. March, April and October: Sundays 1400-1630.* 🍵 ⊞ ✝

43a Clapton Court Gardens (tel. Crewkerne 0460 73220 or 72200). One of Somerset's finest gardens: collection of rare and unusual trees and shrubs in formal and woodland settings; display of spring bulbs. Plant shop. *23 March to 20 October: Sunday to Friday 1400-1700.*

43b Parnham House. (tel. Beaminster 0308 862204). 14 acre garden: Yew Terrace comprising topiary of 50 clipped yews; balustraded ladies terrace; formal garden at East Court; Italian garden, glade and wilderness. *April to October: Sundays, Wednesdays and Bank Holidays 1000-1700. Also Tuesdays and Thursdays by appointment.* 🍵 ⊞ ⊓ 🔱⊤

43b Mapperton. Terraced and hillside garden surrounding a Tudor and Jacobean mansion: daffodils, formal borders and specimen shrubs and trees; orangery; 18th century stone fish ponds and summerhouse. *10 March to 10 October: weekdays 1400-1800.*

43c Melbury House. Large garden with very fine arboretum; wide variety of shrubs; beautiful deer park. *Early July to early September: certain Thursdays only 1400-1800.*

43i Abbotsbury Gardens (tel. Abbotsbury 030 587 387). 16 acre 18th century garden: fine collection of rhododendrons, azalias, camellias; wide variety of unusual tender trees and shrubs. Plant shop. *Mid-March to mid-October: daily 1000-1730.* 🐾

44c Athelhampton (tel. Puddletown 030 584 363). 10 acres of formal garden architecture: walled gardens, fountains and pools, dovecote, river and

wild gardens. *Early April to mid October Wednesdays, Thursdays and Sundays; Good Friday and Bank Holidays; also August Tuesdays and Fridays; 1400-1800.* 🍷🏛

44e Weymouth. The corporation's gardeners create impressive floral displays in gardens all along the promenade, especially at **Greenhill Gardens** and **Nothe Gardens.**

45c Poole: **Compton Acres Gardens,** Canford Cliffs Road (tel. 0202 78036). 15 acre garden, reputed to be one of the finest in Europe, overlooking Poole Harbour; includes Japanese, Italian, rock and water gardens, woodland and a subtropical glen. Plant shop. *April to end October: daily 1030-1830.*

47c Rosemoor Garden Charitable Trust. Started in 1959, the garden includes rhododendrons, ornamental trees and shrubs, primulas, roses, an arboretum, scree and raised beds with alpine plants. Plant shop. *April to end October: daily dawn to dusk.*

48a Roborough: Bickham House (tel. Plymouth 0752 72166). Shrub garden, camellias, rhododendrons, azaleas, cherries, bulbs and trees. *May to July: Sundays 1400-1800.* 🍷

50a Knightshayes Court (tel. Tiverton 088 42 4665). Large woodland garden overlooking River Exe. Contains shrub garden with rarities, fine specimen trees, formal terraces and summerflowering borders. *April to 31 October: daily 1100-1800.* 🍷🏛

50g Killerton (tel. Hele 039 288 345). 15 acres of spectacular hillside gardens sweep down to large open lawns. Walks through fine collection of rare trees and shrubs, including magnolias, azaleas, cork oak and conifers. *Daily during daylight hours.* 🍷 �m 🏛 ℹ

50h B3174: Fernwood Gardens. 2 acre woodland with a wide selection of flowering shrubs, conifers and bulbs, selected to give colour over a long period. *1 April to 30 September daily.*

51h Dalwood Hill. See 42a.

52a Barrington Court. Garden laid out in 1920s by Gertrude Jekyll: lily, iris and rose gardens with wall shrubs and borders. *Wednesdays only: 1015-1215, 1400-1600 (1800 in Summer).* 🏛

52b East Lambrook Manor (tel. South Petherton 0460 40328). A bog garden and herb garden are features of the notable grounds designed by the late Mrs Margery Fish, well-known gardening writer. Many unusual plants. *Daily: 0900-1700.* 🏛

52c Tintinhull House. Beautiful 4 acre formal garden with mixed shrub and herbaceous borders, immaculate lawns, flagstone paths and water garden. *April to September: Wednesdays, Thursdays, Saturdays and Bank Holidays: 1400-1800.* 🏛

52c Montacute House (tel. Martock 093 582 3289). Fine example of Jacobean garden, which slopes from the house through a series of yew hedges and stone terraces. *April to October: Wednesday to Monday 1230-1800 (or sunset).* 🍷📺🏛⌐

52c Brympton: Brympton d'Evercy (tel. West Coker 093 586 2528). 10 acre formal garden with daisy, potpourri, herbaceous and shrub beds, extensive lawns, vineyard and lake. *1 May to late September: Saturday to Wednesday 1400-1800.* 🍷🏛⌐↓T

52d Forde Abbey. See 42c.

52e Clapton. See 43a.

52h Parnham House. See 43b.

52i Mapperton. See 43b.

53d Melbury House. See 43c.

53e Minterne House (tel. Cerne Abbas 030 03 370). Large shrub garden set in wooded valley; contains many varieties of Himalayan and Chinese rhododendrons, magnolias, azaleas and rare trees. *April to June; Sundays and Bank Holidays 1400-1800; also by appointment.*

53h Frampton: Hyde Crook (tel. Maiden Newton 030 02 204). 14 acres of woodland garden with flowering trees and plants; Japanese cherries; orchid house. *February and March Sundays; April Saturdays, Sundays and Mondays; May Sundays and Mondays; 1400-1900.*

55b Tapeley Park Gardens (tel. Instow 0271 860528). Beautiful Italian garden; walled kitchen garden. *Easter to October: Tuesday to Sunday and Bank Holidays 1000-1800.* 🍷🏛⌐

55e Rosemoor. See 47c.

55i Bickham House. See 48a.

56b Castle Hill (tel. Filleigh 059 86 336). Ornamental garden, large shrub and woodland garden and arboretum. *By appointment only.* 🏛

56g Bickham House. See 48a.

57f Combe Head Arboretum (tel. Bampton 039 83 287). Collection of many unusual trees shrubs, climbers, conifers and roses in 25 acres. *By appointment only.*

57i Knightshayes Court. See 50a.

58b Golden Farm: Gaulden Manor (tel. Lydeard St Lawrence 098 47 213). Medium-sized garden with bog plants, primulas and herb garden. Plant shop. *May to September Thursdays, Sundays and Bank Holidays 1400-1800.* 🍷🏛

59a Hestercombe House (tel. Taunton 0823 87222 or 87223). Garden, originally planned by Sir Edwin Lutyens and Gertrude Jekyll, is being restored: pools, borders and terraces; fine views. *May to September: Thursdays 1200-1700. Free.*

60a Mildeney Place (tel. Langport 0458 251229). Large landscaped garden with fine trees and a water garden. *Bank Holiday Mondays; also June to end September Wednesdays; 1400-1730.* 🏛

60c Lyte's Cary. Fine Elizabethan-style garden. Sir Henry Lyte based his *Niewe Herball* on the garden. *March to end October Wednesdays and Saturdays 1400-1800.* 🏛✝

60d Barrington Court. See 52a.

60d East Lambrook. See 52b.

60e Tintinhull House. See 52c.

60e Montacute House. See 52c.

60g Wayford. See 43a Clapton.

60i Brympton. See 52c.

61b Hadspen House (tel. Castle Cary 0963 50200). 6 acre Edwardian garden around an 18th century house. Shrubs, shrub-roses and tender wall plants. Plant shop; no dogs. *All Tuesdays and Thursdays 1000-1700; also April to end October Sundays 1400-1700.*

61e Wilkin Throop: Stowell Hill. Collection of flowering shrubs, including rhododendrons, azaleas and magnolias. *May only: Saturdays 1100-1900; Sundays 1400-1900.*

62g Croyde: Langtrees. A modern 1 acre garden with many unusual plants and a silver foliage collection. *May to September: Friday afternoons; also certain other days.*

62i Marwood Hill (tel. Barnstaple 0271 2528). Extensive collection of flowering shrubs; rock and alpine garden in quarry; small lake with waterside planting; rose and bog gardens; greenhouse with Australian plants. Plant shop. *Daily: dawn to dusk.*

63d Arlington Court (tel. Shirwell 027 182 296). Terraced garden and lake in extensive grounds. *April to end October: daily 1100-1800; November to March (free): dawn to dusk.* 🍷♣📺🏛✝🐾❧

64e West Porlock: Underway Gardens. An excellent and well established collection of uncommon specimen trees, shrubs, herbaceous and bulbous plants in a fine setting.

64f Ellicombe Gardens. Pleasant formal gardens with pools and some very good ironwork.

64f Dunster Castle (tel. 064 382 314). Terraced garden of rare shrubs. *Early April to end September Sunday to Thursday 1100-1700; October Tuesdays, Wednesdays and Sundays 1400-1600.* 🦌🏛⌐

65h Golden Farm. See 58b.

68b Ammerdown House. Famous yew gardens designed by Sir Edwin Lutyens. Also contains an orangery, terraces, statuary, some ornamental foundations and a lime avenue.

68c Rode: Tropical Bird Gardens (tel. Beckington 037 383 326). 17 acres of woodland, flower gardens and ornamental lake. *Daily 1030-1900 (sunset in winter).* 🍷🐦

68c Orchardleigh House. Large garden with a terrace and views over the park and lake; also an interesting old kitchen garden.

68d Oakhill Manor (tel. 0749 840210). 8 acres of gardens in an estate of 45 acres. *Easter to 31 October daily 1200-1800.* 🍷🏛⌐☆

68g Hadspen House. See 61b.

68i Stourhead House and Pleasure Gardens (tel. Bourton 074 784 348). One of Europe's finest landscaped gardens, laid out from 1741-50 by Henry Hoare's son. Magnificent 20 acre lake, temples, grottoes, rare trees and shrubs. *Daily 0800-1830 (sunset if earlier).* ♣🏛

69d Longleat House (tel. Maiden Bradley 098 53 551). Park landscaped by Capability Brown with formal gardens; Azalea Drive; Garden Centre. *Easter to September: daily 1000-1800. Rest of year: daily 1000-1600.* 🍷🏛🐦⌐☆

70f Clevedon Court. 18th century terraced garden, rare shrubs. *April to end September: Wednesdays, Thursdays, Sundays and Bank Holiday Mondays 1430-1700.* 🍷🏛

70g Weston-super-Mare. Among the winter gardens and public parks along the sea front is a unique fragrance garden for the blind.

71 Bristol: Zoological Gardens, Clifton Down (tel. 0272 38951). Delightful flower garden, founded in 1836, with a collection of trees and shrubs; rock garden, tropical house and rose garden. *Daily from 0900 (1000 Sundays).* 🍷🐦

71b Henbury: Vine House (tel. 0272 503573). 2 acre garden with trees, shrubs, water and naturalised garden. *By appointment only.*

72e Bath: Botanical Gardens, Royal Victoria Park. Over 5,000 species of plants from all over the world.

72b Dyrham Park. 17th century garden and terraces; orangery. *April, May and October Saturday to Wednesday; June to September Saturday to Thursday; 1400-1730.* 🍷♣🏛⌐

72e St Catherine's Court (tel. Bath 0225 858159). Fine garden and landscaped park retaining some original Tudor features. *Early April to end September weekends and Bank Holidays: conducted tour 1430 (for 2½ hours).* 🍷🏛

72h Widcombe: Prior Park (east of Bath). Masterly piece of landscaping created over a valley, at the bottom of which is a Palladian bridge crossing waters formed from old ponds. *May to September: Tuesdays and Wednesdays (August Monday to Thursday).*

72i Claverton: Claverton Manor (tel. Bath 0225 60503). Replica of George Washington's flower garden at Mount Vernon; fine specimen trees and pleasant lawns and borders form the rest of the garden. *End March to end October: Tuesday to Sunday 1400-1700; also Bank Holidays and Bank Holiday Sundays 1100-1700. Other times by appointment.* 🍷📺🏛↓T

72i Bradford-on-Avon: The Hall. Large garden beside River Avon with lawns, fine trees, herbaceous and rose borders. No dogs. *Daily 0900-1700. Free.*

73a Sheldon Manor (tel. Chippenham 0249 3120). Formal garden with very old yew trees; many rare and interesting trees and shrubs. *End March to September: Thursdays, Sundays and Bank Holidays 1400-1800.* 🍽 🏛

73d Corsham Court (tel. 0249 712214). Park and gardens laid out by Capability Brown and Repton; some rare flowering trees, flowering shrubs. *All year: Sundays, Wednesdays and Thursdays; mid-July to mid-September daily (except Mondays and Fridays): 1100-1230, 1400-1800 (1630 in winter).* 🏛

73e Bowood (tel. Calne 0249 812102). Pleasure grounds and gardens of 100 acres include Capability Brown's lake, a cascade, grottoes and an orangery. *Good Friday to end September: Tuesday to Sunday and Bank Holidays 1200-1800.* 🍽 🖼 🏛

73g Holt: The Courts. Topiary gardens with lily pond and arboretum. *April to end October: weekdays 1400-1800.*

ᛗ Historical Sites

> Ruined fortifications from prehistoric to modern times, including the remains of many castles (those preserved in good order are listed on pages 88-89); also the sites of Roman camps, ancient tombs, battlefields, monuments, etc.

19b Zennor Quoit. Stone Age tomb of 7 stones, each 10 ft high and topped with a 6 yard slab.

19b Enclosure: Remains of an Iron Age settlement of about 100BC.

19c John Knill Monument. Huge granite mausoleum built by an 18th century mayor of St Ives who wanted to be remembered. In accordance with his wishes, 10 young girls dance around it singing Psalm 100 on 25 July every five years.

19c Trencrom Hill Fort. Scant remains of early Iron Age fort, with dry stone fortifications on a natural rampart.

19d St Just: Plain-an-Gwarry (Place of the Plays), by Bank Square. 50 yd round amphitheatre where miracle plays were performed in the Middle Ages.

19e Chun Castle. Good example of an Iron Age hill fort and smelting house.

Chun Quoit, nearby, is a large burial chamber of stone slabs.

19e Men an Tol. Group of Neolithic standing stones, including one with hole thought to cure children of Rickets.

Men Scryfa (Inscribed Stone), nearby, is a large monolith bearing a Latin inscription to "Rialobran the Son of Cunoval".

Nine Maidens is a stone circle.

19e Lanyon Quoit. Much visited stone megalith now looking like a giant 3 legged table, but once a Neolithic chamber tomb covered by an earth mound. The top slab measures 17 ft by 9 ft and is 18 in thick. *Free.*

19e Madron Well. Nearby are the remains of a Baptistry wrecked by Cromwell's troops in the Civil War.

19e Settlement: Carn Euny. Site of an Iron Age village with 66 ft long underground hiding hole. *Daily from 0930 (Sundays from 1400).*

Blind Fiddler, nearby, is an outstanding Bronze Age standing stone, one of many prehistoric sites, caves, Celtic crosses, etc., in the immediate area.

19f Chysauster Settlement. Iron Age village of eight oval dry stone huts grouped around an open courtyard, surrounded by a 15 ft thick wall. Also animal pens and typical Cornish hiding hole. *Daily from 0930 (winter Sundays from 1400).*

19g Sennen Cove: Table Men. Large rock on which King Arthur is said to have held a banquet to celebrate defeating the Danes.

19h Treryn Castle. Iron Age fortified headland with remains of many earth and stone defences.

19h Crosses: impressive Celtic granite cross with carved crucifixion scene.

19h The Pipers: a pair of 14 ft stone pillars set 120 ft apart.

Merry Maidens, nearby, is a circle of 19 Bronze Age stones, supposedly maidens turned to stone as a punishment for dancing on a Sunday.

20c Pixie's Hall. Mysterious cave 30 ft long, 5 ft wide and 6 ft high.

Glossary of terms

Stone Age (or Paleolithic): characterised by the first use of tools, including stone axes, etc. Normally taken to date from about 650,000 to 8000 BC.

Neolithic: late Stone Age, characterised by the use of polished tools, usually flint; the first domestic animals and the beginning of agriculture. From about 8000 to 4000 BC.

Bronze Age: the first use of metal for tools and weapons (also to time of ancient Troy). From about 4000 to 800 BC.

Iron Age: officially the age in which we still live, it began about 800 BC.

Prehistoric: a general term covering all the above Ages; often used on these pages to describe sites whose precise origins are hard to date.

Mediaeval (or Middle Ages): an ill-defined historical period, usually taken to run from about 1000 AD (the fall of Rome; the Norman Conquest of England) to about 1500 (the start of the Tudor era in Britain).

20f Trelowarren: Halligey Fogous. Cornish hiding hole of about 100BC.

21b Falmouth: Killigrew Monument, Arwenack Street. Erected in 1737 to commemorate the family who developed much of Falmouth in the 17th century.

21d Dennis Head. Ruins of a fort built by Henry VIII to protect the flanks of Pendennis Castle (21b).

21g Three Brothers of Grugith. Bronze Age stone tomb.

22b Tresco: Block House near Old Grimsby. Built to house an artillery battery during the 16th century. *Any time.*

Castles: King Charles' Castle, built in the mid 16th century to defend the coast and extended during the Civil War. *Any time.*

Cromwell's Castle, nearby, was built in the mid 17th century to protect New Grimsby with artillery. *Any time.*

22b Samson: remains of many cottages in use before the island ceased to be inhabited in the mid 19th century. Also numerous burial chambers.

22b 22c St Mary's: there are over 150 prehistoric burial chambers on the island, along with many other ancient sites. Three notable sites have been marked on the map.

Bants Carn, in the north west corner of the island, is a Bronze Age burial mound with entrance passage and chamber. Nearby stone hut remains were occupied in Roman times. *Any time.*

Innisidgen (to the north east) and Porth Hellick (south east) are both sites of ancient burial chambers.

22e Gugh: there are many standing stones, burial chambers and stone tombs on this island.

22h Zennor Quoit. See 19b.

22i John Knill Monument. See 19c.

23f St Agnes Beacon: 3 burial chambers atop a 600 ft high hill.

23h Camborne: Richard Trevithick statue, outside the town library, honours the man born here in 1771 and who designed the first steam-powered passenger vehicle to carry passengers. He also invented many devices which revolutionised deep shaft mining throughout Britain.

23i Carn Brea. Much fortified 738 ft summit, with remains of an Iron Age hill fort, a Roman fortress and a 15th century castle. Also many ancient hut circles and a 90 ft high monument erected in 1837. Fine views.

23i Gwennap Pit. Methodist 'cathedral' first used by John Wesley in 1762 and still used for a major gathering on Whit Monday and for occasional services in Summer. The natural amphitheatre seats 20,000 people, but Wesley's sermons attracted as many as 30,000.

Lanyon Quoit (19e)

24a Towan Head: Huer's House. Castellated watchtower from which a man called the Huer alerted the fishing fleet when pilchards were sighted in Newquay Bay.

24b Porth: Iron Age fort remains on Porth island.

24c Castle Downs: Castle-an-Dinas. Remains of an Iron Age British fort built around the 703 ft summit.

24d St Piran's Round. Hilltop fort and 130 ft amphitheatre dating from about 200BC. Was used for the first meeting of the Cornish Gorsedd druids in 1946. It has now been revived as a mediaeval open air theatre, where Cornish plays old and new are performed.

24f Grampound: one pier survives of the Roman bridge from which the town took its name (Grand Pont).

24h St Clement: the church contains a splendid inscribed stone dating from about 580AD.

24i Veryan Round Houses. Regency homes built with no corners in which the Devil might hide. The conical roofs are also topped with crosses to help drive him away.

25c Lostwithiel: the old bridge over the River Fowey, with 9 arches and passing alcoves, dates from about 1300.

25c Castle Dore. Well preserved, 220 ft wide prehistoric fortification, said to be where the Knights of the Round Table met and where Tristam and Isolde are buried. It was the scene of fierce fighting during the Civil War battle for Lostwithiel in August 1644; Charles I rested here before accepting the surrender of the Roundhead forces.

25c Boconnoc: group of Bronze Age barrows on Braddock Down. The site of the main battle for Lostwithiel during the Civil War is nearby.

25d St Austell: 1 mile north on the Bodmin road are the Holy Well of Mencuddle (Stone in the Wood) and the nearby Stone Chair, cut from a single piece of granite and said to date from Druid times.

25f Fowey: St Catherine's Castle. Remains of 1540 fortification built by Henry VIII to defend Fowey harbour — a chain went across the estuary to Polruan Castle to stop enemy shipping — it helped repel Dutch raiders in 1666. St Catherine's was restored in 1855. *Daily 0900 to dusk. Free.*

Rashleigh Mausoleum. Two granite arches surrounded by iron railings. Contains the graves of William Rashleigh and his family and was erected in 1867.

25g The Dodman. The whole point is a cliff castle, cut off by a deep ditch known as the Balk. On the summit is a tiny, 19th century watch-house, used by coastal patrols against smugglers and wrecks; also an 1896 granite cross erected as a landmark for shipping.

26a Boconoc. See 25c.

26b St Keyne Well, said to have healing properties. Also, whichever of the husband or wife drank first would be master over their household. The water is now stagnant and must not be drunk.

26b Duloe: 37 ft diameter Bronze Age burial circle of 8 giant quartz stones.

26b Tregarland: St Cuby's Well. Small ante chamber for well basin which is now in Duloe Church. Legend has it that when a farmer tried to pull the basin away with an ox, the beast died.

26b West Looe River: St Nuns Well. Dedicated to the mother of St David and built into a bank between hedges, although its basin is missing. According to legend, when the basin was dragged away by a farmer, it detached itself and miraculously flew back to its place.

27a Trematon Castle. Roofless remains of the 13th century keep, plus some walls are all that remain of this early motte castle, mentioned in the Domesday Book.

27a Fort Tregantle. Military barracks built as a national monument after the Napoleonic wars. *Closed when red flags fly.*

27b Plymouth: The Hoe, where Drake played his famous game of bowls while the Spanish Armada approached. Magnificent views.

Smeaton's Tower, The Hoe. The third lighthouse to stand on Eddystone Rock (9½ miles south of Rame Head), it was dismantled in 1882 and rebuilt here. *May to early October daily.*

Mayflower Steps, off Madeira Road. Tablets commemorating many famous sailing events, notably the departure of the Pilgrim Fathers to America in 1620.

Tintagel Castle (36a)

28h Bolt Tail: remains of an Iron Age promontory fortress.

29a Totnes East Gate. Built in the 15th century as the eastern boundary of the town, it divides Fore Street and High Street.

29c Brixham: The Brixham Cavern, 107 Mount Pleasant Road. Inhabited from Stone Age to Roman times, this 600 ft cave was rediscovered in 1858 and has been skillfully lit to show prehistoric bones, plus stalagmites and stalactites. *Mid April to September, Sunday to Friday 1000-1800.*

29e Dartmouth Harbour: Bayard's Cove Castle. Built in the 16th century to protect the inner harbour. *Any time.*

30c Cliff Castle. Iron Age fortified headland with defences built by local tribesmen.

30g Towan Head. See 24a.

30h Porth. See 24b.

30i Castle Downs. See 24c.

31b Tregeare Rounds. Ancient ramparts also known as Castle Dameliock and mentioned in "Morte d'Arthur" as Castle Terrible, which was fortified by the then Duke of Cornwall against Uther Pendragon.

31b Castle Goff. Ancient earthwork with even larger fortification to the north.

31c Slaughter Bridge. With nearby Camelford said to have been Camelot, this is the legendary site of King Arthur's last battle, when he defeated and killed his nephew Modred, only to die later of his own wounds.

31c Fernacre Stone Circle. Good example of prehistoric standing stones.

Brown Willy, nearby, is the highest peak in Cornwall and has several prehistoric 'beehive' huts and a great cairn on its summit.

31d Wadebridge Bridge. Built in 1468 this is the main feature of the town. It spans 320 ft over 17 arches and although twice widened in modern times, the original character has been preserved. Said to be the oldest main road bridge in Britain.

31d Ulcagnus Tomb. Inscribed stone to the son of Severus dating from Roman times.

31f King Arthur's Hall. Remains of an ancient British encampment.

31f Bury Castle. Iron Age earthworks.

31g Burial Chamber: Giant's Quoit. Fine Cromlech on Pawton Farm property.

31h Castle Canyke. Extensive, well-preserved prehistoric earthworks.

31i Boconnoc. See 25c.

32c Launceston South Gate. Two pointed arches from the mediaeval walls of the town; also some ramparts of the 13th century castle.

32e The Hurlers. Line of 3 Bronze Age stone circles and nearby round barrow. *Any time. Free.*

32h King Doniert's Stone. Carved with Irish motifs

recording the death by drowning of a Cornish king in 872AD.

32h Trethevy Quoit. Famous Neolithic tomb consisting of six huge boulders holding up a seventh, which has a mysterious little hole in one end. *Any time. Free.*

32h St Cleer's Well. Restored well supposed to cure madness.

32i Cadson Bury. Ancient British camp on isolated hill.

33c Lydford Castle. The site was first fortified by Alfred in the 9th century as protection against the Danes; the stone keep whose remains survive was built by the Normans in 1195. The castle was best known for its use as a Stannary Court and 'Tinners' Prison' until about 1800. In early times this court was so harsh that men were said to have been hung in the morning and tried in the afternoon! *Any reasonable time. Free.*

33c Watern Oak Bronze Age Village. Unenclosed village with numerous hut circles.

33f Merrivale. This area is rich in prehistoric remains, including hut circles, a long avenue of upright stones, burial chambers and one of the finest Bronze Age cists (hollow stone coffins) on Dartmoor.

34a Watern Oak. See 33c.

34b Broad Down: Broadun Ring. Prehistoric pound with 4 ft wall enclosing a group of hut circles. Splendid views.

Broadun Pound. At 12 acres, the largest prehistoric enclosure on Dartmoor, with several circles of huts within. Thought to have housed sheep or cattle.

34b Postbridge: famous mediaeval stone clapper bridge spanning 45 ft with three flat granite slabs. Used to transport tin to the Stannary Towns.

34b Challacombe Stone Avenue. Long row of upright stones, thought to have formed a ceremonial route in the Bronze Age.

34c Easdon Tor. Two groups of prehistoric hut circles and a cairn.

34c Grimspound. Foundations of 24 dry stone huts and outer wall, thought to date from before 1000BC and one of the earliest such settlements on Dartmoor. It covers 4 acres and the outer wall was over 9 ft thick.

34c Hamel Down: well preserved group of Bronze Age burial chambers.

34d Merrivale. See 33f.

34e Dartmeet Bridge. Granite clapper bridge similar to that at Postbridge (34b).

34f Holne Chase: remains of a late Iron Age earthwork; also two mediaeval bridges over the River Dart.

34f Hembury Camp. Ancient hilltop castle with bank and ditch defences in a strategic location.

35g Totnes. See 29a.

35h Berry Pomeroy Castle. Cleared, but not restored ruins of a castle started in the 12th century and expanded in the 14th. During Elizabethan times, a lavish mansion was built within the castle walls, but its completion was interrupted by the Civil War, when much damage was done by Roundhead forces, and the site was abandoned in 1688. Sited in an inaccessible wooded valley. Remains include the 3 storey gatehouse and hexagonal towers. *Daily.*

36a Tintagel Head: Tintagel Castle.   Legendary site of King Arthur's court, although not actually built until some 600 years after his death. Its construction was undertaken in about 1145 by Reginald, Earl of Cornwall, an illegitimate son of Henry I. In those days the rocky headland on which most of the building stands was linked to the mainland by a narrow causeway "which three armed men shall be able to defend against the whole power of the kingdom", according to a contemporary historian. The castle was greatly expanded in the mid 13th century by a brother of Henry III and was owned by the Black Prince in the 14th century. After his death it fell into disrepair, although it was used as a prison during the late 14th century. The sea has now destroyed the causeway and the cliffs which once supported the drawbridge, leaving the massive gatehouse on the mainland and the rest of the ruins—including battlements and traces of some interior buildings—on the isolated peninsula, which is reached by a vigorous climb. Plenty remains to stimulate the romantic imagination, however, and the location is enhanced by a 40 ft waterfall and by Merlin's Cave, which runs right through the castle rock at sea level. *Daily from 0930 (winter Sundays from 1400).* ✝

36c Hendra. Several groups of grave mounds and stone tombs, all prehistoric.

36d Tregeare Rounds. See 31b.

36e Castle Goff. See 31b.

36e Slaughter Bridge. See 31c.

36f Fernacre Stone Circle. See 31c.

36h King Arthur's Hall. See 31f.

36h Bury Castle. Iron Age earthworks.

37e Launceston. See 32c.

37g The Hurlers. See 32e.

38c Okehampton Camp. Remains of an Iron Age hill fort, thought to have been a frontier post.

38e Lydford Castle. See 33c.

38f Watern Oak. See 33c.

38i Merrivale. See 33f.

39a Stone Circle: this ring of stones near Scorhill dates from the early Bronze Age and is thought to have been used in religious ceremonies.

39b Spinsters Rock. Reconstructed example of a communal Stone Age tomb built of upright stones.

39b Cranbrook Castle. Iron Age hill fort of ditch and bank construction built 1100 ft above the River Teign.

39d Broad Down. See 34b.

39d Postbridge. See 34b.

39e Challacombe Stone Avenue. See 34b.

39e Grimspound. See 34c.

39e Hamel Down. See 34c.

39e Easdon Tor. See 34c.

39g Dartmeet Bridge. See 34e.

39h Holne Chase. See 34f.

39h Hembury Camp. See 34f.

40b Exeter: Undergound Passages, Princesshay off High Street. Aqueducts built in the 13th century to carry local spring water. *Tuesday to Saturday 1400-1700.*

Roman Walls. Built during the Roman occupation between 50AD and 200AD, the best portions are off Southernhay, Northernhay and Bartholomew Street. *Any time.*

Rougemont Castle, Northernhay Park. Built on a hill of red volcanic rock, which gave it its name. Its position beside the city walls was considered so impregnable that no keep was thought necessary, a theory proved correct by centuries of unsuccessful attacks. Parts of the original Norman gateway and a Saxon tower remain, but most of the building dates from the 18th century. ▣

41a Woodbury Castle. Iron Age hill fort with two ramparts separated by a deep ditch.

41c Blackbury Castle. Oval shaped, 4 acre earth hill fort dating from the Iron Age with a complicated entrance on the south side.

42c Lamberts Castle. Prehistoric British earthwork said to have been named after King Canute, who adopted the name Lambert when converted to Christianity as King of England.

42d Shute House. Remains of a manor house dating from 1390/1870, with castellated tower, Gothic windows and gatehouse. *Exterior: April to end October Mondays, Wednesdays, Fridays and Sundays 1400-1800; Free. Interior by appointment only.*

42d Beer: Old Quarry. Used from Roman times until late in the 19th century, it provided white stone for many famous buildings, including Exeter Cathedral.

42f Lyme Regis: The Cobb Harbour is 600 ft long and dates from the 13th century. Famous as the scene of Louisa Musgrove's fall in Jane Austen's "Persuasion".

Buddle Bridge has 14th century arches.

43d Eype Down: prehistoric earthwork.

43e Eggardon Hill. Fine Iron Age hill fort covering 36 acres, with 3 banks and ditches. Two Bronze Age round barrows within.

43f Martin's Down: Poor Lot Barrows. Fine group of Bronze Age burial mounds. *Any time.*

43i Kingston Russell Stone Circle. 80 ft Bronze Age circle of 18 stones. *Any time.*

43f Nine Stones. Remains of a prehistoric circle of standing stones. *Any time.*

44a Nine Stones. See 43f.

44b Dorchester: Maumbury Rings.   Stone Age stone circle adapted by the Romans as an amphitheatre seating up to 10,000 people. It was still in use late in the 18th century for public hangings.

44e White Horse. Carved in the chalk in 1808 in honour of George III.

44e Chalbury Fort. Iron Age defences.

44e Preston: Jordan Hill Roman Temple. Foundations of a small rectangular temple. *Any time.*

44e Sandsfoot Castle. Blockhouse built in 1539 by Henry VIII to defend Weymouth Bay. Walls, gate tower and garrison quarters remain, although much has slipped into the sea.

44f Poxwell Stone Circle. Miniature Stonehenge, with stones only 3 or 4 ft high. The oldest known religious site in Dorset.

44h Rufus Castle, Portland. Remains of 12th century fortifications, built by William II (Rufus). *Free.*

45d Lulworth Castle. Built in 1588 by the Weld family, it burnt down in 1929. Beware of fallen masonry. *Sundays.* ✝

45e Tyneham Village. Ghost village taken over by the War Office and used for military exercises since 1943. *Easter, Whitsun, August and Christmas only.*

45e NT: Creech Grange Arch. Crenellated stone screen erected in the 18th century simply to provide a suitable skyline view for the inhabitants of Creech Grange, the house in the valley below. Magnificent views.

45f Corfe Castle (tel. 092 93 442). Devastated remains of what was once one of the most impressive castles in Britain. The site, high on a ridge dominating the village, was fortified in Saxon times, but the present fortress was built in Norman times. It repulsed a seige by King Stephen, but later became a favourite residence of English sovereigns, including Henry I, John and Henry III, all of whom extended it. The fortifications were completed by Edward I in 1280 and Corfe then remained a centre of royal administration until it was sold by Elizabeth I in 1635 to the Bankes family. During the Civil War they supported the Royalists and in 1643, while her husband was away, Lady Bankes led the defenders in beating off a well-equipped, 500-strong Roundhead army. In 1646, however, Cromwell's forces returned and, after a fierce fight, succeeded in

Corfe Castle (45f)

44b Maiden Castle. The most famous hill fort in Britain, this is also one of the largest earthwork systems in Europe: the massive triple ramparts, rising to over 80 ft, cover more than 2 miles and enclose some 120 acres. The site was first occupied by Bronze Age man in about 2000BC, and the defences were started in the Iron Age, about 300BC. The name derives from 'Mai-Jun', Celtic for "the stronghold on the plain". During the Roman invasion, it was the capital of the Durotriges, who succumbed to Vespasian's 2nd Legion in 43AD. After the battle, the Romans reduced much of the castle and they later built a temple on the site. *Any reasonable time. Free.*

infiltrating a body of their troops into the castle disguised as friendly forces. When the castle fell, Parliament decided that it should be completely demolished (rather than just 'reduced'): gunpowder and mines were employed, but the Norman fortifications were so stout that much still remains, including parts of the keep and several other towers. *March to October daily 1000 to dusk, November to February PM.*

45f Rempstone: complete prehistoric stone circle.

46e Stamford Hill. Site of the famous Civil War battle on 19 May 1643, when the Roundhead army

despite holding the top of the 200 ft hill, were driven off by Royalists under Sir Bevil Grenville.

47c Great Torrington Castle. Scant remains of Norman fortress on a site with excellent views.

48c Colleton Barton. Gatehouse dating from the Middle Ages, although the present house is 17th century.

48c Chulmleigh: Stone Castle. Motte and bailey remains of mediaeval defences.

48f Eggesford House. Remains of an Elizabethan manor, once the seat of the Earls of Portsmouth, but uninhabited since 1913. Immediately north of the building are two prehistoric earthworks.

49f Cadbury Castle. Iron Age earth hill fort with magnificent views. Not to be confused with the Somerset site of the same name (61a).

50c Wellington Monument. 175 ft obelisk standing at the highest point of the Blackdown Hills, built in 1817 to commemorate the Duke of Wellington. Climb the 235 steps to the top for fantastic views.

50g Killerton (tel. Hele 0329 288 345). Iron Age hill fort on the Dolbury. *Daily in daylight hours.*

50i Hembury Fort. Excellent example of an Iron Age hill fort, described by experts as "the grandest monument to the military skills of the Britons in Devon". The oval defences enclose 8 acres within double ditches and banks, which were supplemented by wooden palisades.

51b Brown Down: Robin Hood's Butts. Two groups of Bronze Age burial mounds. The northern group comprises 5 round barrows, each 50-90 ft diameter and 5-7 ft high, in a beech copse; the southern group is much less visible, with only 4 surviving mounds.

51b Castle Neroche. Remains of an 11th/12th century Norman earth-work castle. ♣

51g Honiton: St Margaret's Hospital. Two sets of thatched cottages built as a leper hospital about 1000 years ago.

51h Shute House. See 42d.

52b Hamdon Hill Fort. One of the largest in Britain, covering 200 acres in an L shape. Used in Iron Age and Roman times. Has a modern inn within it.

52g Lamberts Castle. See 42c.

52i Eggardon Hill. See 43e.

53b Sherborne Old Castle. Remains of a fortified residence built in 1107-35 by the Bishop of Salisbury and modified in 1592 by Sir Walter Raleigh, who lived here. It was destroyed by Cromwell's forces in 1645. *Daily from 0930 (winter Sundays from 1400).*

53e Batcombe Hill: Cross & Hand. Oddly shaped prehistoric monolith whose purpose is uncertain. In Thomas Hardy's novel "Tess of the D'Urbervilles", the heroine is made to swear an oath on this stone.

53h Cerne Giant. Famous figure of a naked man holding a club, cut into the chalk hillside. It is 180 ft long and 167 ft wide and is thought to be a fertility symbol dating from about 500AD. On the hilltop above is an enclosure where the Rites of Spring were performed, while as recently as the 19th century local women believed that a night spent sleeping on the hill would cure barrenness.

54e Clovelly Dykes. Iron Age hill fort with three sets of banks and ditches.

55c Barnstaple: Norman Castle. Scant remains of a typical motte and bailey fort built after the

Normans captured the town in 1068. Now a public open space. *Anytime. Free.*

Long Bridge. Built in the 13th century on 16 arches. Much original stonework remains despite repeated widening in modern times.

55e Bideford: Torridge Bridge. Built in 1535 to replace an oak bridge which had stood since 1285, it spans 677 ft on 24 different sized arches.

Victoria Park. Contains 8 cannon believed to have come from the Spanish Armada.

55e Great Torrington. See 47c.

56h Colleton Barton. See 48c.

56h Eggesford House. See 48f.

56h Chulmleigh: Stone Castle. See 48c.

57a Withypool Hill Stone Circle. Well preserved Bronze Age group of about 40 small stones spanning 120 ft.

57b Winsford Hill: Wambarrows. Group of three small Bronze Age barrows at the northern end of the hill.

Caractacus Stone, at the eastern end of the hill, is a 5th century standing stone inscribed to "The Nephew of Caractacus".

57b Tarr Steps. Stone clapper bridge over the River Barle, thought to be the oldest bridge in England.

57b Dulverton: Barle Bridge. Ancient packhorse bridge.

58b Elworthy Barrows. Remains of an Iron Age camp.

58f Wellington Monument. See 50c.

59a Ruborough Camp. Prehistoric site later used by the Romans as a fort. Now overgrown with trees.

59g Brown Down: Robin Hood's Butts. See 51b.

59h Castle Neroche. See 51b.

60b Hood Monument. Column erected in 1831 in honour of Admiral Lord Hood (1724-1816), who served with Nelson. The column is topped by ships sails.

60b Dundon Hill Fort. 10 ft wall of earth and stones from Iron Age camp.

60e Long Load Bridge. 15th century stone bridge with four triple arches over the River Yeo.

60e Pill Bridge. 17th century packhorse bridge over the River Yeo.

60e Hamdon Hill Fort. See 52b.

60f Ilchester: Mace. The oldest mace in England is preserved in the Town Hall.

Roman Remains. A well preserved section of the town walls can be seen in fields to the east of the town.

61a Castle Cary: circular stone lock up behind the market hall, dating from 1779.

61a Cadbury Castle. An 18 acre hill fort popularly believed to be the site of King Arthur's Camelot. Extensive excavations have revealed that the site was inhabited before 3300BC and that it was fortified by Iron Age, British and Anglo-Saxon tribes. During the 11th century it was defended against the Danes by Ethelred the Unready, and most of the surviving structure dates from this period. Excellent views. Guides in summer during excavations.

61d Sherborne Old Castle. See 53b.

61i Sturminster Newton. 15th century bridge with 6 arches and a notice promising "Transportation for Life" to anyone damaging it.

62a Lundy Island: Marisco Castle. Remains of a 13th century castle with walls 9 ft thick. Access by boat from Ilfracombe (tel. 0271 62687). Advance booking essential. *May to end September daily. No cars.*

62f Combe Martin: 12th century tithe barn.

62h Braunton Tower. 19th century folly built to celebrate the end of the Corn Laws. ⌂

62i Barnstaple. See 55c.

63c Old Barrow. Early Roman fort built in 48AD to keep watch on the Silures tribe of South Wales; it was abandoned in 52AD after Caractacus and the Silures had been defeated.

63d The Beacon. The old stagecoach road between Minehead and Ilfracombe can be followed as a path; there are also traces of a Roman signal station used to guard against invasion.

63e Lynton: Rhenish Tower, the Breakwater. The original was built in 1855 to supply a retired colonel with seawater for his bath. It was swept away by the famous flood in 1952 and the current structure is a replica.

63e Chapman Barrows. Bronze Age burial site.

63h Squallacombe: Setta Barrow. Good example of a round Bronze Age burial mound, 96 ft wide and 6½ ft high with intact circle of retaining stones.

63i Cow Castle. 3 acre earth fort with unusual defences including a ditch inside the rampart.

64d Porlock Stone Circle, south of Hawkomb Head, is a Bronze Age site about 80 ft across with 10 standing and 11 fallen stones, all quite small.

64d Chetsford Water: Alderman's Barrow. Round mound 87 ft wide and 4 ft high, used since the 13th century to mark one of the bounds of Exmoor Forest.

64e Selworthy: tithe barn dating from the 14th century with interesting window arch and animal symbols on the wall.

64e Dunkery Hill: Joaney How & Robin How. Two cairns over 70 ft wide, Robin being 10 ft high, Joaney half that. Their names are thought to derive from Robin Hood and Little John.

64f Dunster: Yarn Market, High Street. Octagonal building erected by the Luttrells of Dunster Castle in 1609 and restored in 1647, it was used for selling locally woven cloth. *Any time.*

Gallox Bridge, at the southern end of the village, is a stone packhorse bridge.

Old Dovecote. Built in the 12th century as part of the priory. Still has its rare revolving ladder for reaching the nesting boxes. *Easter to mid October daily 1000 to dusk. Free.*

Conygar Tower, just north of town, is an 18th century folly built as a lookout tower. The circular stone building can be seen for miles around.

64g Cow Castle. See 63i.

64g Withypool Hill Stone Circle. See 57a.

64h Winsford Hill. See 57b.

64h Tarr Steps. See 57b.

65f Storgursey Castle. Remains of an 11th century fortification destroyed during the Wars of the Roses now overgrown.

65h Trendle Ring. Iron Age circular hill fort enclosing 2 acres.

65h Elworthy Barrows. See 58b.

65i Dowsborough Castle. Iron Age hill fort of 7 acres containing Bronze Age round barrow.

66c Brent Knoll Hill Fort. Iron Age earthworks covering 4 acres which was still occupied in Roman times.

66d Stogursey Castle. See 65f.

66g Ruborough Camp. See 59a.

66i Sedgemoor. Site of the last major battle fought on English soil, when in 1685 the Duke of Monmouth's rebellion against James II was crushed in a fierce hand to hand fight.

67a Tynings Farm: remains of a Neolithic long barrow and several Bronze Age round barrows.

67a Cheddar: the site of Saxon and mediaeval palaces can be seen in the grounds of the Kings of Wessex Secondary School. Finds from the site are in Taunton Museum.

67b Roman Lead Mining Settlement. Scant remains of lead mining activities, plus a small amphitheatre. It is occasionally possible to discern the street plan of the settlement in the adjacent ploughed field.

67b Priddy Circles. Four earth rings, each 200 yd across, stretching in a line for about 1 mile. Their origin is unknown.

67b North Hill: Priddy Nine Barrows. Group of Bronze Age burial mounds, one of which yielded several finds now in Bristol City Museum.

67c East Harptree: Richmont Castle. Remains of a Norman fortification captured by Stephen in 1138 and demolished in Tudor times.

67c Devil's Punchbowl. Notable mainly as a swallow hole, where a stream disappears underground, it also marks the start of a section of footpath following the old Roman road from Uphill to Old Sarum: the path runs south east to Priddy Circles (see below).

67c Stock Hill: Hunter's Lodge Inn Barrows. Bronze Age site spanning both sides of the road, with 130 ft bell barrow to the north and a 150 ft earthwork to the south.

67d Lake Village. Site of Iron Age swampland community, whose houses were thatched daub-and-wattle buildings on central wooden poles. The lake, now drained, once covered 5 miles.

67d Meare: Abbot's Fish House. Restored 14th century building once used to salt and store fish caught in nearby Abbot's Fishpool, which was drained in the 18th century. The Fish House has recently been re-roofed by the Department of the Environment. *Any time. Free.*

The Manor House, nearby, was the summer residence of the Abbots of Glastonbury and dates from the 14th century.

67e Site of Lake Village. Ancient British village, with small mounds marking the site of huts which once stood on a huge timber island.

67f Maesbury Castle. Prehistoric earth fort with 2 banks and a ditch enclosing 7 acres.

67f Pilton: The Great Tithe Barn of Glastonbury Abbey, over 100 ft long with a beamed roof.

The Manor House, nearby, was a summer house of the Abbot of Glastonbury and has a square dovecote.

67h Glastonbury Tor. Dramatic hilltop thought to have been used for pagan ceremonies and having legendary connections with the stories of King Arthur.

67h Ponter's Ball. 1 mile linear earthwork thought to have been part of the outer defences of Glastonbury.

67h Hood Monument. See 60b.

67h Dundon Hill Fort. See 60b.

68b Tedbury Camp. Prehistoric earth fort with ramparts still up to 15 ft high.

68d Maesbury Castle. See 67f.

68d Beacon Hill Barrows. Group of one dozen round burial mounds, including one topped with a boundary stone.

68d Shepton Mallet: Shambles. Remains of a 15th century wooden shed which housed the local meat market.

Market Cross. Famous monument erected in 1500, with paved floor, 6 arches, pinnacles and 50 ft spire.

68g Castle Cary. See 61a.

68h Bruton Dovecote. 3 storey building on a hill above the town, all that now remains of the local priory.

Pulteney Bridge (Bath)

69b Bratton Castle. Iron Age camp with nearby 18th century white horse cut into the chalk downs.

69f Codford Circle. Prehistoric site 617 ft across.

70f Clevedon: Walton Castle. Remains of 17th century fortifications.

70f Cadbury Camp. Iron Age fortification covering 6 acres; also used in Roman times. Not to be confused with the famous Cadbury Castle (61a).

70g Worlebury Hill. British hill fort covering 10½ acres, where local Saxons inflicted a heavy defeat on the Romans in 577AD.

70i Banwell Fort. Rectangular earthwork containing raised earth and stone cross, the purpose of which is a mystery. Nearby is an octagonal tower built in 1840 as a monument to Lord Auckland, Bishop of Bath and Wells.

70i Dolebury Warren: fine Iron Age hill fort covering 20 acres, although the internal earthworks are thought to be those of a 17th century rabbit warren.

71 Bristol: The Exchange, Corn Street. 18th century building housing a corn market. Outside are four 'nails' — flat topped brass pillars on which merchants used to seal their bargains. Thus the saying "cash on the nail".

University Tower, Queen's Road. Huge octagonal tower housing the 10 ton Great George Bell.

Old City Gate, Nelson Street. Incorporates statues of Brennus and Belinus, the legendary founders of Bristol. ✝

71b Lawrence Weston: Kingsweston Roman Villa, Long Cross. Remains of small, late Roman country house, including mosaics and a display of Romano-British building techniques. Key from R Hazell, The Kiosk, Barrowmead Drive, Lawrence Weston.

71f Hanham. 15th century tithe barn with unusual towered porch.

71g Tynings Farm. See 67a.

71g Roman Lead Mining. See 67b.

71h Chew Magna: fine bridge over the River Chew is 15th century. Also, near the church, what was the 16th century court house is open to the public.

71h East Harptree. See 67c.

71i Stanton Drew Stone Circles. The most important prehistoric monument in Avon, consisting of 3 Bronze Age circles, 2 avenues of standing stones and a burial chamber. The largest circle is 120 ft wide, with 24 stones of about 6 ft. Thought to be a smaller version of Stonehenge. *Monday to Saturday.*

72e Bath: Roman Baths, Abbey Churchyard (tel. 0225 61111). Remains of Aquae Sulis, the largest Roman baths complex in Britain and the only one with hot water springs. *Daily 0900-1800 (but November to March Sundays 1100-1700).* 🍴 📷

Pulteney Bridge, built by Robert Adam in 1770, is lined with shops on both sides. It crosses the Avon on 3 arches, with a central Venetian window. *Any time. Free.*

Cleveland Bridge, built in 1827, has neo-Grecian toll houses at each end.

City Walls, Upper Borough Walls. A section of mediaeval wall can be seen on the north side of the street.

Watchman's Sentry Box, Norfolk Crescent. The only one left, it was erected in 1793 and restored in 1896.

72g Stantonbury Hill Fort. Iron Age fortification whose north side is part of Wansdyke (see below).

Wansdyke. Single bank and ditch stretching 50 miles from Hampshire, across Marlborough Downs and North Somerset to Dundry Hill (71e). The name derives from Woden's Dyke, one of the functions of the god Woden being to oversee tribal boundaries; thus Wansdyke is thought to have marked the border between Mercia and the West Saxons. It is the longest feature of its kind in Britain.

72h Stoney Littleton Long Barrow. The finest prehistoric tomb of its kind in Avon, it is 107 ft long, 13 ft high and includes a passage grave some 50 ft long. Restored in 1858, the interior is open to the public. *Any reasonable time.* Keys — and candles — from Stoney Littleton Farm.

72i Bradford-on-Avon: Barton Tithe Barn. One of the best preserved in the country, with 167 ft granary, timber joists and stone tiled roof. It was built in the 14th century for the Abbess of Shaftesbury. *Any time. Free.*

Avon Bridge. Halfway across the 14th century bridge is a tiny chapel, which in the 17th century was converted to a lock-up.

72i Farleigh Hungerford Castle. Built as a fortified house in 1370 by Sir Thomas Hungerford, first Speaker of the House of Commons, who was said to have kept his wife locked in the castle tower for many years. Now largely ruined, although the moat, two inner courts and towers can be seen. Sir Thomas is buried in the 14th century chapel. *Daily from 0930 (winter Sundays from 1400).* 📷

73b Wick Hill Monument. Pillar erected in memory of Maud Heath, who in 1474 left her life savings to build a 4 mile causeway from here to Chippenham, so bypassing a muddy path along which she had had to walk. The stone causeway can be seen nearby.

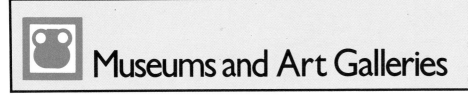

Museums and Art Galleries

Collections of almost every size and kind are listed here, other than those of a purely industrial nature, which are described in the section on Industry Past & Present on pages 103-105. Many stately homes also contain fine collections of objets d'art and these are detailed under Historic Buildings (pages 90-94).

19b Zennor: **Wayside Cottage Folk Museum** (tel. St Ives 073 670 6945). Archeology, domestic, agriculture and mining items, plus a cottage kitchen with open hearth. *May to October: daily 0930 to dusk. Free.*

19c St Ives: **Barbara Hepworth Museum,** Trewyn Studio, Barnoon Hill (tel. 073 670 6226). Photographs, letters and sculptures in the cottage studio where Dame Barbara lived and worked for 25 years. *Monday to Saturday 1000-1630 (later in summer); also July and August Sundays 1400-1800.*

Town Museum, The Harbour. Converted pilchard cellar with model ships, costumes, fire brigade history, a Cornish kitchen display and items on mining and fishing. *June to end September daily.*

Barnes Museum of Cinematography, 44 Fore Street (tel. 073 670 5860). A comprehensive history of moving pictures, starting with ancient puppets and moving through magic lanterns, illuminated panoramas, rotating zoetropes and other such devices, with cinematographic exhibits in the very last room. *Easter to mid October daily 1100-1300, 1430-1700; also July to September daily 1900-2100.*

Penwith Galleries. Exhibitions of painting, sculpture and crafts, much of it by local artists. *Monday to Saturday.*

Old Mariners Church, Norway Square (tel. 073 670 5582). Exhibitions by the St Ives Society of Artists. *Summer: daily 1000-1230, 1400-1630. Winter: daily AM.*

19f Crowlas: **Age of Steam** (tel. Cockwells 073 674 631). Museum containing relics and models; also a picture gallery, all in an 18 acre steam park with steam organs, traction engines and many children's amusements. *Easter to October: daily from 1030.* 🍽 🚻 🖐

19f Penzance: **The Museum of Nautical Art,** 19 Chapel Street. Four decks of a 1730 man o' war, complete with guns; also hundreds of items brought up by divers from the many shipwrecks in the area, including such famous vessels as *Association* and *Colossus,* the latter containing 2500 year-old pottery. *May to September: daily 1000-1300, 1400-1600; also 1900-2100 in season.*

Penlee House, Penlee Park, off Morab Road (tel. 0736 3625 or 2341). The history and development of the Penwith region from ancient times, with items of military, fishing, tin mining and theatrical history; model of Chrysauter Iron Age village (see page 79); fine natural history collection; art gallery; children's quizzes. *Monday to Saturday (not Bank Holidays) 1230-1630. Free.*

Royal Geological Society of Cornwall, Municipal Buildings, Alverton Street. The library and museum of this, the second oldest geological society in the world (founded 1814), offer displays of rocks and fossils, local minerals and old maps. *May to September.*

19f Newlyn: **Passmore Edwards Art Gallery,** on the Penzance road (tel. 0736 3715). Permanent display of work by the famous Newlyn School of painters, who worked in the town from 1883 to about 1930. Also work by modern West Country artists. *Monday to Saturday 1000-1700.*

20a Goldsithney: **World of Entertainment,** B3280 (tel. Marazion 0736 710679). Unique collection of mechanical music machines, including an automatic Wurlitzer organ, music boxes, phonographs and even a self-playing violin. Also a 19th century magic lantern show, restored amusement machines (fortune telling, strength testing, etc.). All indoors.

Live demonstrations. *Easter to 30 September: weekdays 1030-1730, Sundays 1400-1730.* 🍽

20f Helston: **Folk Museum,** Old Butter Market (tel. 032 65 2480). Collections of archeological, industrial, domestic and farming items, including a cider press, mill and reconstructed rooms *Weekdays 1030-1230, 1400-1630 (but closed Wednesdays PM). Free.*

21b Falmouth: **Council Chamber,** Municipal Offices, The Moor. Fine collection of old documents connected with the town.

Public Library, The Moor. Good selection of books about Cornwall; also exhibition of drawings and paintings.

Maritime Museum, Church Street. Models and relics of the Falmouth 'packets' — the famous mail boats (see page 103); also an art centre and gallery. *Monday to Saturday (not Bank Holidays).*

22b Tresco: **Valhalla Museum,** Tresco Abbey (tel. Scillonia 0720 22849). Figureheads, carved ornaments and other relics from wrecked ships dating back to the 17th century. *Monday to Saturday 1000-1600.*

22e Hugh Town: **Isles of Scilly Museum.** Exhibits showing the history of the islands since the Stone Age, including a fully rigged pilot gig and many remains from shipwrecks. *April to mid October: Monday to Saturday. Rest of year: Wednesdays only.*

22h Zennor. See 19b.

22i St Ives. See 19c.

23h Pool: **Camborne School of Mines Museum,** Trevenson (tel. 0209 714866). Extensive geological collection of minerals and ore specimens. *Weekdays 0900-1630.*

23h Camborne: **Public Library and Museum,** The Cross. Extensive collection of Stone Age tools and weapons; also prehistoric pottery, snuff boxes, old china, mineral specimens and photographs. *Monday to Wednesday and Fridays 1500-1700; Saturdays 1400-1600.*

23h Treskillard: **Carriage Museum.** Old carriages and horse drawn vehicles, some of which can be ridden in behind heavy horses. *Easter to October daily.*

24b Newquay: **Motor Museum.** Early bicycles and rare vehicles from 1900 to 1935. Working Victorian peepshows; 1912 seaside scene. *Easter, then Spring Bank Holiday to October daily.*

Trenance Cottages, Trenance Park. Collection of antiques and curios from all over the world. *May to September daily.* 🍽 ✂ 🖐

24h Truro: **County Museum and Art Gallery,** Royal Institution of Cornwall, River Street (tel. 0872 2205). Excellent museum with a really wide range of exhibits: archeology (including prehistoric weapons), natural history, industry; a world famous mineral collection; fine pottery, porcelain and pewter; Japanese ivories. Also displays of old master's drawings and a range of paintings. *Monday to Saturday (but not Bank Holidays): April to September 0900-1700; October to March 0900-1300, 1400-1600. Free.*

25d Mevagissey: **Town Museum,** East Quay (tel. 072 684 3568). Converted boatbuilders; workshop built in 1745 and specialising in maritime, agricultural and industrial exhibits, including a 6 ton granite cider press and a Cornish kitchen. *Easter to end September: daily from 1030.*

25e Charlestown: **Shipwreck Centre** (tel. St

Austell 0726 3332). Situated in a conserved 18th century harbour village, the Centre contains the complete wreck of the *Grand Turk,* plus displays showing the causes of wrecks and what happens to their remains. Boat trips arranged. *Easter daily, then Thursdays and Sundays to mid May: 1200-1730. Mid May to end September: daily 1030-1730 (2100 in July and August). October: Thursdays and Sundays 1030-1730.* 🍽

25f Fowey: **Noah's Ark Folk Museum,** Fore Street. Set in the oldest house in Fowey, it has a dozen rooms depicting Cornish scenes such as a photographic studio, kitchen, wash house, merchant's room, etc. Also a marine section with underwater scene, model schooner and ship's tools; early diving equipment; children's toys. *Mondays, Tuesdays and Thursdays to Saturday.*

Fowey Museum, Town Hall. Former council chamber now containing pictures, documents and other relics of the town's history.

26b St Keyne Station: **Paul Corin Music Museum,** Old Mill (tel. Liskeard 0579 43108). Outstanding collection of automatic music machines, including organs, pianos, music boxes and a violina, many of which are very rare. All housed in lovely hall and played daily. *Easter week, then May to September: daily 1030-1300, 1430-1700; also March, April and October Sundays PM.*

26b Looe: **Cornish Museum,** Lower Street, East Looe. Collection of magic and witchcraft items; also displays of local arts, crafts, folklore, industry and fire fighting, all housed in an old fish cellar. *Spring Bank Holiday to 30 September: daily 1000-2100.*

Guildhall Museum, Higher Market Street, East Looe. Restored building with displays of local history, including old town maces and pillory stocks. *April to September: Sunday to Friday.*

26d Polperro: **Smugglers' Museum,** Talland Street. Two life sized tableaux, one depicting the smugglers of old for which the village became notorious; the other showing modern smuggling methods. Also many relics of past and present crimes. *Easter to late October: daily 1000-1900.*

27a Sheviock: gallery with pictures, sculpture and antiques. *Daily.*

27b Plymouth: **City Museum and Art Gallery,** Drake Circus, off North Hill (tel. 0752 68000 ext 4378). Collections of silver, porcelain, natural history, archeology and history; diaries, family portraits and other relics of Sir Joshua Reynolds; famous collection of old master's drawings; model ships. *Monday to Saturday 1000-1800 (2000 Friday); Sundays 1500-1700. Free.*

The Prysten House, off Royal Parade (tel. 0752 61414). Contains an impressive model of Plymouth as it was in 1620; also the *Mayflower Story Room,* an exhibition of old printing and a herb display. *Monday to Saturday 1000-1600.* 🏠

The Merchant's House, 33 St Andrew Street (tel. 0752 68000 ext 4378). Museum of Plymouth history up to 1670. *Monday to Saturday 1000-1800; Sundays 1500-1700.* 🏠

28f Kingsbridge: **Cookworthy Museum,** Old Grammar School, 108 Fore Street (tel. 0548 3235). The 1670 school rooms have been converted into a memorial to William Cookworthy, the Quaker who started the local china clay industry. Also: Victorian kitchen and scullery, agriculture gallery, shipbuilding tools, costumes, photographs and local history displays. *Easter to mid October: Monday to Saturday 1000-1630.*

28i Salcombe: Overbecks Musem, Sharpitor, 1½ miles south of town. Interesting variety of exhibits, with sections on local shipbuilding, agricultural history, 19th century photographs, a children's room with dolls and dolls' house furniture, and a collection of moths and butterflies, birds' eggs, shells and animals. *1 April to 31 October daily 1100-1300, 1400-1800.* ✿ ⌂

29a Totnes: The Elizabethan House, 70 Fore Street (tel. 0803 863821). Houses the town museum, with a wide range of exhibits connected with the town and its inhabitants. Displays cover furniture, household objects, toys, dolls, costumes, archeology, documents and computers. *Christmas for 3 weeks, then April to October: Monday to Saturday 1030-1300, 1400-1730.* �**m** 🏛

Devonshire Collection of Period Costume, 10A High Street (tel. 0803 862423). Selections from the extensive collection are shown with accessories throughout the summer, with displays changed annually. *June to 30 September: weekdays 1000-1600; Sundays 1400-1700.* 🏛

Totnes Motor Museum, The Quay (tel. 0803 862777). Collection of vintage, sports and racing cars, many of which are still raced; they include Talbot Lago and Viosin cars. Also engines, motor bikes and automotive miscellany, all dating from 1922 to 1966. *Easter to October daily 1000-1800.*

Guildhall Museum, off High Street (tel. 0803 862147). Exhibits include Saxon coins minted locally, a list of over 600 past Mayors from the 14th century onwards, and a plaque to John Wells, the Totnes explorer who crossed Australia. *Easter to September: weekdays 0930-1300, 1400-1700. October to March: by appointment.* 🏛

29b Dartmouth: Town Museum, The Butterwalk (tel. 080 43 2923). Former merchant's house built in 1640, with original panels and ceilings, now housing historic and maritime exhibits, including over 140 model ships depicting the age of sail; also paintings and photographs. *Monday to Saturday: May to October 1100-1700; November to April 1415-1600.* 🏛

Henley Museum. Interesting relics of Dartmouth's past, plus pictures and other records of more recent history. *Monday to Saturday.*

29c Brixham: Museum. Displays depicting the history of the local fishing industry, once the most prosperous in South Devon; also geology, archeology and local history. *Spring Bank Holiday to September: daily (Sundays PM). Rest of year: Wednesdays and Sundays: PM only.*

30f Padstow: Institute Museum. Photographs and nautical items from the town's maritime history, also domestic and industrial tools and documents. *May to mid September Monday to Saturday.*

30h Newquay. See 24b.

31b Delabole Slate Quarry (tel. Camelford 084 02 2242). Small museum depicting 400 years of continuous working at the quarry. *Easter, then May to September weekdays: 1000-1800.* ↓T

31b Camelford: North Cornwall Museum, The Clease (tel. 084 02 3229). Voted the best small museum in England in 1978, this restored cottage offers a fascinating collection of tools used by craft and tradesmen in the 19th century; also an exhibition gallery. *1 April to 30 Setember Monday to Saturday 1030-1700.* ↓T

31d Wadebridge: Cornish Motor Museum. Includes a giant engine known as 'The Iron Maiden'.

31h Bodmin: Military Museum, The Keep, Victoria Barracks (Tel. 0208 2810). Medals, uniforms, weapons and other relics of the Duke of Cornwall's Light Infantry. *1 April to end February weekdays (not Bank Holidays): 0900-1230, 1400-1645. Free.*

Town Museum, 13 Rock Lane (tel. 0208 4159). Local history exhibition. *Telephone first.*

32c Launceston: Lawrence House Museum, Castle Street (tel. 0566 2833). Georgian House in the care of the National Trust, part of which

contains a remarkable collection of antiquities. *April to end September: weekdays 1430-1630; also Mondays, Wednesdays, Thursdays and Saturdays 1030-1230. Free.*

32g Dobwalls: Thorburn Museum and Gallery (tel. 0579 20325). Memorial exhibition of paintings, drawings, books, photographs and letters by Britain's finest painter of birds, Archibald Thorburn (1860-1935). This large barn, which won the Museum of the Year title in 1977, contains over 120 of his original works. Half price admission for visitors to adjacent Railroad Park (see page 106). *Easter for 10 days, then 1 May to end September daily: 1030-1800. Other times by appointment.* 🦽

32h St Keyne Station. See 26b.

33h Buckland Abbey. Once the home of Sir Francis Drake, it is now a museum in his honour, with a splendid model of his round-the-world ship *The Golden Hind*, the famous Drake's Drum, his sword and other relics; there is also a Folk Gallery, with West Country crafts, restored Elizabethan and Georgian rooms and a fine collection of silverware. Shrub and herb gardens and a mediaeval tithe barn in the grounds. *Good Friday to end September: Monday to Saturday and Bank Holidays 1100-1730; Sundays 1400-1730. Rest of year: Wednesdays and weekends 1400-1630.* 🐛 ✝

33i Yelverton: The St Tudy Paperweight Centre, Buckland Terrace, Leg-o-Mutton (tel. 082 285 4250). Probably the largest collection in existence, with over 800 glass paperweights, mostly French. *Good Friday to end October, also December: Monday to Saturday 1000-1700. Free.*

34i Buckfast: House of Shells, off A38 (tel. Buckfastleigh 036 44 3452). Enormously varied collection of mollusc containers from all over the world; also displays of shell art—painting, engraving, etc. *Easter to mid October daily 1000-1800 (1900 July and August).*

35c Dawlish: Town Museum. Local history, Victoriana, dolls and toys. *May to September daily.*

35d Ashburton: Town Museum, 1 West Street (tel. 0364 52298). American Indian relics; also local items, weapons, costumes, tools and geology specimens. *Mid May to end September: Tuesdays and Thursday to Saturday 1430-1700. Free.*

35g Totnes. See 29a.

35i Torre Abbey Mansion, The Kings Drive (tel. 0803 23593). Local authority museum and art gallery with interesting pictures and furniture. *April to October daily 1000-1300, 1400-1730.* ✿ 🏛

35i Torquay: Natural History Museum, Babbacombe Road (tel. 0803 23975). Archeology, folk life and natural history of Devon; also relics from Kents Cavern and other caves, including an exhibition of extinct mammals. *Monday to Saturday 1000-1645.*

36b Boscastle: Museum of Witchcraft and Black Magic (tel. Buckfastleigh 036 44 3452). One of the largest in Europe, it contains such grisly items as the skeleton of a witch executed in 1589, the thigh bone of a Tibetan sorcerer, paintings by a devil worshipper and samples of ointments and magic powders. Witches' altar room. *Easter to mid October daily 1000-2100.*

36e Delabole Slate Quarry. See 31b

36e Camelford. See 31b.

37e Launceston. See 32c.

39i Ashburton. See 35d.

40b Exeter: Royal Albert Memorial Museum, Queen Street (tel. 0392 56724). Extensive permanent collections include: important English paintings, ceramics and glass, silverware, costumes, natural history, anthropology, industry and technology. Star exhibits include the shield of the Apache chief Cochise. *Tuesday to Saturday (not Bank Holidays): 1000-1730. Free.*

Maritime Museum, The Quay (tel. 0392 58075). The world's largest collection of working boats, with about 100 craft afloat, ashore and inside.

Many can be boarded. There are Arab dhows, Irish curraghs, Welsh coracles, Burmese sampans, Red Indian canoes, Iraqi reed boats, Portugese beach craft, the world's oldest working steamboat, vessels from the TV series "Onedin Line" and much more. *Daily 1000-1700 (1800 in summer).* 🐛 ↓T 🚣

The Devonshire Regiment Museum, Wyvern Barracks (tel. 0392 76581 ext 268). The history of the regiment from its foundation in 1685 to its amalgamation with the Dorset Regiment in 1958. Weapons, uniforms, documents and medals. *Weekdays (not Bank Holidays) 0900-1630. Free.*

Rougemont House Museum, Castle Street (tel. 0392 56724). Mainly relics of prehistoric, Roman and mediaeval archeology. *Tuesday to Saturday: 1000-1300, 1400-1730. Free.* **m**

40c Topsham: Town Museum, 25 The Strand (tel. 039 287 3244). The sail loft of a 17th century gabled house containing pictures, tools and other relics depicting the history and trade of Topsham. *Mondays, Wednesdays and Saturdays: 1400-1700. Free.*

40f Dawlish. See 35c.

41a Bicton Countryside Museum (tel. Colaton Raleigh 0395 68465 or Budleigh Salterton 039 54 3881). Comprehensive range of old agricultural vehicles, including tractors and waggons; also a gipsy caravan. Hall of Transport has early steam and electric cars as well as petrol models. *1 April to 31 October daily 1000-1800.* 🐛 ⌂ 🦽

41b Sidmouth: Town Museum, next to parish church (tel. 039 55 2946 or 2357). Georgian house containing lace, ceramics, toys, Victoriana and prints of old Sidmouth. *Easter for 10 days, then Spring Bank Holiday to end September: Monday to Saturday 1030-1230, 1430-1630; Sundays PM.*

41d Budleigh Salterton: Fairlynch Arts Centre and Museum, Fore Street (tel. 039 54 2666). An 18th century house with mainly local exhibitions changed annually. Smuggler's Cellar, local history display, costumes, lacemaking displays. *Easter to end October daily 1430-1700 (also Monday to Saturday AM in July and August).*

42f Charmouth: Barney's Fossil and Country Life Exhibition. Superb collection of prehistoric fossils collected from the local beach, which is world famous for its fossils. *Easter to September daily.*

42f Lyme Regis: The Philpot Museum, Bridge Street. Old prints, documents, fossils (some very large), coins, relics from the Monmouth Rebellion, local history and a 1710 fire engine. *Easter to 30 September: daily 1000-1300, 1430-1730. October to April: weekends 1030-1230, 1430-1630; Tuesdays AM; Thursdays PM.*

43d Bridport: Town Hall, South Street. Collection of paintings by a local artist depicting scenes from the town's history. *Written permission only: Borough Offices, 32 South Street.* Also in the town hall are numerous records and documents, including a 1268 will.

Museum & Art Gallery, The Chantry, South Street (tel. 0308 22116). Tudor house with displays mainly depicting local history: rope and net making, archeology, agriculture, natural history, costumes, paintings and Roman relics. Also a famous collection of dolls in historical and national dress. *Weekdays 1000-1230; also 1 June to 30 September Monday to Wednesday and Fridays 1330-1800.*

44b Dorchester: Dorset County Museum, High West Street (tel. 0305 2735). Impressive museum covering the region's geology, archeology, natural history and history. Includes finds from nearby Maiden Castle and from Roman Dorchester; Stable Gallery has agricultural and domestic machinery; Thomas Hardy's reconstructed study has many of his original manuscripts, notebooks, drawings and other relics; regular concerts, lectures and film shows. *Weekdays 1000-1700; Saturdays 1000-1300, 1400-1700.*

The Dorset Military Museum, The Keep, Bridport Road (tel. 0305 4066). The history of the

Dorset Regiment from 1660, with weapons, medals, uniforms, pictures and battlefield relics. Also many foreign items, including Adolf Hitler's desk and relics of Clive of India. Well stocked reference library. *Monday to Saturday 0900-1300, 1400-1700 (but closed Saturday PM in winter).*

44e Weymouth: **Local History Museum,** West Ham Road (tel. 030 57 74246). Displays illustrating transport, royal visits, shipwrecks and domestic life. *Summer: Monday to Saturday 1000-2000 (1700 Tuesdays and Saturdays). Winter: Tuesday to Saturday 1000-1300, 1400-1700.*

44h Easton: **The Hardy and Portland Museum,** 217 Wakeham (tel. 0305 821804). Avice's Cottage in Hardy's novel "The Well-Beloved", it now contains items of local and natural history, including paintings, prints, photographs and relics of the stone industry and the prison service. *Easter to September: Monday to Saturday 1000-2000 (1700 Tuesdays and Saturdays). October to Easter: Tuesday to Saturday 1000-1300, 1400-1700.*

45a Bovington Camp: **The Tank Museum** (tel. Bindon Abbey 0929 462721 ext 463). The museum of the Royal Armoured Corps and the Royal Tank Regiment, it contains over 140 wheeled and tracked armoured fighting vehicles from 11 nations, the largest collection of its kind in the world. Also displays of armament, engines and equipment. *Daily 1000-1200, 1400-1600.*

45b Wareham: **Town Museum.** Local history and archeology; also photographs and relics of Lawrence of Arabia. *Easter to end September weekdays.*

Trinity Art Gallery. Variety of British and continental art. *June to end September daily; rest of year Fridays and weekends.*

45c Poole: **Guildhall Museum,** Market Street (tel. 020 13 5323). Georgian house now housing displays of Poole life in the 18th and 19th century. *Monday to Saturday 1000-1700; Sundays 1400-1700.*

Maritime Museum, Paradise Street, Poole Quay (tel. 020 13 5323). Nautical items from prehistoric to modern times displayed in the 15th century Town Cellars. *Times as for Guildhall Museum (above).*

Scalpen's Court, High Street (tel. 020 13 5323). Exhibition covering the development of Poole from prehistoric times until the 19th century, mostly with archeological items. *Times as for Guildhall Museum (above).*

Allen's Rock and Gem Centre, Poole Quay. Fascinating specimens, including fluorescent and polished stones. *January and February Saturdays; March to December Tuesday to Saturday.*

RNLI Lifeboat Museum, Poole Quay. Paintings, photographs, medals, documents, models and other relics of the service. *Weekdays.*

45f Corfe Castle: tiny museum in 1680 building containing village relics, including dinosaur footprints 130 million years old. *Daily 0900-1800 (later in summer). Free.*

45f Langton Matravers: **Parish Museum.** *Weekdays AM.*

46e Bude: **Historical and Folk Museum.** Old blacksmith's forge now housing models, maps, photographs and drawings illustrating the development of the town. *Easter to Spring Bank Holiday: weekends. June to September: daily.*

47c Great Torrington: **Town Hall Museum.** Georgian building housing displays of local history and a collection of Clinton pictures. *May to October daily.*

47d Thornbury: **Devon Museum of Mechanical Music,** Mill Leat (tel. Milton Damerel 040 926 378 or Shebbear 040 928 483). Tremendously varied collection of music machines, ranging from tiny music boxes to an 8 ton fairground organ. Everything can be played for visitors. *Easter to October daily 1400-1700.*

48a Beaford **Arts Centre,** Greenwarren House. Permanent exhibition of paintings, photographs, prints and some sculpture. Evening and residential courses in art and crafts. Travelling theatre group. *Weekdays.*

50a Tiverton: **Town Museum,** St Andrew Street (tel. 088 42 56295 or 2446). Restored 19th century school housing an outstanding collection of local exhibits, including a Victorian laundry, a costume gallery and a war room. *Monday to Saturday (not Bank Holidays): 1030-1300, 1400-1630. Free.*

51c Hatch Court (tel. Hatch Beauchamp 0823 480208). Includes a small Canadian military museum.

51f Chard: **Town Museum.** Restored Elizabethan cottage containing exhibits depicting local history and industry. *June to September: Monday to Saturday.*

Cromwell Tank,
Bovingdon Tank Museum (45a)

51g Honiton: **Allhallows Public Museum,** High Street (tel. Farway 040 487 307). Displays of lace and lacemaking (for which the town is famous); also a reconstructed Devon kitchen; 100,000-year-old animal bones found when the by-pass was built; Stone and Bronze Age tools; wartime relics. *May to September daily 1000-1700.*

52c Montacute House (tel. Martock 093 582 3289). Collection of Elizabethan and Jacobean portraits from the National Gallery; also fine examples of tapestry, heraldic glass and furniture. *April to October: Wednesday to Monday 1230-1730 (sunset if earlier).*

52c Yeovil: **Borough Museum,** Hendford Manor Hall (tel. 0935 5171; Saturdays only tel. 0935 24774). History, archeology and specialised collections of firearms, costumes, glass, engravings and maps. *Monday to Wednesday, Fridays and Saturdays: 0930-1300, 1400-1700. Free.*

53b Sherborne: **Abbey Gate House Museum,** Church Lane (tel. 093 581 2252). Local geology and history, a model of the Norman Castle as it was, photographs of the town from 1850, Roman relics, a Victorian dolls' house and a natural history section. *1 April to 31 October: Tuesday to Saturday 1030-1230, 1500-1630: Sundays 1500-1700. 1 November to 31 March: Tuesdays, Saturdays and Sundays (times as above).*

55b Appledore: **North Devon Maritime Museum,** Odun House, Odun Road (tel. Bideford 023 72 6042). Models, photographs and paintings illustrating every aspect of local nautical history, including shipwrecks and rescue work. Also a reconstructed 1900 kitchen. *Easter to 30 September daily 1430-1730; also Tuesday to Friday 1100-1300.*

55c Barnstaple: **The North Devon Athenaeum,** The Square (tel. 0271 2174). Archeological and geological specimens from throughout North Devon; also coins, butterflies, maps and an extensive specialist library. *Weekdays 1000-1300, 1415-1800; Saturdays AM. Free.*

St Anne's Chapel Museum, St Peter's Churchyard, High Street (tel. 0271 72511 ext 272). Former 14th century chapel now housing mainly local exhibits, including paintings, coins, firearms and ceramics. *1 June to mid September: Monday to Saturday 1000-1300, 1400-1700. Children free.*

55e Bideford: **Town Museum.** Collections of pottery, maps and shipbuilding tools. *Monday to Saturday.*

Burton Art Gallery, Victoria Park, Kingsley Road (tel. 023 72 6711). Permanent and visiting exhibitions of painting and other art. *Weekdays 1000-1300, 1400-1700; Saturdays 0945-1245. Free.* Also in Victoria Park are eight Spanish cannon, from ships of the Armada.

55e Great Torrington. See 47c.

56f South Molton: **Borough Museum,** The Guildhall (tel. 076 95 2501). Local history items, including a 1750 cider press; a fascinating collection of ancient fire engines, one of them dating from 1736; also pewter, weights and measures, documents. *Monday to Saturday: 1100-1230, 1430-1630. Free.*

57i Tiverton. See 50a.

59d Taunton: **Somerset County Museum,** Taunton Castle (tel. 0823 3451 ext 286). Large museum with impressive range of collections, including sections on archeology, geology, palaeontology, natural history, silver, ceramics, costumes and local arts and crafts. Also houses the museum of the Somerset Light Infantry (1685-1959), with weapons, medals, uniforms and battlefield relics. *1 April to 30 September: Monday to Saturday (not Bank Holidays) 1000-1700. 1 October to 31 March: Tuesday to Saturday 1000-1700.*

59e Hatch Court. See 51c.

59i Chard. See 51f.

60e Montacute House. See 52c.

60f Yeovilton: **Fleet Air Arm Museum** (tel. Ilchester 0935 840551 ext 521). The story of aviation at sea since 1903 is told with models, paintings, photographs, uniforms and medals connected with the Royal Naval Air Service and the Fleet Air Arm. Over 40 actual aircraft on display. *Monday to Saturday 1000-1730; Sundays 1230-1730.*

60i Yeovil. See 52c.

61d Sherborne. See 53b.

62e Ilfracombe: **Town Museum,** Wilder Road (tel. 0271 63541). Collections of botany, birds, reptiles, insects, engravings, pictures, maps, weapons, ships' models, pewter, stones, clocks, Victoriana, Egyptology. *Daily 1000-1700 (1300 in winter).*

Art and Crafts Exhibition, The Pavilion, The Promenade (tel. 0271 64864). Pictures and other art by local artists. Profits to charity. *Late April to end September daily 1000-2230. Free.*

62f Combe Martin: Motor Cycle Collection, Cross Street. British machines old and new, including a Brough Superior thought to have belonged to Lawrence of Arabia; also old signs and other motor cycle memorabilia. *May to end September: daily 1000-1800 (later in July and August).*

62g Croyde: Gem Rock and Shell Museum (tel. 0271 890407). Unique museum and workshop where semi-precious stones and shells from all over the world can be seen both on display and being worked on by skilled craftsmen. *March to October. daily 1000-1700 (2200 in July and August).*

62h Braunton: District Museum. Displays connected with local shipping, farming, industry and home life. *May to October: Monday to Saturday.*

Studio Ceramics, East Street (tel. 0271 812714). Pottery and lustre ware made from local clays. *Tuesday to Friday 0930-1700. Free.*

62i Barnstaple. See 55c.

63b Lynton: Lyn and Exmoor Museum, St Vincent's Cottage. 16th century building containing over 1000 items of local history, including scale models and photographs of the Lynton-Barnstaple Railway, which closed in 1935. Exmoor kitchen with open fireplace. *April to September: weekdays 1000-1230, 1400-1700; Sundays PM.*

63d Arlington Court (tel. Shirwell 027 182 296). Impressive country house with collections of model ships, shells, pewter, furniture, dresses, costumes, snuff boxes and other objets d'art; paintings include a William Blake watercolour; stables house a collection of horse-drawn carriages. *1 April to end October: Tuesday to Sunday and Bank Holiday Mondays 1100-1730.* 🐀 ⊞ ✝ 🐾

63f Malmsmead Museum: includes a reconstructed 17th century kitchen.

64d Malmsmead Museum: see 63f (above).

66b Burnham-on-Sea: small museum of Victoriana.

66h Bridgwater: Admiral Blake Museum, Blake Street (tel. 0278 56127). Birthplace in 1598 of Admiral Blake, this 15th century house now contains relics of the admiral; also items from the Battle of Sedgemoor, watercolours, local history and archeology. *Daily (not Bank Holidays): 1000-1300, 1400-1700 (Tuesdays AM only). Free.*

67a Axbridge: King John's Hunting Lodge, Market Place. Tudor house restored by the National Trust, now containing displays of archeology and local history, including old stocks, a bull-baiting anchor, a 1627 moneychanger's table, coins, flints, photographs and animal bones. *April to end September 1400-1700. Free.* ⊞

67a Cheddar: Gough's Cave Museum (tel. 0934 742343). Collection of Stone Age weapons and tools; a 12,000-year-old skeleton; flints, amber and engraved stones. *Easter to October daily 1000-1730.* 🐀 ☆

Motor and Transport Museum, at the foot of Cheddar Gorge. Veteran and vintage cars, motor cycles, bicycles and tricycles, all dating from 1898. *Daily 1000 to dusk.*

67b Wookey Hole: Cave Museum (tel. 0749 72243). Relics of some of the earliest men in Britain, including human and animal bones, jewellery and cooking utensils; also Celtic and Roman items, all found in the caves. *Daily: April to September 1000-1800; October to March 1000-1630.* 🐀 ⊨ ↓T ☆

Lady Bangor's Fairground Collection (tel. 0749 72243). The largest collection of its kind in Europe, it comprises colourful relics from the days of steam roundabouts—everything was made, mostly by hand, between 1870 and 1939. *Open as museum (above).*

67e Wells: Town Museum, Cathedral Green (tel. 0749 73477). Local history, prehistoric cave relics, fossils, rocks, minerals, coins and natural history. *Monday to Saturday: April to September 1000-1800; October to March 1400-1600. Sundays: June to September 1430-1730.*

67e Glastonbury: Tribunal, High Street. Collection of prehistoric items from Lake Village, including dug-out canoe, pottery, ornaments and weapons. *Daily from 0930 (Sundays PM).*

New Abbey Museum, Abbey Gatehouse (tel. 0458 32267). Includes a fine model of the abbey as it was in 1539. *June to August: daily 0900-1930. Rest of year: daily from 0930.* ✝ ↓T

68c Beckington: Min Lewis Pram Museum (tel. 037 383 531). Collection of old nursery furniture, Victorian toys, dolls and, of course, prams. *Saturday to Thursday.*

68c Frome: Town Museum. Exhibits and records of the town and the surrounding villages. *March to October: Wednesday to Saturday. Rest of year: Wednesdays and Saturdays only.*

68d Shepton Mallet: Town Museum, Market Place. Tiny building with prehistoric, Roman, mediaeval and natural history collections. *Weekdays.*

69a Phillips Countryside Museum, off A361 south of Southwick (tel. Westbury 0373 822238). Natural history and forestry items; also a collection of birds eggs which can be viewed with prior permission. *Daily 1000 to dusk* 🐀 🍀

69e Warminster: The Weapons Museum, School of Infantry, north east of town (tel. 0985 214000 ext 2487). *By appointment only.*

70f Nailsea Moor: Clevedon Country Museum, Moor Lane (tel. 0272 872 867). Exhibition gallery and craft displays at a working craft centre. *Whitsun and Summer Bank Holidays only: 1000-1730.* 🐀 ↓T

70g Weston-Super-Mare: Woodspring Museum, Burlington Street (tel. 0934 21028). Located in the old workshops of the Edwardian Gaslight Company, the displays include local history, archeology, wildlife, industry, costumes, china, photographs, early cameras and jewellery. Also a transport gallery, with a range of vehicles from penny farthing to autogyro; a reconstructed 1900 dentist's surgery, Victorian seaside holiday display. *Monday to Saturday 1000-1300, 1400-1700. Free.* 🐀 ↓T

71 Bristol: City Museum and Art Gallery, Queens Road, Clifton (tel. 0272 299771). Sections of archeology, geology, natural history, Egyptology, science and transport; also the history of Clifton Bridge. model ships and a collection of Victorian machinery. The art gallery offers a good selection of English, Italian and Dutch masters, sculpture, glass and excellent ceramics. *Monday to Saturday 1000-1700. Free.* 🐀

St Nicholas Church Museum, St Nicholas Street, off Baldwin Street (tel. 0272 299771). Depicts the history of Bristol up to the Reformation; collections of church plate and vestments; 18th/19th century water colours of the city; Hogarth altar piece. brass rubbing. *Monday to Saturday 1000-1700. Free.* ✝

Arnolfini Complex, Narrow Quay, off Redcliff Way. Galleries showing painting and sculpture; also films and music. *Tuesday to Saturday.* 🐀

Royal West of England Academy, Whiteladies Road (tel. 0272 35129). 19th century building housing occasional exhibitions.

72b Dodington House (tel. Chipping Sodbury 0454 318899). House contains a magnificent collection of furniture, paintings and other works of art; Carriage Museum has over 30 carriages; Family Museum includes scale aircraft models. Miniature railway, carriage rides, children's adventureland and many other attractions. *Easter to last Sunday in September: daily 1100-1700* 🐀 ❖ ⊞ 🐾 ↓T

72e Bath: Roman Baths Museum, Abbey Churchyard (tel. 0225 61111 ext 324). Items from the site of the baths complex next door; also gravestones,

pewter, tools and other relics from this and other Roman sites. *Daily 0900-1800 (winter Sundays 1100-1700).* 🐀 ⋒

Museum of Costume, Assembly Rooms, Alfred Street, off Lansdown Road (tel. 0225 61111 ext 324). World famous collection, one of the largest in the world, with fashions from the 17th century to modern times displayed in period rooms and settings; also toys, dolls and jewellery. *November to end March: Monday to Saturday 1000-1700; Sundays 1100-1700. Rest of year: daily 0900-1800.* 🐀 ⊞

Costume and Fashion Research Centre, 4 The Circus (tel. 0225 61111 ext 324). An extension of the Museum of Costume (above), with an extensive reference library and a collection of costumes for study. *Weekdays 1300-1700 by appointment only.*

Carriage Museum, Circus Mews (tel. 0225 25175). Britain's largest collection of over 30 horse drawn vehicles, ranging from a State Coach to a lowly Hansom Cab and including such oddities as a Victorian hearse. Also a display of harnesses and tackle. Carriage rides in summer. *Summer: Monday to Saturday 0930-1800, Sundays 1000-1800. Winter: Monday to Saturday 1000-1700, Sundays 1100-1700.*

Holburne of Menstrie Museum, Sydney Gardens (tel. 0225 66669). Outstanding collection of old master paintings (including work by Gainsborough, Reynolds and Stubbs), also silver, porcelain, glass, furniture and a 20th century Craft Study Centre. *Monday to Saturday 1100-1700; Sundays 1430-1800.* 🐀

Geology Museum, Bath Library, 18 Queen's Square. Collection of mainly local specimens. Library also offers numerous temporary exhibitions. *Monday to Saturday (not Bank Holidays).*

Burrows Toy Museum, The Octagon, Milsom Street. Books, games, dolls and other toys.

Victoria Art Gallery and Library, Bridge Street, near Pulteney Bridge (tel. 0225 61111 ext 324). Changing exhibitions of glass, ceramics, watches, coins, drawings, prints and paintings. *Weekdays 1000-1800; Saturdays 1000-1700.*

Museum of Bookbinding, Manvers Street, near Spa Station. Displays depict the history and art of bookbinding.

72i Claverton: The American Museum, Claverton Manor (tel. Bath 0225 60503). Furnished rooms decorated in period style; also fascinating collections depicting aspects of American society, including red indians, the Shaker religious sect, the conquest of the west and maritime history, with special lighting and sound effects. Displays of painting, glass, metalwork, costumes, folk sculpture, etc, comprising the best collection of American decorative art in Europe. *End March to end October: Tuesday to Sunday 1400-1700; also Bank Holidays and Bank Holiday Sundays 1100-1700. Other times by appointment.* 🐀 ⊞ ↓T

72i Farleigh Hungerford Castle Museum (tel. 022 14 4026). Weapons and armour, mostly dating from the Civil War; 15th century wall painting; 17th century stained glass. *Daily from 0930 (winter Sundays from 1400).* ⋒

73d Lacock: Fox Talbot Museum of Photography (tel. 024 973 459). Old cameras, slide shows and other relics of the great pioneer of photography who invented the negative/positive process. His original prints are not on show as they would fade. *March to October daily 1100-1800.* ⊞ ✝

73e Bowood House, Calne (tel. 0249 812102). Georgian house with exhibitions of paintings, sculpture, costumes, ceramics and furniture. Also the laboratory where Joseph Priestley discovered oxygen in 1774. *Good Friday to end September: Tuesday to Saturday 1400-1800; Sundays and Bank Holidays 1200-1800.* 🐀 ⊞

73e Spye Park House: Stables Museum (tel. Lacock 024 973 247). Large collection of carriages, harness and tackle, model fire engines, military relics and local history. *Sundays 1400-1700. Free.*

Castles

Only complete military fortifications or substantially complete ruins are included here; lesser remains are listed as Historical Sites (pages 79-83). Where castles also have notable interiors, further details can be found in the section on Historic Buildings (pages 90-94).

19f St Michael's Mount (tel. Marazion 0736 710507). The Mount was first fortified in 1190, at which time it was in the middle of a forest some miles from the sea. The present defences were laid down in the 14th century. The castle saw much heavy fighting in the 1549 Cornish Revolt, and again during both the Civil War and the Wars of the Roses during both of which it changed hands on several occasions. The guns on the 230 ft high summit were last fired at a pirate ship in 1812. The castle is still lived in and was much modified during the 17th, 18th and 19th centuries. It contains about 60 rooms, many linked by passages carved through the solid granite rock. Less visible features include a light railway which carries stores through a tunnel from the base of the rock. Access by causeway at low tide; ferry at high tide (take single tickets only). Limited space on Mount, so delays at peak periods. *April to end May Mondays, Wednesdays and Fridays; June to end October as above plus Tuesdays; 1030-1645. Also November to end March Mondays, Wednesdays and Fridays by hourly guided tours only 1100-1600 (weather and tide permitting).*

21b Pendennis Castle. One of a chain of forts built by Henry VIII to protect the South Coast from the French in the late 16th century, Pendennis was completed in 1544 to defend Falmouth harbour (with St Mawes, on the opposite side of the estuary, described below). It was extended by Elizabeth I in 1595 after Spanish raids in the area, but the only actual attack on the castle came from the land during the Civil War: from March to August 1646 the garrison held off Cromwell's army, being the last-but-one (Raglan held out for two days longer) Royalist stronghold to surrender. The Tudor defences—designed to withstand cannon-fire—consist of a circular keep and two rings of walls, all well preserved and with the original portcullis and drawbridge surviving. *Daily from 0930 (winter Sundays from 1400).*

St Mawes Castle. Completed in 1543 as part of Henry VIII's coastal defenses (see Pendennis, above). One of the best-preserved Tudor castles, it never saw action: with defences, albeit massive, aimed entirely to sea, its garrison chose instant surrender when beseiged in the Civil War. The central tower is surrounded by defensive walls shaped like a clover leaf (or a Tudor rose?) with entry via the stalk. *Opening times as for Pendennis.*

22e Star Castle, Hugh Town. Built on The Garrison headland in 1571 on the orders of Elizabeth I, who feared the Spanish might seize the Scilly Isles as a naval base. Built in the shape of an 8-pointed star with 96 loopholes and a moat.

25c Restormel Castle. The site was first fortified in wood just after the Norman Conquest, but a stone gatehouse was added about 1100. In 1264 the castle was surrendered to Simon de Montfort, after which much of the existing stonework was installed. Despite being in poor condition at the time, it was garrisoned by the Roundheads in 1644, but fell to the Royalists. The site then became overgrown but has since been thoroughly cleared to reveal ruins in surprisingly good condition. Almost perfectly circular, the castle stands on an artificially-raised hill surrounded by a 60 ft wide moat. *Daily from 0930 (winter Sundays from 1400).*

25g Caerhays Castle. Striking 'mock' castle restored by John Nash in Gothic style in 1802. Privately owned, but visible from the road. *Not open.*

27b Plymouth: Citadel, The Hoe. Built by Charles II in the 17th century and incorporating all the then-latest ideas of defensive strategy. It covers 33 acres and its limestone-and-granite walls are 20 ft thick in places, but it saw very little action. *Daily.*

29a Totnes Castle. Built in the 11th century by Judhael, who led the Norman conquest of South-West England, it is an excellent example of Norman castle design, with central keep and huge motte. Little remains of the original structure, the site having been much modified in the 13th, 14th and 15th centuries. *Daily from 0930 (winter Sundays from 1400).*

29e Dartmouth Castle. Built in 1480 to protect the harbour entrance, it was the first fortress in Britain designed specifically to withstand artillery. Radical features included a heavy chain stretching across the river to Kingswear Castle (which is not open to the public) to deter enemy shipping. During the Civil War it was captured by the Royalists after a seige of 1 month; they held it for 3 years until Roundhead forces stormed it in 1646. *Daily from 0930 (winter Sundays from 1400).*

30f Padstow: Prideaux Place, Fentonluna Lane. Castellated home, previously known as Gwarthandrea, built in 1585 on the site of a monastery. Privately owned, but visible for many miles around. *Not open.*

31a Doyden Castle. Built around 1830, this 'folly' takes the form of a miniature castle perched on the cliff edge. Shaped like a long octagon, it was used by a Wadebridge merchant for parties.

31i Restormel Castle. See 25c.

32c Launceston: Dunhevet Castle. The site was first fortified soon after the Norman Conquest, the wooden fort being replaced in the mid 13th century by the existing stonework, despite the apparent strategic unsuitability of the hilltop location (no sea or river supply route). A shell keep was surrounded by a circular wall and the gap was roofed in to provide a firing platform. Its original military career was brief and it was overgrown by 1409; during the Civil War, however, it was fought over—and captured—by both sides on several occasions. After that it became a prison, in 1656 holding George Fox, founder of the Quakers. *Daily from 0930 (winter Sundays from 1400).*

Restormel Castle (25c)

St Michael's Mount (19f)

the work of the Courtenays, Earls of Devon. The Great Hall is over 50 ft long and there is also an armoury, guard room, Stuart farmhouse wing, moat and gardens. *Easter to late September: Wednesdays, Sundays and Bank Holiday Mondays; July to end October daily except Saturday; 1400-1700.*

50a Tiverton Castle (tel. 088 42 3200). Small Norman castle started in 1106 by the first Earl of Devon, by order of Henry I. It was a Royalist stronghold during the Civil War, but fell to Roundheads under General Fairfax. Remains include two towers and gatehouse. Furnished rooms, Joan of Arc Gallery, St Francis Chapel and fascinating clock collection. *Easter, then May to late September daily 1430-1730.* ●

53b Sherborne Castle (tel. 093 581 3182). Built for Sir Walter Raleigh in 1594 and enlarged in 1625. Family home of the Digbys since 1617. The central block of the castle is Norman. *Easter Saturday to last Sunday in September: Thursdays; weekends and Bank Holiday Mondays 1400-1800.* ● � ⌂

Tiverton Castle (50a)

35c Powderham Castle (tel. Starcross 062 689 243). Home of the Earls of Devon for over 600 years, the oldest parts of this castle date from 1390, although most of the building dates from 1760-1860. It was damaged during Civil War skirmishes, but has been restored. *Easter Sunday and Monday, then mid April to mid May Sundays; then to end September daily; 1230-1730.* ● 113 ⌂

35g Totnes Castle. See 29a.

35h Compton Castle (tel. Kingskerswell 080 47 2112). Fortified manor house built in 1320, extended in 1440 and 1520 and restored since 1930. The defences were included to help protect Paignton from French raiders, each entrance having a portcullis and the whole house and garden being surrounded by a 24 ft high curtain wall. It is still the home of the Gilbert family, whose ancestors included Sir Humphrey Gilbert, one of Britain's great Elizabethan sailors. *April to end October; Mondays, Wednesdays and Thursdays 1000-1145, 1400-1645.* 113

37e Launceston: Dunhevet Castle. See 32c. ●

38c Okehampton Castle. Originally a Norman stronghold on a spur overlooking the river, most of the existing granite and shale castle was built early in the 14th century. It remained in the hands of the Courtenay family until 1538, when the owner was beheaded and the castle dismantled by the king. Restoration was started at the end of the 19th century and today one can see much of the original defences, the keep, Great Hall and chapel. *Daily from 0930 (winter Sundays from 1400).*

39b Castle Drogo, Drewsteignton (tel. Chagford 064 73 3306). The last castle built in England, this remarkable granite building was only completed in 1930. It stands 900 ft up overlooking the wooded gorge of the River Teign and was built as a private house, with luxurious unmilitary interior and formal gardens. *April to end October daily 1100-1730.* ●

40f Powderham Castle. See 35c.

44h Portland Castle. Built in 1540 as part of Henry VIII's coastal defences (see 21b Pendennis), it is probably the best preserved of all, although some of the surviving buildings date from the 17th and 18th centuries. The Portland Stone fortification is still lived in. *April to September weekdays 0930-1900 (1730 April); Sundays 1400-1900 (1730 April).*

46e Bude Castle. Quaint little building in the town centre dating from 1850 and now housing the council offices.

49f Bickleigh Castle (tel. 088 45 363). Although the majority of the surviving stonework dates from the 15th century, the castle was built on the site of a Norman fort—the thatched chapel within dates from about 1090. The mediaeval defences were

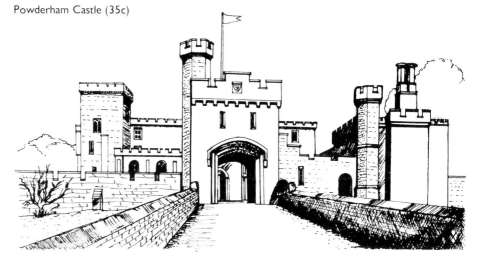

Powderham Castle (35c)

57i Tiverton Castle. See 50a.

59d Taunton Castle (tel. 0823 3451 ext 286). 12th century Norman castle with massive walls, Great Hall 120 ft long and notable gatehouse added in 1495. After the defeat of the Duke of Monmouth at Sedgemoor in 1685, the Great Hall was the scene of Judge Jeffrey's Bloody Assize. *1 April to 30 September Monday to Saturday; 1 October to 31 March Tuesday to Saturday; 1000-1700.* ■

61a Compton Castle. Not to be confused with the older castle of the same name in Devon (35h), this is a 19th century Gothic fantasy.

61d Sherborne Castle. See 53b.

62f Watermouth Castle (tel. Ilfracombe 0271 643879). Neo-Gothic castle built in 1825 with banqueting hall, minstrels' gallery, dungeons, small museum, etc.; part of a family entertainment centre with many other attractions. *Whitsun to end September: weekdays 1030-1700, Sundays 1400-1700. October: limited opening.* ● ⛵ ☆ ✛

64f Dunster Castle (tel. 064 382 314). The wooded ridge on which it stands dominates the town and has been fortified since Saxon times, and parts of the existing castle date back to the 13th century, notably the fine gatehouse. Most of the castle was rebuilt in the 16th century, however, with Gothic additions in the 19th century. Dunster has led a peaceful existence, apart from the Civil War: it was taken by the Royalists in 1642 and then, after a siege of 150 days in 1645, by the Roundheads. Fortunately, a subsequent order to dismantle it was never carried out, and the castle is still occupied by

the descendants of those who lived there 600 years ago. *Early April to end September Sunday to Thursday 1100-1630; October Tuesdays, Wednesdays and Sundays 1400-1530.* ♠ ✿ 113 ⌂

67f Wells Bishop's Palace (tel. 0749 78691). Official residence of the Bishops of Bath and Wells, the palace was built in the 13th century, fortified in the 14th and much extended in the 15th. Parts of the palace, the Bishop's Chapel, the banqueting hall and the undercroft all date from the earliest period; the fortifications, including the moat and the gatehouse, are still intact; while the later parts of the palace include the present Bishop's residence, state rooms and the Long Gallery, with its pictures of past Bishops. *Easter, then May to October Sundays (daily in August); PM.*

68e Nunney Castle. Built in 1373 by the local knight, with more of an eye to prestige than to defensive strategy, this small castle is most unusual. It is a tall rectangular structure with a large tower at each corner, roofed in the style of a French Chateau and surrounded by one of the deepest moats in Britain. It saw action only once, during the Civil War, when in 1645 the Roundheads used cannon to swiftly breach the north wall, the remains of which finally fell down in 1910. The site has been well restored since. *Daily from 0930 (Sundays PM). Free.*

72h Midford Castle. Built in 1775 in the shape of a cloverleaf, supposedly to celebrate the gambling success of one whose game was based on a lucky ace of clubs. Beautifully sited in wooded grounds.

Historic Buildings

Including stately homes, historic houses and non-military buildings with interesting architectural features. Some castles which boast fine interiors have their rooms described here, although their military histories will be found in the section on Castles (pages 88-89).

19e Castle Horneck (Iron Castle). An 18th century mansion in wooded surroundings, now a Youth Hostel. Half a mile SW is **Trereife House**, a splendid 17th century mansion.

19f Penzance: **The Egyptian House**, Chapel Street. Flamboyant facade created in about 1830 and recently restored. National Trust shop. *1 March to end December Monday to Saturday 0900-1700.*

20b Godolphin House (tel. Germoe 0736762409). Part Tudor, part Elizabethan manor with unique front of granite colonnades added in 1635. Kings Room said to have been used by Charles II after his escape from Pendennis. *May and June Thursdays 1400-1700; July, August, September Tuesdays and Thursdays 1400-1700.*

23f Harmony Cottage, birthplace in 1761 of Cornwall's best-known painter, John Opie.

24b Trerice (tel. Newquay 063 73 5404). Small Elizabethan manor rebuilt in 1571. Fine fireplaces and plaster ceilings; hall window with 576 panes of glass; collection of oak and walnut furniture. Interesting garden. *1 April to end October daily 1100-1730.* 🖛

24c St Columb Major: Glebe Cottage, next to the churchyard of St Columba, dates from 1638.

24d Harmony Cottage. See 23f.

24f Trewithen, Probus (tel. St Austell 0726 882418). Fine Cornish house built in 1720 and occupied by the same family ever since. Furniture, pictures and relics of Sir Stamford Raffles, first governor of Singapore. Guided tours. *April to July Mondays and Tuesdays 1400-1630.* �֍

25f Fowey: Place House. Home of the Treffry family rebuilt in 1457, 1740 and early in the 19th century. Highly ornamented, with many 16th century items and a chair used by Elizabeth I.

25c Lostwithiel: Guildhall. Built in 1740 and containing the borough regalia, 1670 silver mace and charters dated from 1189 to 1885. Call at municipal offices opposite. Sited in the town's main street, which contains fine examples of many periods of English architecture.

26b Looe: Thomas Bond's house. Finely panelled 17th century home of the man who was town clerk of both Looes for 40 years.

Guildhall. 16th century with gabled porch, exterior stair, pillory and old magistrates' bench.

Market House. Six sided with bell turret, now converted to a shop.

27a Antony House, Torpoint (tel. Plymouth 0752 812191). Finest Georgian house in Cornwall, built of silver granite in 1711-21, with red brick wings attached by colonnades. Original panelling, fine furniture, china, needlework and paintings (including work by Reynolds). The site has been occupied by the Carew family since 1492. Guided parties only. *April to end October: Tuesdays, Wednesdays, and Thursdays; also Bank Holiday Mondays; 1400-1730.*

Bath Pond House, ½ m from Antony House, was built in 1784 and has extensive grounds. *Written appointment only: The Secretary, Antony House.*

27b Mount Edgcumbe. This 16th century mansion overlooking Plymouth Sound was damaged by bombs during the Second World War, but has since been partly restored, with fine furniture and pictures. Philip of Spain promised the estate to the commander of the Spanish Armada if he defeated Drake in 1588. *May to end September Mondays and Tuesdays 1400-1800. Free.* 🖛 �֍

27 Plymouth: Elizabethan House, 32 New Street (tel. 0752 68000 ext 2006). Situated in Plymouth's historic Barbican area, this merchant's house was built in the 16th century and has been well restored. Furnishings are Elizabethan and Jacobean. *Monday to Saturday 1000-1300, 1415-1630 (1800 in summer); also summer Sundays 1500-1700. Free.*

The Prysten House (priest's house), off Royal Parade (tel. 0752 61414). The oldest house in the city, it was built in 1490 to accommodate visiting clergy. Its grey stone exterior is little changed and it retains a 'Door of Unity' into the next door St Andrew's Church. *Monday to Saturday 1000-1600.* 🖾 ✝

The Merchant's House, 33 St Andrew Street (tel. 0752 68000 ext 4378). Large 16th/17th century town house furnished in contemporary style *Monday to Saturday 1000-1800; Sundays PM.* 🖾

Guildhall, off Royal Parade. Built in 1870-1874, it was extensively damaged by bombs during the Second World War, but was restored and re-opened in 1959.

27c Saltram House (tel. Plymouth 0752 336546). A large and remarkable George II mansion, built to incorporate the remains of earlier Tudor and Stuart homes. Magnificent interior, with salon and dining room by Robert Adams, and many original furnishings. Collections of pottery, porcelain and paintings (including work by Reynolds, Rubens, Breughel and others). Kitchen, stables with exhibition and shop, garden with 18th century octagonal summer house and orangery. Private rooms open Thursday PM only. *1 April to end October: Tuesday to Sunday and Bank Holiday Mondays 1230-1730.* 🖛 ✖

28e Flete. Elizabethan manor house restored in 1876, with timber panels and floors. *May to September Wednesdays and Thursdays 1400-1700.*

29a Totnes: Tudor House, 10A High Street (tel. 0803 862423). Beautifully restored residence now housing an extensive costume collection. *June to 30 September: weekdays 1000-1600; Sundays PM.* 🖾

Elizabethan House, 70 Fore Street (tel. 0803 863821). Four storey, half timbered, gabled merchant's house dating from about 1575, with a cobbled courtyard and an interesting interior now housing a museum. *Christmas for 3 weeks, then April to October: Monday to Saturday 1030-1300, 1400-1730.* 🅼 🖾

Guildhall, off High Street (tel. 0803 862147). Home of the council chamber since 1624, this colonnaded 16th century building also houses the local magistrates' court and a museum. *Easter to September: weekdays 0930-1300, 1400-1700. October to March by appointment.* 🖾

29b Dartmouth: Agincourt House, Lower Ferry (tel. 080 43 2472). This former merchant's house is one of the oldest in Dartmouth. Built in 1380, it has twice been restored (1671 and 1966) and now houses an antique shop and museum. *Daily all year. Free.*

Butterwalk. Row of four shops with projecting timbered houses (supported by granite columns) dating from 1635. Damaged by bomb in 1943, they were restored in 1954. 🖾

29c Paignton: Oldway (tel. 0803 550711). Magnificent mansion with 115 rooms built in 1873 by American sewing-machine millionaire Isaac Singer. Modelled on Versailles, with ballroom, marble staircase, miniature hall of mirrors, etc. Used as a civic centre by Torbay Borough and therefore closed for council use occasionally. *May to September:*

Monday to Saturday 1000-1300, 1415-1715; Sundays 1430-1730. October to April Monday to Friday only, as above. Free. 🖛 ✖

Kirkham House, Kirkham Street. Restored 15th century house with interesting architecture. *April to September: weekdays 0930-1900 (1730 in April); Sundays 1400-1900 (1730 in April).*

29g Widdicombe House. Early 18th century with added Georgian wing. Picture gallery, also water gardens by Capability Brown.

30f Padstow: Abbey House, North Quay. 15th century home which had an underground passage leading to the monastery.

Raleigh Court, South Quay. 16th century building used by Sir Walter Raleigh when collecting dues to which he was entitled as Warden of Cornwall.

30i St Columb Major. See 24c.

31e Pencarrow (tel. St Mabyn 020884369). Georgian mansion of about 1776, built in Palladian style; fine Inner Hall with marble pillars and cantilever staircase; music room with Rococo ceiling; superb collection of 18th century paintings, including 11 by Sir Joshua Reynolds; English, French and Oriental furniture and china. *Easter Saturday to 30 September, Tuesday to Sunday and Bank Holiday Mondays 1330-1700 (1100-1700 in summer).* 🖛 ✖ 🎏

31h Lanhydrock (tel. Bodmin 0208 3320). Extensive 17th century mansion built in 1634, most of which was rebuilt in 1881 after a major fire. Beautifully-furnished rooms, including 116 ft long gallery whose barrel ceiling is plastered with scenes from the Old Testament. Extensive 1881 kitchen, 17th century picture gallery and family portraits from the 17th to 20th centuries. Fine 1651 gatehouse. *1 April to end October daily 1100-1730.* 🖛 ♣ ✖

32b Trewint: John Wesley Shrine. Small cottage dedicated to the founder of Methodism, who stayed here during preaching tours in 1742 and 1762. Two rooms have been preserved in the style of that period.

32d Bolventor: Jamaica Inn. Scene of Daphne du Maurier's famous novel about smuggling. Now a hotel and restaurant. 🖛

32f Trecarrell (tel. Coads Green 056 682 286). Restored manor hall and chapel of 1488. *By appointment only.*

33g Cotehele (tel. St Dominick 0579 50434). Magnificent mediaeval house, built between 1485 and 1627 and little changed since. Constructed of grey granite round three courts, it contains furniture, tapestry, needlework and armour, all of which has always been in the house. Also, at Cotehele Quay, the restored Tamar sailing barge *Shamrock* and a small maritime museum can be seen. With extensive grounds, the estate requires at least a full day to cover. Certain rooms in the house have no electric lighting. *April to end October, Tuesday to Sunday and Bank Holiday Mondays 1100-1730; November to 23 December, Hall of House only 1100-1700.* 🖛 ✖ 🥄🍴 🖾

35b Ugbrooke (tel. Chudleigh 0626 852179). Fine 18th century house by Robert Adam, his first castle-style design. Grand library, interesting chapel, outstanding collection of Elizabethan embroidery and needlework, restoration portraits and other paintings. *Spring Bank Holiday Sunday and Monday, then June to September Sunday to Thursday; 1400-1730.* ✖

35c Powderham Castle (tel. Starcross 062 689 243). Home of the Earls of Devon for over 600 years, the oldest parts date from 1390, although most of the building dates from 1760 to 1860. The ground floor rooms are open to the public and include: Banqueting Hall, Music Room (in blue and gold, containing a small organ), Marble Hall (with fine tapestries) and the Grand Staircase leading to the private apartments, which can be visited Thursday PM only. Fine pictures include family portraits of the Courtenays. Deer park in grounds. *Easter Sunday and Monday, then mid April to mid May Sundays; then to end September daily; 1230-1730.* ☛ ⚑ ⌂

35e Bradley Manor. Small, roughcast 15th century manor house with great hall, buttery, screens passage and Perpendicular chapel; 13th century undercroft in south wing. Excellent example of domestic Gothic architecture. No indoor photography. *Early to end September Wednesdays 1400-1700. Other times by written appointment only.*

35g Totnes. See 29a.

35h Compton Castle (tel. Kingskerswell 080 47 2112). Fortified manor house built in 1320 and extended in 1440 and 1520. Restored since 1930. Original kitchens, restored Great Hall, courtyard and chapel are on show. *April to end October Mondays, Wednesdays and Thursdays 1000-1200, 1400-1645. Other times by appointment.* ⚑

35h Paignton. See 29c.

35h Cockington Court (tel. Torquay 0803 67230). Elizabethan house with Georgian front. ✟ ⚵ ☺

35i Torquay: Torre Abbey Mansion, The Kings Drive (tel. 0803 23593). Constructed from the abbey ruins in the 18th century. Collections of 17th century silver, 18th century glass, also paintings. **Tythe Barn** nearby is known as Spanish Barn because the crew of the Spanish flagship were imprisoned there after the Armada. *April to October daily 1000-1300, 1400-1730.* ▣

36d Tintagel: Old Post Office. Former 14th century manor house with large hall, converted to a letter receiving office in the 19th century and now restored as such. National Trust Shop. *1 April to end October: Monday to Saturday 1100-1300, 1400-1800 (sunset if earlier); Sundays 1400-1800. December to February: key from caretaker.*

King Arthur's Hall. Modern building built with 50 different kinds of Cornish stone and opened in 1933. It is decorated with scenes from Arthurian legend. Headquarters of the Fellowship of the Knights of the Round Table.

36g Pencarrow. See 31b.

36i Bolventor: Jamaica Inn. See 32d.

37h Trecarrell. See 32f.

40b Exeter: Guildhall, High Street (tel. 0392 77888). Thought to be the oldest municipal building in Britain, it dates back at least to 1160. The main structure dates from 1330, with the Tudor frontage added in 1593 and straddling the pavement. Fine displays of portraits, silver and city regalia. *Opening times subject to council functions. Monday to Saturday 1000-1730. Free.*

Custom House, Quay Hill (tel. 0392 74021). Brick built in 1681 and little changed. Fine plasterwork ceilings. *Visits by arrangement with HM Customs & Excise, but casual callers usually accepted.*

Tuckers Hall, Fore Street. Ancient hall of the Incorporation of Weavers, Fullers and Shearmen, founded in 1471 and still in existence. Was a one-storey chapel until divided horizontally in the 16th century. Upper floor features fine timbered roof and oak-panelled chamber. *June to September, Tuesdays, Thursdays and Fridays; October to May, Fridays.*

Mol's Coffee House, Cathedral Close (tel. 0392 74312). Three storey building of uncertain origin with upper windows styled like those at the rear of an Elizabethan galleon. Now an art shop.

West Street. Row of 15th century houses, including one which in 1961 was moved intact from a site 50 yards away.

St Nicholas Priory, The Mint, Fore Street (tel. 0392 56724). The mediaeval guest house of the Benedictine monastery, with massive pillars, vaulted roof, Norman crypt and 15th century kitchen. Displays of furniture, wood carving and pewter. The only such building to have survived the Dissolution and be restored. *Tuesday to Saturday 1000-1300, 1400-1730.* ✟

40b Haldon Belvedere, also known as Lawrence Castle: a tower built in 1788 by Sir Lawrence Palk, governor of Madras, to remind him of the beauties of the Orient. Marble spiral stairs from India, given by the Nizam of Hyderabad. Excellent views of surrounding moors from top. Lived in by a local farmer. *Open occasionally.*

40e Ugbrooke. See 35b.

40f Powderham Castle. See 35c.

40g Bradley Manor. See 35e.

41d A la Ronde, Summer Lane, Exmouth (tel. 039 52 45514). This unique house at first appears round, but is actually a 16 sided (hexadecagonal) building with all the rooms radiating from a central, 35 ft high wall. It was built in 1798 by the Misses Jane and Mary Parminter and is still owned by the same family. A curious combination of elaborate design and practicality, it includes a Regency gallery and staircase lined with thousands of shells, collages of sand and seaweed and a feather frieze around the drawing room. The windows, from which there are fine views, are diamond shaped. *Easter to end October: Monday to Saturday 1000-1800; Sundays 1400-1900.*

Point-in-View, nearby, is a pretty group of buildings including a miniature chapel and almshouses.

41d Hayes Barton, East Budleigh. Birthplace in 1552 of Sir Walter Raleigh. Elizabethan-style farmhouse with stone chimneys and reed thatch in excellent condition. *June to September Monday to Friday.*

42c Forde Abbey (tel. South Chard 0460 20231). Founded by Cistercian Monks in 1138 and enlarged in 1500, it was converted to a private house in 1650 for Cromwell's Attorney General. The present family have lived there since 1864. Contains five famous Mortlake tapestries. *Easter Sunday and Monday; then May to September Sundays, Wednesdays and Bank Holiday Mondays; 1400-1800.* ☛ ❈

42d Colyton: Vicarage. Early 16th century with Tudor front and the badges of Henry VIII and Catherine of Aragon over the porch.

Church House. 15th century stone building which once served as the local Grammar School.

Court House. Said to be one of those used by 'Hanging Judge' Jeffries.

42e Uplyme: old hotel with 1,000-year old oak beam and quaint 13th century passage.

42f Charmouth: Queen's Arms Hotel. Once the guest house for Forde Abbey (42c 52d), it includes a fine Gothic window and interesting walls, ceilings and fireplaces. Used by Catherine of Aragon and by Charles II.

42f Lyme Regis: Tudbold Almshouses, near the Parish Church, were built in 1548 with funds by Thomas Tudbold and rebuilt in 1867.

Marder Almshouses. Paid for by Captain Nicholas Marder in 1892, these six almshouses stand in old Coombe Street.

43b Parnham House (tel. Beaminster 0308 862204). Attractive Tudor mansion, one of the best in Dorset. Strode Bedroom with giant four-poster, Oak Room with linen-fold panelling and ancient plasterwork—where Churchill and Eisenhower met to plan D-Day—plus exhibitions of modern furniture, arts and crafts. *April to October Wednesdays, Sundays and Bank Holidays 1000-1700 (but closed one Sunday in June).* ☛ ❈ ⚵

44b Higher Bockhampton: Hardy's Cottage (tel. Dorchester 0305 2366). Birthplace in 1840 of Thomas Hardy, the famous West Country novelist. The small thatched cottage, in one acre of garden, was built by his great-grandfather and is virtually unchanged. *Exterior can be viewed March to end October daily 1100-1800; interior by appointment only.*

44b Wolfeton House (tel. Dorchester 0305 3500). Manor house dating from 14th century, originally moated. Outstanding mediaeval and Elizabethan interior, with excellent wood and stone work, fireplaces and ceilings, Great Hall and stairs. Furniture and pictures from 17th century. Mediaeval gatehouse; also chapel and cider house. *Early May to 30 September: Sundays, Tuesdays, Wednesdays and Bank Holiday Mondays; August: daily except Saturdays; 1430-1800.*

44b Dorchester: Court House, High West Street (tel. 0305 5211). Scene in 1834 of the trial of the six Tolpuddle Martyrs, condemned to 7 years at Botany Bay in Australia for daring to demand a wage rise. The small court room belies the fame and importance of the case, which did so much to further the cause of trade unionism. *Summer weekdays 1000-1200, 1430-1600: winter weekdays AM. Free.*

King's Arms, High East Street. Fine Georgian inn, with pillared porch and bowed windows.

44b Came House, near Winterbourne Came. Built in the 18th century with columned frontage; interior features nice fireplaces and plasterwork. *By appointment only: Major N D Martin.*

44c Athelhampton (tel. Puddletown 030 584 363). Magnificent mediaeval house, a family home for over five centuries. One of the finest examples of

Montacute House (52c)

15th and 16th century residences in Britain. The Great Hall has a timbered roof, oriel window, heraldic glass and linenfold panelling. Also: Tudor Great Chamber, State Bedroom, wine cellar, thatched stables, secret passages, 15th century dovecote. The house is said to be the site of Athelstan's Palace; it is Thomas Hardy's 'Athel Hall'. *Early April to mid October Wednesdays, Thursdays and Sundays; Good Friday and Bank Holidays; also August Tuesdays and Fridays; 1400-1800.* 🍵 ❋

44e Weymouth: 2 and 3 Trinity Street. Tudor cottages restored with contemporary furniture typical of a 17th century sailor's home. *April to October: Wednesdays, Saturdays and Bank Holidays.*

Pilgrim House, Hope Square. Rebuilt in the 18th century, with original fire insurance plaque on the outer wall.

45a Cloud's Hill. Cottage owned by Lawrence of Arabia after he re-joined the RAF in 1925. Contains furniture and other memorabilia. No photography. *April to end September: Wednesday to Friday, Sundays and Bank Holiday Mondays 1400-1700; October to March Sundays only 1300-1600.*

45c Poole: Scalpen's Court, High Street (tel. 020 13 5323). Excellent 15th century town house with display of Poole history. *Monday to Saturday 1000-1700; Sundays 1400-1700.* ▣ ⬆T

45e Creech Grange. Tudor House with collection of furniture and paintings. *Summer months: Wednesdays, Thursdays and Sundays; PM.*

45e Barneston Manor. Stone-built 13th century manor house. *May to September Sundays.*

45e Smedmore House (tel. Corfe Castle 0929 480717). 17th and 18th century manor still occupied by the family who built it. Dutch furniture, Dresden china, antique dolls; walled garden. *Early June to mid September Wednesdays only 1415-1700.*

46e Ebbingford Manor, nr. Bude (tel. 0288 2808). Small 12th century Cornish house, originally a royal manor of the Duchy of Cornwall estate. Fine Tudor chimneys, restored Tudor chapel and small museum. *Early June to mid September: Tuesdays, Wednesdays and Thursdays; July to September as above plus Sundays; 1400-1730.* 🍵 ♣

46e Bude: Vicarage. Unusual building in which no room has right-angled walls.

47b Wear Giffard. Manor house built in 1454 and in good condition despite much damage by Cromwell's forces during the Civil War. Great Hall has outstanding hammerbeam roof. Lavish carving and linenfold panels throughout. *April to early September.*

47c Great Torrington: several buildings of note include the 17th century Black Horse Inn, the Victorian Market House, and the Georgian Town Hall ▣

49d Easton Barton. Fine example of a late mediaeval home, built about 1500 and hardly altered since.

49i Thorverton: delightful village with four centuries of architecture, including 16th century wattle-and-daub thatched cottages, a 1661 former parsonage and many others. The oldest house in the village is opposite the church.

50a Knightshayes Court (tel. Tiverton 0884 24665). This remarkable house is one of the few surviving examples of the work of William Burges. Built 1870-74, it has an ornate Victorian frontage and contains a collection of Old Masters. *April to 31 October daily 1330-1730.* 🍵 ❋

50a Tiverton: Blundell's. The original building of the famous grammar school, built in 1604 by a local wool merchant. The school moved on in 1882, but this stone building is preserved by the National Trust. The school features in "Lorna Doone".

Almshouses. Several examples of 16th century Tudor almshouses, including John Greenway's in Gold Street and Waldron's, on the other side of the River Exe.

50b Holcombe Rogus: Holcombe Court. Excellent example of Tudor house with fine woodwork by local craftsmen and a collection of 18th century furniture.

Church House. 16th century, with oak mullioned windows.

50c Wellington: The Squirrel Inn. Residential hotel over 400 years old.

The Three Cups, Mantle Street. Dates back at least to 1694.

50e Cullompton: The Manor House Hotel and Walronds House, both early 17th century, are among the few buildings which survived a great fire in 1839.

50g Killerton (tel. Hele 0329 288 345). Rebuilt in 1778 on the foundations of a much earlier house. Contains a splendid costume collection shown in rooms furnished in different styles. *April to end October daily 1100-1730.* 🍵 ❋ m

50i Cadhay, Ottery St. Mary (tel. 040 481 2432). Charming Elizabethan manor house built in 1550 and modified until the 18th century. A good example of domestic architecture from that period. Contains the "Court of Monarchs"—statues of Henry VIII and his children—in the Long Gallery. *Spring and Summer Bank Holidays; mid July to late August Wednesdays and Thursdays; 1400-1800.*

51c Hatch Court (tel. Hatch Beauchamp 0823 480208). Palladian-style Bath stone mansion of 1755 with curved wings, impressive stone staircase, early 19th century decoration and good collections of furniture, china and paintings. *July to September Thursdays 1430-1730.* 🍵 ▣

51g Honiton: Marwood House. Built in 1619 by one of Elizabeth I's doctors.

52a Barrington Court. Lovely Tudor mansion built 1514-20 in an E-shape. Gothic and Renaissance features, with restored interior. Nearby 1790 stable block. *Wednesdays only 1015-1215, 1400-1800 (1600 Easter).* ❋

52a Hinton House. Large building with parts dating back to the 17th century, but with many more recent additions.

52b East Lambrook Manor (tel. South Petherton 0460 40328). A 15th century home built of local Ham stone, extended in 16th century. Old panelling and period furniture. *March to October Thursdays 1400-1700.* ❋

52b Martock: Treasurer's House. Small 13th/14th century house with mediaeval hall and kitchen. *Written appointment only: The Tenant, Treasurer's House, Martock.*

52b Stoke sub Hamdon: Priory. A complex of buildings of Ham Hill stone, built in the 14th and 15th centuries to house the priests of the chantry of St Nicholas. The chantry itself is gone, but the Great Hall and screens passage remain. *Daily 1000-1800. Free.*

52c Tintinhull House. Small 17th century house with pedimented facade added in 1700. *April to end September: Wednesdays, Thursdays, Saturdays, and Bank Holiday Mondays; 1400-1800.* ❋

52c Montacute House (tel. Martock 093 582 3289). Tudor residence, built 1588 to 1601 from local Ham Hill stone on H-shape groundplan. Many Renaissance features, including plasterwork, chimneys and heraldic glass; fine 17th and 18th century furniture. *April to October: Wednesday to Monday 1230-1730 (sunset if earlier).* 🍵 ❋ ▣ ⌂

52c Brympton d'Evercy (tel. West Coker 093 586 2528). Norman mansion house with Tudor and Stuart additions, thoroughly restored by the owners. Contains the longest straight staircase in England. Felix dress collection. *1 May to late September Saturday to Wednesday 1400-1800.* 🍵 ❋ ⌂ ⬆T

52d Forde Abbey See 42c.

52h Parnham House. See 43b.

53a Yeovil: Newton Surmaville. Early 17th century manor house near the railway station.

53b Sherborne Castle (tel. 093 581 3182). Built by Sir Walter Raleigh in 1594 and enlarged in 1625. Home of the Digby family since 1617. Red Drawing Room has 17th century decorated ceiling and famous picture of Elizabeth I; Elizabethan Hall and Jacobean Oak Room show contemporary architecture and furniture. Fine pictures by Van Dyck, Gainsborough, Reynolds and others. 20 acres of Cability Brown gardens and 50 acre lake. *Easter Saturday to last Sunday in September: Thursdays, Saturdays, Sundays and Bank Holiday Mondays 1400-1800.* 🍵 m ⬛

53b Ven House, Milborne Port. Queen Anne mansion.

53b Purse Caundle Manor (tel. Milborne Port 0963 250400). Mediaeval manor house with original beamed and arched Great Hall and appropriate furniture. *Early March to 31 October: Wednesdays, Thursdays and Bank Holidays; 1400-1700.*

54d Hartland: 18th century mansion built on the ruins of a 12th century abbey and incorporating the abbey cloisters.

55b Tapeley Park, Instow (tel. 0271 860528). Remarkably sited overlooking the Atlantic, this William & Mary mansion has been owned by the Christie family since 1854 (John Christie founded the famous opera festival at Glyndebourne). Superb Italian plasterwork ceilings; also interesting furniture, glass, china and pictures. Guided tours. *Good Friday to late October: daily including Bank Holiday Mondays, but closed other Mondays; 1000-1800.* 🍵 ❋ ⌂

55c Barnstaple: Three Tuns Inn (tel. 0271 3637). Dating from 1450, this former merchant's house retains much of the decoration of a 15th century home.

Queen Anne's Walk, the Strand. Low colonnaded exchange building completed in 1609 when it was used by ship owners and shop keepers to discuss their business. Deals were completed by placing money on the Tome Stone, which is still in position.

Butcher's Row. A complete street of striking shops, all of which were once butchers. Opposite is the Pannier Market, scene of a market every Friday.

Penrose Almshouses were built in the 17th century.

55e Wear Giffard. See 47b.

55e Great Torrington. See 47c.

56b Castle Hill (tel. Filleigh 059 86 227). Palladian mansion built 1729-40 and home of the Fortescue family for centuries. Fine furniture, tapestries, porcelain and pictures. Conducted tours only. *By appointment only.* ❋

57i Knightshayes Court. See 50a.

57i Tiverton. See 50a.

58b Gaulden Manor (tel. Lydeard St Lawrence 098 47 213). Small red sandstone manor house dating from 12th century, immortalised by Thomas Hardy. Magnificent plaster ceiling in the Great Hall; oak screen to the 'Chapel'; fine furniture. *May to early September Thursdays and Sundays; also Easter Sunday and Monday; Spring and Summer Bank Holiday Mondays; 1400-1800.* 🍵 ❋

58c Cothelstone Manor. Fine Jacobean manor house beseiged during the Civil War. Gatehouse where 'Hanging Judge' Jeffreys hanged two supporters of the Duke of Monmouth after the latter's defeat at Sedgemoor in 1685. *By appointment only.*

58e Holcombe Rogus. See 50b.

58f Wellington. See 50c.

59d Taunton: Tudor House. Fore Street. Built in 1578, it is a splendid example of contemporary domestic architecture, with gales and half-timber construction.

Almshouses: two sets, one founded in 1635 by Robert Gray, with groups of tall triple chimneys; the other founded in 1615 by Richard Huish, a London merchant.

59e Hatch Court. See 51c.

60a Midelney Manor, Drayton (tel. Langport 0458 251229). Originally the island manor of the Abbots of Muchelney, this 16th to 18th century home has been in the hands of the Trevilian family since the Dissolution. 17th century Falcons Mews with converted interior. *Bank Holiday Mondays; also June to end September Wednesdays; 1400-1730.* ✿

60c Lytes Cary. 15th century manor house with Great Hall and 16th century great chamber with plaster ceiling and linenfold panelling. Home of the Lyte family for 500 years. *March to end October Wednesdays and Saturdays 1400-1730.* ✿ ✝

60d Muchelney: Priest's House. Late mediaeval thatched house with a large Gothic hall window. Originally the home of secular priests serving the local parish church. *By written appointment only; the tenant.*

60d Barrington Court. See 52a.

60d East Lambrook Manor. See 52b.

60e Martock. See 52b.

60e Tintinhull House. See 52c.

60e Montacute House. See 52c.

60g Hinton House. See 52a.

60i Brympton d'Evercy. See 52c.

60i Yeovil. See 53a.

61e Sherborne Castle. See 53b.

61e Ven House. See 53b.

61e Purse Caundle Manor. See 53b.

62f Combe Martin: The Pack of Cards. 300-year-old inn said to have been built by a card player, as it has four floors, 13 doors per floor and 52 windows.

62f Chambercombe Manor, Ilfracombe (tel. 0271 62624). Small manor house built in 1500, but incorporating parts dating back to the 12th century. Beautiful period furniture, armour and porcelain in 9 show rooms. Associations with smuggling and shipwrecking. Bricked-up room opened in the 19th century revealed the skeleton of a young woman now said to haunt the room. One of England's oldest inhabited houses. Pleasant gardens. *Easter Sunday to end September: Monday to Friday 1030-1300, 1400-1730; Sundays 1400-1700.* ☕

62i Youlston Park, Shirwell (tel. 027 182 200). Georgian house which includes the mediaeval beamed roof of an earlier building; 18th century stucco ceilings, fine staircase, Chinese decorations and collection of Victoriana. Woodland garden and lake. *May to September, Tuesday to Sunday, 1400-1800.* ☕

62i Barnstaple. See 55c.

63d Arlington Court (tel. Shirwell 027 182 296). Plain white Regency house with Doric porch, but with gorgeous interior. Built in 1822, it is unusual in having been unchanged since, most of the contents also being original. It is a superb example of the English country house and includes bedrooms and nursery in original condition; White Drawing Room with the carpet that was fitted when it was built; and several fascinating collections. Carriage rides. *1 April to end October: Tuesday to Sunday and Bank Holiday Mondays 1100-1730.* ☕ ♣ ✿ ▣ ♠

63e Lynton: Watersmeet House. Fishing lodge built in 1832 in a very attractive location. Now run by the National Trust as an information centre and shop. *April to end October daily 1100-1800. Free.* ☕

Dunster Castle (64f)

64f Dunster Castle (tel. 064 382 314). Although the site has Saxon origins and the gatehouse is 13th century, the residential part of this castle is largely Elizabethan, much of it done in 1589 by George Luttrell, whose family have lived here for over 600 years. The Gothic additions date from the 19th century, when a major reconstruction was undertaken. The notable interior includes plaster ceilings and a fine carved elm staircase dating from the 17th century; a set of 16th century leather hangings in the Banqueting Hall and a collection of family portraits. *Early April to end September: Sunday to Thursday 1100-1630; October Tuesdays, Wednesdays and Sundays 1400-1530.* ✿ ▦ ⌂

65d Bardon Manor, Washford (tel. 098 44 217). Unspoilt 14th century manor house with Saxon fireplace, collection of Mary Queen of Scots' papers and exhibitions of painting and handicrafts by locals. Said to be haunted. *June to September daily 1030-1730.*

65f Dodington Hall (tel. Nether Stowey 027 873 281). Fine Elizabethan house with timbered minstrels' gallery.

65f Nether Stowey: Coleridge Cottage (tel. 027 873 662). Home of Samuel Taylor Coleridge from 1797 to 1800; he wrote "The Ancient Mariner" here. Parlour only is shown. *April to end September Sunday to Thursday 1400-1700; other dates by written application only.*

Stowey Court. Part 15th century manor house with fine 18th century garden house.

65g Nettlecombe Court (tel. Washford 098 44 320). Ancestral home of the Raleigh and Trevelyan families. Mixture of Elizabethan and Georgian architecture, with two Adam-style drawing rooms. *By appointment only: March to October, Thursdays only.* ♣ ♠

65h Combe Sydenham Hall (tel. Stogumber 098 46 284). Romantically situated Elizabethan manor house, once the home of Elizabeth Sydenham, wife of Sir Francis Drake. *Mid June to end August weekdays 1100-1630.*

65h Gaulden Manor. See 58b.

65i Cothelstone Manor. See 58c.

66g Barford Park (tel. Spaxton 027 867 269). Small, stone and red-brick country seat in Queen Anne style, with rooms furnished to period. Still lived in. *May to end September Wednesdays and Thursdays 1400-1800, or any time by appointment.* ✿

67a Axbridge: King John's Hunting Lodge, Market Place. Elizabethan merchant's house having no connection with King John. Extensively restored in 1971, it now houses a museum. *April to end September daily 1400-1700. Free.* ▣

68b Mells Manor. Tudor house with gabled roofs and mullioned windows, built in H-shape. The rhyme of "Little Jack Horner" (dating from 1770) is said to have been based on an untrue story that the title deeds to Mells Manor were sent to Henry VIII in a pie but were stolen en route.

68c Norton St Philip: The George. Stone and timber inn dating from the 15th century and believed to be the oldest in England.

68d Oakhill Manor (tel. 0749 840210). Attractive country estate with furnished mansion house. Many attractions in grounds. *Easter to early November daily 1200-1800.* ☕ ✿ ⌂ ☆

68i Stourhead Tel. Bourton 074 784 348). Palladian villa built by Colen Campbell in 1722 and standing in 2,500 acres of ground. Chippendale furniture, fine picture collection, many other art treasures. *April, September and October: Mondays, Wednesdays, Saturdays and Sundays; May to August: daily (closed Fridays); 1400-1730 (sunset if earlier). Other times by appointment.* ♠ ✿ ℹ

69a Chalcot House, Westbury. Small Palladian manor of the 17th century. *August daily 1400-1700.*

69d Longleat House (tel. Maiden Bradley 098 53 551). Home of the Marquess of Bath, this is one of Britain's great historic houses. Built in Renaissance style between 1566 and 1580, it was modernised early in the 19th century and has been scrupulously preserved since. The decoration is Italian-style and is on a grand and lavish scale, although the house is actually lived in. There are fabulous State Rooms, with ornate ceilings and appropriate furniture, paintings and books; restored Victorian kitchens (open summer only); a fine library and much else besides. Many attractions in the extensive grounds, quite apart from the famous Safari Park. *Easter to end September: daily 1000-1800. Rest of the year: daily 1000-1600.* ☕ ✿ ♠ ⌂ ☆

69i Phillips House, Dinton (tel. Teffont 072 287 208). Neo-Greek house built in 1816. Now used as a YWCA conference centre. *Limited viewing: April to end September Wednesdays 1415-1730 (sunset if earlier). Other times by written appointment.*

Tintinhull House (52c)

69i Phillips House, Dinton (tel. Teffont 072 287 208). Neo-Greek house built in 1816. Now used as a YWCA conference centre. *Limited viewing: April to end September Wednesdays 1415-1730 (sunset if earlier). Other times by written appointment.*

70f Clevedon Court. Early 14th century manor house incorporating a 12th century tower and a 13th century hall. It was further modified in the 16th and 17th centuries. Most notable feature is a large reticulated window lighting the chapel, but the house contains fine collections of Nailsea glass and of pottery by Elton. William Thackeray wrote part of "Vanity Fair" here and also modelled 'Castlewood' in "Henry Esmond" on Clevedon. *April to end September: Wednesdays, Thursdays, Sundays and Bank Holiday Mondays 1430-1700.* 🐦 ❊

70f Nailsea Court. Stone-built 16th and 17th century manor house set in 27 acres of National Trust land.

70i Congresbury: very fine 15th century vicarage with moulded beams.

71 Bristol: Georgian House, 7 Great George Street (tel. 0272 299771). Built in 1789 and showing furniture and fittings of that period, plus a fascinating plunge bath and a fine 18th century harpsichord. *Monday to Saturday 1000-1700.*

Red Lodge, Park Row (tel. 0272 299771). Late 16th century house with 18th century modifications, including impressive staircase. Oak carvings and furniture from both periods. *Monday to Saturday 1400-1700. Free.*

St Vincent's Priory, Clifton (tel. 0272 39621). Small Gothic revival house built over caves which were once a Christian sanctuary. Unusual figures on the facade; chimneypiece illustrating David and Goliath; coloured glass Christian symbols; Pompeiian murals in first-floor music room. *July and August weekends 1415-1800. Other times by appointment.*

The Royal Fort, Woodland Road. Merchants house dating from the 18th century, with fine plasterwork.

71b Blaise Castle, Henbury (tel. Bristol 0272 506789). An 18th century house containing reconstructions of 18th/19th century farmhouse kitchen and Victorian drawing room. *Monday to Saturday 1400-1700. Free.* ┧T

Blaise Hamlet, west of Henbury. Nine gabled cottages built 1810-11 around a village green, all

designed by John Nash in a profusion of different styles.

71b Leigh Court, Abbots Leigh. Neo-classical house built in 1814, but based on a much older building, in which Charles II sheltered.

71d Barrow Court. Jacobean mansion standing in splendid gardens.

72b Dodington House (tel. Chipping Sodbury 0454 318899). Built 1796-1813 on the site of Norman and Tudor remains, this was the last great house built in classical style. The major state rooms and family apartments (it is still lived in) are on show, along with a magnificent double staircase and collections of furniture, paintings and other art works. Many other attractions in 700-acre grounds. *Easter to last Sunday in September daily 1100-1700.* 🐦 ♣ ▣ 🐦 ┧T

72b Dyrham Park. Mansion of Bath stone built between 1691 and 1702 and remarkably unchanged. It was designed for the Secretary of State to William of Orange and shows Dutch influence in panelling, floors and ceilings. Original furnishings, as recorded in the original housekeeper's inventory; Dutch paintings and a collection of pottery. *April to October daily (but closed Thursdays in April, May and October and closed Fridays throughout): 1400-1730.* 🐦 ❊ ⊓

72c Castle Combe: Manor House Hotel (tel. 0249 782206). Mediaeval manor (1664) with antiques in the public rooms and some four-poster beds. The village was used in the film of "Dr Doolittle". 🐦

72e Bath: No 1 Royal Crescent (tel. Bath 0225 28126). In a city famed for its Georgian architecture, the 30 houses of Royal Crescent stand out as supreme examples of the Palladian style, built between 1767 and 1744 by John Wood the Younger as the climax of his father's plans for a complete city designed along classical lines. No 1 was completely restored in 1970 with rooms decorated and furnished as they would have been in the 18th century. *First Tuesday in March to last Sunday in October: Tuesday to Saturday 1100-1645, Sundays 1400-1645.*

Prior Park College, Combe Down (tel. 0225 832752). Magnificent Palladian mansion built by John Wood the Elder in 1735. Six column central porch, pavilions on either side and notable Palladian bridge in the grounds. Now a Roman Catholic public school. *May to September Tuesdays and Wednesdays; August Monday to Thursday; 1400-1800.*

Assembly Rooms, Alfred Street, off Lansdown Road (tel. 0225 61111). Designed in 1769 by John Wood the Younger with magnificent rooms, including 100 ft long ballroom with Corinthian columns and 5 chandeliers. Bombed in 1942, it was rebuilt in 1956-61 and fully restored in 1979. Occasionally closed for Bath City Council functions. *November to end March: Monday to Saturday 1000-1700;*

Sundays 1100-1700. Rest of year: daily 0900-1800. 🐦 ▣

72e St Catherine's Court (tel. Bath 0225 858159). Small Tudor house built on earlier remains, with excellent furniture and needlework collection. Connections with Henry VIII and Elizabeth I. Conducted tour (2½ hours including tea) starts 1430. *Early April to end September weekends and Bank Holidays.* 🐦 ❊

72h Hinton House, Hinton Charterhouse. 18th century mansion incorporating parts of the lodge and gatehouse of the nearby Carthusian priory, whose 13th century remains are the second oldest of their kind in Britain.

72h Norton St Philip. See 68c.

72i Claverton: Claverton Manor (tel. Bath 0225 60503). Greek revival house high above the Avon valley, with 18 rooms furnished to show life in the 17th to 19th centuries, the furniture having come from the USA. *End March to end October: Tuesday 1400-1700; also Bank Holidays and Bank Holiday Sundays 1100-1700. Other times by appointment.* 🐦 ❊ ▣ ┧T

72i Bradford-on-Avon: Church House. Early 16th century house built as a cloth hall by a rich weaver.

The Hall, Holt Road. Built in 1610 and a fine example of Elizabethan architecture.

72i Westwood Manor. Lovely 15th century stone house with late Gothic and Jacobean windows and Jacobean plasterwork. Modern topiary garden. *April to end September Wednesdays 1430-1800.*

73a Chippenham: Town Hall. 15th century building with fine timbers.

73a Sheldon Manor (tel. Chippenham 0249 3120). The oldest manor house in Wiltshire, this Plantagenet home dates from 1282 and has always been lived in. Panelled rooms, oak staircase and many interesting items. *Thursdays, Bank Holidays and August Wednesdays 1400-1800; Sundays 1230-1800.* 🐦 ❊

73d Corsham Court (tel. 0249 712214). Elizabethan mansion of 1582 with additions by Capability Brown and Nash. Georgian State Rooms with furniture by Chippendale and others; famous collection of Old Masters; Georgian bath house; 15th century garden house; imposing pedimented gateway. *All year: Sundays, Wednesdays and Thursdays; mid July to mid September: Tuesday, Wednesday, Thursday, Saturday, Sunday; also during Bath Festival and on Bank Holiday Mondays; 1100-1230, 1400-1800 (1630 in winter).*

Hungerford Almshouses, in Corsham village, feature unusual baroque pediments. Next door is an old school with original seating and 1668 master's desk.

73d Lacock Abbey. 13th century building converted to a country house in 1539, with half-timbered gables. Tudor octagonal tower and stable court and 1754 Gothic hall. *June to end September daily; April, May and October Wednesday to Sunday and Bank Holiday Mondays; 1400-1730.* Situated in Lacock Village, which is National Trust owned and which has no building later than 18th century. ▣ ✝

73e Bowood House, Calne (tel. 0249 812102). Large Georgian house dating from 1754 with orangery, picture gallery, chapel, sculpture gallery, and exhibition rooms. Doric chapel and Palladian Mausoleum designed by Robert Adam in 1761. The present building, home of the Earl of Shelburne, was once dwarfed by the Big House, demolished in 1955. Adventure playground. *Good Friday to end September: Tuesday to Saturday 1400-1800, Sundays and Bank Holidays 1200-1800.* 🐦 ❊ ▣

73g Great Chalfield Manor. Moated, late-Gothic house built around 1480, with original Great Hall and screen. Well restored, with much of architectural interest. *Mid April to late September Wednesdays only 1200-1300, 1400-1700.*

Claverton Manor (72i)

Religious Places

Cathedrals, churches, chapels, abbeys and monastries in use are open all year unless marked otherwise; if a church is locked enquire at the vicarage for the key. Also included here are holy wells, ecclesiastical ruins and other places of religious significance.

19b Zennor: church restored in 1890; it has a Norman window, 14th century font and a pew-end carving of the "mermaid of Zennor".

19c St Ives: St Ia. The 119 ft high 15th century tower dominates the town. Other features include a fine roof and bench-end carvings.

19d St Just: 14th century church restored in 1865, featuring a sundial above the south porch and a 5th century Greek-inscribed stone.

19e Madron: a mainly mediaeval church with 15th century wagon-roofs, richly carved screen and Norman font.

19e Sancreed: tree-shaded church which has a chancel roof carved with 64 different oak medallions.

19f Gulval: beautifully situated church with an abundance of sub-tropical plants and trees in the churchyard.

19f St Michael's Mount. Once the home of Celtic saints and a shrine to St Michael, the Mount was granted to the Abbey of Mont St Michel by Edward the Confessor. As an alien priory it was suppressed in 1425, becoming a garrisoned fortress; in 1660, after the Reformation, the monastic buildings were secularised. The 12th century church with 15th century rose windows is austere and impressive; the 15th century Lady Chapel was converted into drawing rooms in the 18th century. *Sundays only: 1030 for 1100 service.*

19h St Buryan: ancient church with granite arcades and 15th century screen.

20a Lelant: St Una. Church with a mixture of Norman and Perpendicular architecture, including sundial above the south porch and a staircase to a rood loft.

20e Breage: St Breaca. Built in the 15th century, the church contains some unusual items, including a Roman milestone, a Celtic cross and some finely restored wall-paintings.

20e Helston: St Michael. Built in the 15th century the church contains the grave of Henry Trengrouse (1772-1854), a pioneer in rocket-fired lifesaving devices.

20f Mawgan: a 13th to 15th century church with a fine tower. Nearby Mawgan Cross is reputed to be 1,000 years old.

20f Church Cove: St Winwalloe. Isolated 15th century church with separate 13th century tower built into the rock. Features include a Norman font and an attractive wagon roof.

20i Mullion: St Melan. Mainly 15th century church with rare dog or cat door at the foot of the ancient south door; also a 15th century font.

20i Landewednack: the most southerly church in Great Britain, it combines Norman and Perpendicular architecture.

21a Budock Water: St Budock. 15th century church containing box pews, a cut-down screen and many monuments to local families.

21b Mylor: surmounted by a small tower, the church has fine Norman doorways, font and Elizabethan chancel with a carving of the Crucifixion.

21b St Just: built in 1261, the church has a 15th century tower and font. Churchyard is full of sub-tropical plants and trees.

21b Falmouth: Parish Church. Features an unusual oblong tower, a memorial to the 14th Earl of Glencairn—a friend and benefactor of Robert Burns—and a high standard of singing.

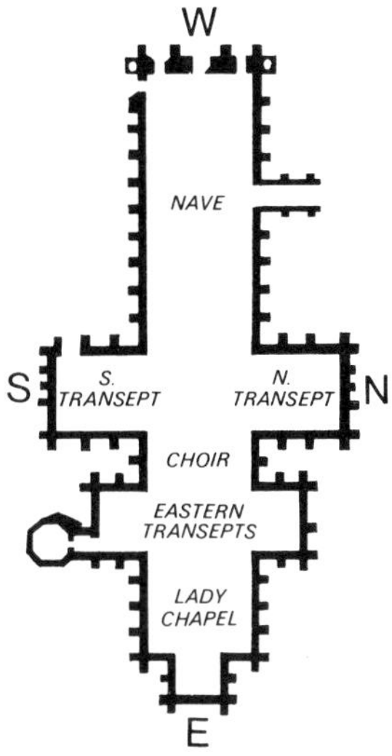

Glossary of Terms

Shown here is the ground plan of a typical mediaeval cathedral. Most of the cathedrals and churches described here were started and/or completed during the mediaeval period, and their general layout will be similar.

Apse. Vaulted recess, usually at one end of the choir.
Barrel Vault. Semi-circular vault in the roof; also known as a tunnel vault.
Fan Vault. Chamber whose supporting ribs spread out in the shape of an open fan.
Lancet Window. High narrow window with sharply pointed arch.
Lady Chapel. Usually named for its dedication to the Virgin Mary. See plan.
Misericord. Small hinged wooden seat, used in the choir stalls to give some support to a person standing up; often elaborately carved.
Rood Loft. Loft or gallery built above a rood screen (see below).
Rood Screen. Separates the nave from the chancel or choir; incorporates a large rood (crucifix).
Tympanum. A triangular space above the main door, usually highly decorated.
Vault. Arched room or passageway, often underground.

21d Mawnan: 13th century church set in ancient earthworks. Churchyard contains an old headstone with skull and crossbones, believed to be the grave of a pirate.

21d St Anthony: 13th century church with granite tower made from stone only found in Normandy, believed to have been built by shipwrecked Normans. Note small brass chandeliers, each holding 6 candles.

21d Manaccan: partly Norman church famous for a large fig tree, believed to be centuries old, growing out of the south wall.

21d St Keverne: interesting 13th century church with notable bench ends. The tower and spire, 98 ft high, form a well-known landmark.

22b Tresco Abbey. A wall and a few arches are all that remain of 10th century abbey.

22h Zennor. See 19b.

22i St Ives. See 19c.

23g Lelant. See 20a.

24a Crantock: St Carantoc. Norman church but rebuilt in the 14th and 19th centuries. It contains a Norman font, notable stained glass windows, fine bench ends and screen.

24a Cubert: St Cubertus. The 14th century spire is a prominent landmark. Interior includes a Norman font, richly carved pew ends and roof, and a Saxon inscription on a granite pillar.

24a St Piran's Chapel. Founded in 6th century by Celtic monks it is one of Britain's earliest Christian worshipping places. Abandoned and overwhelmed by sand in the 11th century, it was exposed by a storm in 1835 and is now protected by concrete blocks. The 10th century cross to the north is all that remains of a second church, built in 1150 and abandoned in the 15th century.

24b Newlyn East. Norman building on the site of a 12th century church. Features include a Norman font, 16th century bench ends and richly carved choir stalls noted for their mediaeval arrangement.

24c St Columb Major: St Columba. Church with an impressive four-tiered tower over 600 years old. Once proposed for use as the Cornish cathedral it was restored in the 19th century. Good brass rubbings.

24f Probus: SS Probus and Gren. 16th century church with one of the finest towers (125 ft high) in Cornwall. Interior of graceful pillars and arcades lit by 3 large east windows with fine stained glass.

24h Truro Cathedral. Built on the site of the 16th century parish church of St Mary, it was the first Protestant cathedral erected after St Pauls. Work started in May 1880 and was completed in 1910. The parish church's 15th century south aisle was incorporated in the cathedral and provides a strong contrast to the newer work. The architecture of the cathedral is nominally Early English and is constructed almost entirely of Cornish granite. The central tower, a memorial to Queen Victoria, is 250 ft high. The simple interior with its fine reredos shows a skillful mastery of proportion. As an example of the Victorian Gothic revival it is masterly.

24h St Clement: 13th century church which underwent drastic Victorian renovation.

24h Penelewey: Come-to-Good Chapel. Said to be the oldest Quaker meeting place in England, it is a simple thatched building of 1710, one of only three. Built of plain whitewashed rock, it contains a gallery with rough hewn timber as seating. *Key from nearby cottage.*

25a Roche: Tregeagle Chapel. Remains of a 15th century chapel and hermit's cell set on an unusual outcrop of rocks.

St Gonadus. Norman church heavily rebuilt in the 19th century. Contains fine Norman font ornamented with foliage and snakes.

25b Luxulyan: SS Cyriac and Julitta. One of the finest granite churches in Cornwall. The Roman well of St Cyors is nearby.

25c Lothwithiel: St Bartholomew. Church famous for its granite tower crowned by an octagonal spire. Construction was probably started in 1180 but most of it dates from the early 14th century. Features include a large, 5-light east window of Early English period, curious oak alms box made in 1645 and an alabaster carving of the flaying of St Bartholomew.

25c St Winnow: 16th century Perpendicular church in riverside setting. Contains a chancel screen with 31 panels at the base and one of the few Elizabethan pulpits in Cornwall.

25c Golant: St Samson. Interesting 16th century church built on the site of 6th century shrine; holy well by the porch.

25c Lanteglos: St Wyllow. 14th century church with unusual north and south aisles extended to embrace the mediaeval tower to which they give arched access. Also 13th century font and beautiful early 15th century brass of Thomas de Mohun.

25d St Austell: Holy Trinity. 15th century church with an abundance of carved stonework; 100 ft high tower with numerous statues and gargoyles; also an old clock face, outstanding stained glass windows and a late Norman font.

25d Mevagissey: St Peters. Cruciform church dating from 1259, although this has been the site of a religious edifice since the 6th century. Contains a Norman font and interesting monuments.

25f Fowey: St Finn Barr. Church has a 119 ft high tower, built in four stages, has a clock and 8 bells. Notable 15th century wagon roof, Norman font (1150) and pulpit carved from the oak of a Spanish galleon.

26b Duloe: St Cuby. Early English church with a 13th century tower and a low spire added in 1860. Notable screen of black oak and an Elizabethan Communion cup.

26b Looe: St Nicholas. This 14th century building has not always been used as a church. In 1574 it became a Guildhall but was reconsecrated in 1852. Note the sunken vestry and chancel rafters made from the timbers of the Spanish warship *San Jose*, a prize of Nelson at the Battle of St Vincent.

26d Lansallos: St Ildierna. A 15th century church with fine wagon roof, many original pews and slate floors.

26e Talland: church with tall tower sunk into the hillside and connected to the main building by a passage. Collection of old bench ends and beautifully engraved slate headstones.

27a St Germans: St Germanus. Imposing Norman monastic church on the site of a Saxon cathedral. Two west towers with one partly octagonal; magnificent carved door.

27a St Stevens. Large 15th century church with a Norman font and stocks in use until early 19th century.

27 Plymouth: St Andrews, off Royal Parade. Only the tower of the 15th century church remained after the blitz but the rest of the church has been restored and is both simple and impressive. Note the brightly coloured stained glass windows behind the altar. ▣ 🏚

27d Rame Head: Chapel of St Michael. Dedicated in 1397, this tiny chapel is only 21 ft by 9 ft with 3 ft thick walls, four windows and a doorway.

27e Rame: St Germanus. 13th century church with some Norman features, including a carved slate tympanum. Note also the fine roof and carved bench ends.

28e Modbury. Imposingly sited church, one of the few in Devon to have a tower with a mediaeval spire.

28f Kingsbridge: St Edmunds. Church with remarkable 13th century tower.

29a Totnes: St Mary. Wholly rebuilt in the 15th century, this church contains one of the finest stone rood screens in England, plus a gracious 120 ft high tower and a mediaeval stone pulpit.

29a Ashprington. Pleasing 15th century church, despite Victorian restoration. Rare stone coffin table under the lych gate.

29b Stoke Gabriel: SS Mary and Gabriel. 15th century church with 13th century tower. Churchyard contains a yew tree believed to be over 1,000 years old.

29b Dartmouth: St Saviours. 14th century parish church with remarkable wood carving, particularly the rood screen and west gallery. Ancient manual fire engine in the porch.

30f Padstow: St Petroc. 15th century church with 13th century tower. Note the font, window tracery, pulpit and bench ends.

30f Little Petherick: church dating from 14th century, rebuilt in 1858. Fine screen, priest's tombstone, bench ends carved by Belgian refugee, Norman font, Byzantine altar cross and Venetian processional cross.

30h St Mawgan: built in the 13th/14th centuries the church is noted for its fine carvings and an early Christian cross.

30i St Columb Major. See 24c.

31b Lanteglos: St Willow. Isolated 14th/15th century church with fine west tower and fragments of early stained glass.

31d St Endellion: St Endelienta. 15th century collegiate church with early Norman font, 15th century slate shrine, early bench ends and fine wagon roof.

31d St Breock: beautifully situated 13th century church with unusually long nave.

31d Egloshayle: St Helie. 15th century church with fine tower; rugged interior due to lack of plaster; two Celtic crosses near the south porch.

31e Michaelstow: church with remains of an anchorite's cell in the north wall of the chancel; holy well in the churchyard.

31f Blisland: SS Protus and Hyacinth. Norman church with a 15th century granite tower. Richly painted rood screen is set against white walls and slate floors.

31f Temple: a church of the Knights Templar of Jerusalem, it fell into ruin but was restored in 1883. Many crosses and gravestones from the derelict churchyard were used in one of the outbuildings.

31g St Wenn: St Wenna. 15th century church which has a sundial bearing the inscription "Ye know not when".

31h Bodmin: St Petroc. The largest church in Cornwall, it bears traces of Norman work but most of the present building was erected between 1469 and 1471. Fine carvings on the roof, porch, pulpit and lectern. Small 14th century chantry chapel in the churchyard is dedicated to St Thomas à Becket.

31h Lanivet: St Nivet. The church has a simple, tall, granite tower and a churchyard with a number of Celtic crosses. Also in the village is the tower of an ancient priory.

31i Cardinham: St Mewbred. The village is dominated by this 15th century church which has a Norman font, fine carved bench ends and two ancient Celtic crosses.

32a Altarnun: St Nonna. Known locally as 'The Cathedral of the Moor', this church is famous for its 79 carved bench ends depicting Instruments of the Passion. Imposing west tower (109 ft), rood screen and Norman font.

32a Trewint: Wesley's Cottage (tel. Pipers Pool 056 686 561). Small cottage from which Wesley preached in 1744-1762. Now a Methodist shrine; annual Wesley Day service plus Sunday services in summer. *All year daily 0900 to dusk. Free.*

32b Laneast: SS Sidwell and Gulval. Secluded Norman cruciform church enlarged in the 15th century. Note carved bench ends, Norman font, fine rood screen and early pulpit.

32c St Stephen: built in 1259 this church was moved up the hill in 1419; its tower is a well-known landmark. Nail-studded door, round font with fine vine-and-cable pattern and stone coffin in the west wall.

32c Launceston: St Thomas. Criminals who died while imprisoned in the castle are buried here. Church contains a fine font, pillars, panelling and arches.

St Mary Magdalene. Consecrated in 1524, church has exquisitely carved granite exterior. Interior contains magnificent carving on roof, reredos, pulpit and many bench ends.

32e North Hill: St Torney. 15th century church with granite tower and 16th/17th century tombs.

32f Linkinhorne: St Melors. Built on the site of a smaller Norman edifice this church has a magnificent granite tower and porch. Also carved beams and bosses and fragments of wall paintings.

32g St Neot: parish church famous for its 15th/16th century stained glass windows; also ancient churchyard crosses. North west is the holy well of St Neot.

32h Liskeard: St Martin. The church is built in Perpendicular style but has a modern tower (1903). Inside is a 1636 carved pulpit and fine stained windows.

33b Brent Tor: St Michaels. Perched on an isolated hill, this late 14th century church is one of the smallest in England.

33d Callington: St Mary. 15th century church with fine monument to Lord Willoughby de Broke (1452-1502), a Marshall of Henry VII.

33d Dupath Holy Well, west of Callington: an almost complete 16th century chapel built over one of the best ancient holy wells of Cornwall. *Any time. Free.*

33e Tavistock: St Eustachius. Mainly 15th century Perpendicular church with fine carved roof and Elizabethan altar table.

33h Buckland Monachorum: St Andrew. 16th century Perpendicular church with Norman font and Drake family monuments.

33h Buckland Abbey. Cistercian monastery founded in 1278 and occupied by the monks until the Dissolution in 1539. In 1576 it was turned into a home for Sir Richard Grenville, who sold it to Sir Francis Drake in 1581. The house was a Royalist stronghold during the Civil War and was damaged by Parliamentary attacks. *Good Friday to end September: Monday to Saturday and Bank Holidays 1100-1730; Sundays 1400-1730. Rest of year: Wednesdays and weekends 1400-1630.* 🐾 ▣

34f Widecombe in the Moor: St Pancras. Well proportioned 14th century church with a fine 120 ft tower.

34f Buckland in the Moor: small church with unique clock face and elaborately carved rood loft staircase.

34f Ashburton: 15th century church with tall tower containing a peal of 8 bells. Fine modern oak reredos.

34i Buckfast Abbey. Cathedral-size Abbey church, with an impressive 158 ft pinnacled tower, built by the Benedictine monks from 1906-1938. Note the mosaic floor, high altar and Blessed Sacrament Chapel's inch-thick stained glass east window. ▣

34i Buckfastleigh: 13th century church restored in 19th century. Still retains Norman font, Jacobean font cover and pulpit.

35b Higher Ashton: 15th century church of outstanding beauty. Note the carved bench ends, rood and parclose screens, ancient painting of Christ, Elizabethan pulpit.

35c Kenton: late 14th century parish church with 100 ft tower. Contains carved stone arcades and screen, ancient oak pulpit and a double triptych reredos.

35g Torbryan. Attractive 15th century church with exceptional carving on the rood screen. Also a mediaeval *mensa* (stone altar), decorated porch and ancient pulpit.

35g Totnes. See 29a.

35h Cockington: SS George and Mary.   Noted 11th century church.

36a Tintagel Head: ruined Celtic monastery with sophisticated rectangular buildings. *Daily from 0930 (winter Sundays from 1400).* m

36a Tintagel: St Materiana. Partly Norman church containing five-legged Norman font, fine rood screen and a Roman-inscribed stone.

36b Hennet: St Juliot. Restored in 1870 by apprentice architect Thomas Hardy.

36e Lanteglos. See 31b.

36g Egloshayle. See 31d.

36h Michaelstow. See 31e.

36h Blisland. See 31f.

36i Temple. See 31f.

37d Laneast. See 32b.

37d Altarnun. See 32a.

37d Trewint. See 32a.

37e St Stephen. See 32c.

37e Launceston. See 32c.

37g North Hill. See 32e.

37h Linkinhorne. See 32f.

37i Callington. See 33d.

37i Dupath Holy Well. See 33d.

38c Okehampton: All Saints. Only the tower remains of a 15th century church, built on the site of the original Saxon settlement.

38e Brent Tor. See 33b.

38h Tavistock. See 33e.

39a South Tawton: St Andrew.   15th century granite church with impressive west tower. Inside are a Norman font, carved wagon roofs, an outstanding memorial to the Burgoyne family and five-arched arcades of Beer stone.

39b Chagford: St Nicholas. Granite 13th century church in Perpendicular style.

39h Widecombe in the Moor. See 34f.

39h Buckland in the Moor. See 34f.

39i Ashburton. See 34f.

40b Exeter: Cathedral Church of SS Mary and Peter. Built on the site of a Norman cathedral, of which the north and south towers survive, this Gothic cathedral has been little altered for 600 years. Notable features: the west facade, with the largest surviving array of 14th century sculpture in England; the superb 60 ft high Bishop's throne; the oldest carved misericords (1260) in England; a library with 20,000 books and manuscripts; an astronomical clock dated 1478; and the bell in the north tower, which is the oldest (1616) of its weight in Britain.

St Nicholas Priory, The Mint, Fore Street (tel. 0392 56724). Remains of an 11th century Benedictine priory which was extended until the 16th century Dissolution. Also the adjacent Tudor guest house. *Tuesday to Saturday 1000-1300, 1400-1730.*

40d Higher Ashton. See 35b.

40f Kenton. See 35c.

41b Sidbury: Norman/Saxon church with rare Saxon crypt beneath the chancel.

41b Bicton: St Mary. The 14th century tower of the church houses the Rolle family vault.

41c Branscombe: attractive church with Norman tower and nave and 13th century transepts.

41d East Budleigh: All Saints. 13th century church with fine sandstone tower. Noted for a collection of carved bench ends, some among the oldest in England, and for memorials to the Raleigh family.

42a Loughwood Meeting House. Mid 17th century Nonconformist place of worship with plastered barrel ceiling. 18th century interior remains unaltered. *Daily. Free.*

42c Forde Abbey (tel. South Chard 0460 20321). Cistercian monastery founded in 1138 and enlarged by Abbot Chard in 1500. Although it was converted to a private house in 1650, the exterior is remarkably unaltered since its monastic days. *Easter Sunday and Monday; then May to September Sundays, Wednesdays and Bank Holiday Mondays: 1400-1800.* ☛ ✳ ⌂

42d Colyton: St Andrew. Norman church rebuilt in the 15th century with tower crowned by an octagonal lantern. Outstanding 30 ft high west window.

42e Musbury: St Michael. Contains an impressive monument to the Drake family.

42e Combpyne: 13th century church containing ancient tenor bell, tower arch, leper squint, piscina and Early English lancet window.

42f Whitchurch Canonicorum: St Candida. Cruciform church which is partly Norman. Contains 13th century shrine to St Candida, possibly Saxon carvings on the tower and a porch decorated with gargoyles.

42f Lyme Regis: St Michael the Archangel. 16th century church with Norman nave now used as west porch; 17th century oak lectern and Tudor tapestry.

43d Chideock: Perpendicular church with Victorian restoration work. Notable monuments.

43d Bridport: mainly Perpendicular 14th century cruciform church dominated by a fine tower. Notable parvise (room above the porch).

43i Abbotsbury: St Peters Abbey. Ruins of an 11th century Benedictine abbey, including part of the gatehouse and dovecote. Enormous 13th century tithe barn nearby was monk's granary.

St Nicholas. 16th century Perpendicular church. Features 17th century chancel ceiling and pulpit with Civil War bullet holes.

44a Upwey: St Lawrence. 13th century church with Saxon font and fine Flemish glass.

44b Dorchester: St Peter. Mainly 15th century church with 90 ft tower. Notable pulpit, reredos and memorials; Thomas Hardy Memorial Chapel.

44b Stinsford: church has a memorial window to Thomas Hardy, whose heart is buried in the churchyard.

44h Portland: parish church was built and fitted by convicts from the nearby prison.

45a Wool: Bindon Abbey. Remains of a 12th century Cistercian monastery.

45b Wareham: St Martin. Founded in 705AD by the 1st Bishop of Sherborne, the church is only 45 ft long. Notable statue of Lawrence of Arabia in Arab dress.

Lady St Mary. Church of mixed styles, rebuilt in 1882. Note Chapel of Edward the Martyr and 9th century Danish-inscribed stones.

45d Lulworth Castle: Rotunda. The first Roman Catholic church built after the Reformation; George III consented on condition that it did not look like a church. m

45i St Alban's Head: 12th century stone chapel built as a chantry and a beacon for shipping.

46a Morwenstow: St Morwenna. Partly 12th century church with notable oak roofs, Norman arcades and bench-end carving.

Rectory. A 19th century folly built by Rev R S Hawker, the poet; the chimneys are modelled on the towers of the various churches he was connected with.

46e Kilkhampton: St James. Stately church, rebuilt in 16th century, with fine tower and much Norman work. Notable porch, door and bench ends; organ has reversed-colour keys.

46e Poughill: St Olaf. Mainly 14th century church with fine frescoes of St Christopher, recoloured in 1894. Large (1 ft 11 in long) lock, fine carving and impressive east window.

46e Launcells: St Andrew. 15th century church on the site of a Celtic monastery. Notable barrel roofs, mediaeval encaustic (painted with wax colours) tiles and some of the finest carved benches in Cornwall.

46g St Gennys: St Genesius. Norman tower believed to be the oldest in Cornwall.

46h Marhamchurch: church with 14th century embattled tower preserves a rare cresset stone and a fine carved pulpit.

48b High Bickington: 12th century church is only one in the county with two towers. Features famous carved bench ends, Norman font and exceptional choir stalls.

48b Burrington: church with superbly coloured 16th century rood screen and unique wagon roof.

48c Kings Nympton: church is noted for its rare painted ceiling above the chancel. Also: embattled aisle, 15th century rood screen and carved bosses in the wagon roof.

48c Chulmleigh: St Mary Magdalen. 15th century church noted for its rood screen and 38 carved wooden angels on the roof.

48f Eggesford: All Saints. Delightful church containing two outstanding memorials.

48f Lapford: St Thomas of Canterbury.   Mainly 15th century church but with Norman doorway. Collection of very fine woodwork.

48f Brushford: St Nicholas. Mainly Perpendicular church with an attractive chapel built by Sir Edwin Lutyens (1926); 15th century screen and Norman font.

48g Okehampton. See 38c.

48h Honeychurch: remote Norman church well worth a visit. Note 12th century tub font, Elizabethan pulpit and altar rails.

48i Spreyton: St Michael. Well proportioned 15th century church.

49f Cruwys Morchard: Holy Cross. Church contains the finest classical Georgian screen in Devon.

49h Crediton: Holy Cross. 15th century cruciform-shaped red sandstone church. Inside are a Norman font, some fine stained glass and monuments.

50a Tiverton: St George. Early 18th century Classical church with galleried interior.

St Peter. 15th century church with fine tower; splendid carvings, porch and Greenway Chapel with two full length brasses.

50c Wellington: 14th century church occupying a Saxon site.

50e Cullompton: St Andrew. Impressive church with 16th century pinnacled west tower. Features mediaeval coloured screen and a gruesome oak carving called "Golgotha" (Calvary).

50i Ottery St Mary: St Mary. 14th century church modelled on Exeter cathedral. Contains superb carved roofs, 14th century choir stalls, a beautiful altar screen and reredos. Canopied tombs of Sir Otho Grandisson and his lady are outstanding.

51h Loughwood Meeting House. See 42a.

51h Colyton. See 42d.

51h Musbury. See 42e.

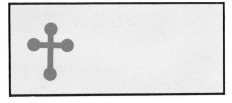

52a Ilminster: St Mary. 15th century church with dominating central tower. Notable brasses and monuments, especially of the Wadham family; 18th century brass chandelier.

52b Martock: great Ham-stone church with notable interior.

52c Yeovil: St John The Baptist. Stately Perpendicular building with massive tower, 13th century crypt and fine 15th century brass lectern.

52d Forde Abbey. See 42c.

52g Whitchurch Canonicorum. See 42f.

53b Sherborne: Abbey Church. Late 15th century Perpendicular church built on site of Saxon cathedral. Contains very fine fan vaulting, a tower bell decorated by Cardinal Wolsey and a Saxon doorway; monuments include those of 13th century monks.

53h Cerne Abbas: St Mary. Mainly 15th century church but with Norman chancel. Fine screen and 14th/15th century wall paintings.

    Cerne Abbey. The gateway and Guest House are all that remain of this fine 10th century monastery.

54d Stoke: St Nectan. Recently restored 14th century church with 130 ft tower, the tallest in Devon. Note richly carved screen.

54e Clovelly: All Saints. Grey stone church with tower housing 6 bells. Norman porch, Saxon font and monuments to the Cary family.

54g Morwenstow. See 46a.

54h Kilkhampton. See 46e.

55c Barnstaple: St Peter. Parish church has fine twisted, lead-covered spire and rich 17th century monuments.

    St Mary. 14th century church built on site of 12th century priory. Remarkably fine Elizabethan woodwork, especially the screen and font canopy.

55c Tawstock: magnificent church in the park of the former Earls of Bath. Of particular note are the north and south transept ceilings of Italian plasterwork. Also: the unique canopied Manorial pew, like a small room; a collection of monuments recognised as one of the best in any church; the 16th century gallery leading to the belfry; and an hour glass attached to the pulpit by swivelling arm.

55e Bideford: St Mary. Largely rebuilt in the 19th century, this Saxon/Norman church has notable memorials to the Grenville family and a Norman font.

56a Swimbridge: St James. 15th century church with mediaeval spire, fine wooden font, carved rood screen and stone pulpit.

56d Chittlehampton: St Urith. Late Perpendicular church with 115 ft tower, stone pulpit, original wood ceilings and 17th century monuments.

56d Atherington: St Mary. Perpendicular Gothic church with tall west tower. Inside are notable locally carved 14th century bench ends, wagon roofs and screen. Also the only complete rood loft remaining in Devon and a rare coffin table beneath the lych gate.

56d High Bickington. See 48b.

56e George Nympton: tiny village church with attractive red brick tower (rebuilt 1673) and unusual manual pipe organ with black notes white and white notes black.

56e Kings Nympton. See 48c.

56f South Molton: St Mary Magdalene. 15th century church, restored in 1865, set in an avenue of lime trees. Inside are a mediaeval stone pulpit and some beautiful figure carving in the nave and chancel.

56h Burrington. See 48b.

56h Chulmleigh. See 48c.

56i Lapford. See 48f.

57a Molland: St Mary. Isolated Perpendicular church with rare unchanged Georgian interior; includes 49 horse-box pews, a fine three-decker pulpit and excellent memorials.

57b Winsford: St Mary Magdalene. 13th/14th century church with 80 ft high tower. Notable Norman font and 13th century lancet window in the chancel.

57b Hawkridge: St Giles. Perched 1,000 ft up on a narrow ridge, this small church has a Norman doorway and font with a 14th century nave and chancel and a Perpendicular tower.

57b Dulverton: All Saints. Large church with 13th century tower.

57c Exton: St Peter. Norman church extensively restored in 1878. 13th century tower and 15th century octagonal font.

57c Brompton Regis: St Mary. Perpendicular church (rebuilt in 1885) with 13th century tower and unusual squint on the chancel arch.

57f Bampton. Well preserved 15th century church.

57h Cruwys Morchard. See 49f.

57i Tiverton. See 50a.

58f Wellington. See 50c.

59d Taunton: St Mary Magdalene. 15th/16th century church with double aisles to the nave and a splendid tower.

    St James. Church with notable tower, rebuilt in the 19th century.

59f Swell: St Catherine. Small, simple 12th century church reached through a farmyard.

59i Ilminster. See 52a.

60a Langport. An architectural curiosity, this 15th century hanging chapel is built over an archway. Notable mediaeval stained glass, 12th century Norman tympanum and tie beam chancel roof.

60c Lyte's Cary. 15th century manor house with 14th century chapel. *March to end October Wednesdays and Saturdays 1400-1730.* ❋ 🏠

60d Muchelney: Abbey. Ruins of a 12th to 16th century Benedictine abbey built on Saxon foundations.

60i Yeovil. See 52c.

61a North Cadbury: St Michael. Classic example of Somerset Perpendicular church, with rare 15th century painted glass in the west window and a collegiate style chancel.

61d Sherborne. See 53b.

61f West Stour. Restored 13th century church.

61f Marnhull: St Gregory. Fine cruciform-shaped Early English church with 15th century pinnacled tower; Gothic font.

61f Sturminster Newton. Perpendicular church with 14th century stone work and a 15th century wagon-beam roof.

62e Ilfracombe: St Nicholas, Lantern Hill. Small chapel dedicated to the patron saint of seafarers; built in the 13th century, it was converted to a lighthouse in 1522 and still shows a red beam.

    Holy Trinity. Norman parish church built on site of Saxon church. Contains one of the finest wagon roofs in West Country; dating from the 15th century it is richly carved and painted (restored 1960).

62f Combe Martin: St Peter ad Vincula. 15th century church with 100 ft tower, beautifully carved rood screen and wall brass dedicated to William Hancock in 1587.

62h Braunton: St Brannock. Originally Norman, this 14th century church has a short leaded spire on a Norman tower. Notable wagon roof and bench ends.

62i Barnstaple. See 55c.

63b Lynton: St Mary. 18th/19th century church with 13th century tower. Notable octagonal Norman font and Bishop's Bible of 1586.

63d Trentishoe: St Peter. Isolated church, the smallest in Devon until the chancel was added in 1861, with a 15th century tower (a regular hiding place for smuggled goods) and a tiny musicians' gallery in the nave.

63d Arlington Court (tel. Shirwell 027 182 296). The estate church, dedicated to St James, was restored and rebuilt in 1844; it contains memorials to the Chichester family. *April to end October: Tuesday to Sunday and Bank Holiday Mondays 1100-1730.*
🍴🅿️❋🖼️🏛️🏠🚶

63e Parracombe: St Petrock. 10th century church with 13th century tower, chancel and east window. Notable Georgian interior with painted chancel screen, 3-deck pulpit and high pews. Musicians' gallery has a pew with hole cut for bass viol's bow.

63f Oare: St Mary. 14th century stone church with embattled west tower. Famous as the setting in R D Blackmore's novel *Lorna Doone* of the shooting of the heroine by Carver Doone. Notable 17th century pews.

64d Culbone: the smallest complete parish church in England; 35 ft long, 12 ft 4 in wide, with seating for 30 it was built during the 15th century. Norman font and Saxon window.

64d Oare. See 63f.

64e Porlock: St Dubricius. 13th century church with heavy Early English tower and truncated spire. Two notable 13th century monuments beautifully carved in alabaster.

64e Selworthy: All Saints. Perpendicular church in delightful surroundings. 14th century tower, Norman font and wonderful tracery on the windows.

64e Luccombe: St Mary. Mainly Perpendicular church with 13th century chancel and 82 ft high embattled tower. Fine brasses and monuments.

64f Minehead: St Michael. Fine 15th century church with 87 ft high tower. Contains richly carved font and screen, 17th century wooden pulpit, rood loft and an interesting brass dated 1440.

64f Dunster: St George. Large, mainly 15th century cruciform church incorporating parts of a Norman church built by Benedictine monks. Features a fine carved rood screen (1498), good early brasses, well carved font (1530) and 15th century wagon roof.

64f Timberscombe: St Petrock. Perpendicular church with fine Dunster screen, carved wagon roofs and mid-15th century door with original ironwork.

64h Winsford. See 57b.

64h Exton. See 57c.

64h Hawkridge. See 57b.

64i Luxborough: St Mary. 14th century church (restored in the 1890s) with an unusual saddle-back roof to its 1350 tower.

64i Brompton Regis. See 57c.

65d Watchet: St Decuman. Perpendicular church with 80 ft high tower and 13th century chancel. Notable tombs and brasses.

65d Old Cleeve: St Andrew. 15th century church with fine Perpendicular tower built about 1530. Notable 15th century font and cover and a brass chandelier of 1770.

65d Withycombe: St Nicholas. Lovely 13th century church with two contemporary effigies, a Norman font and a small 15th century wooden screen.

65d Cleeve Abbey: ruined 13th century Cistercian house noted for gatehouse, dormitory and refectory with traceried windows, timber roof and wall paintings. *All year daily.*

65e Sampford Brett: 13th century church with monument to Richard de Brett, one of Thomas à Becket's assassins.

65f Stogursey: St Andrew. The parish church, containing some fine Norman work, is the only surviving part of a Benedictine priory.

65g Rodhuish: St Bartholomew. Small 14th century chapel with thick limewashed walls and tiny bell turret.

65h Monksilver: All Saints. Mainly 15th century church with Norman window in chancel, rare 17th century bench ends and a poor box with three locks dated 1634.

65h Elworthy: St Martin. Small Perpendicular church with 13th century tower and 15th century painted rood screen.

65i Crowcombe: church has some handsomely carved Tudor bench ends symbolising fertility.

66b Burnham-on-Sea: St Andrew. Church with 14th century, 78 ft high tower leaning 3 ft from vertical. Carved angels by Grinling Gibbons from "Whitehall Altar".

66d Storgursey. See 65f.

66h Bridgwater: St Mary. 13th to 15th century church with slender 75 ft Ham-stone spire, black oak pulpit and Jacobean screen.

66i Westonzoyland: St Mary. 14th/15th century church with magnificent tie-beam roof. Captured rebels from Monmouth's army at the Battle of Sedgemoor were confined here in 1685.

67e Glastonbury Abbey (tel. 0458 32267). The oldest Christian sanctuary in Britain, legend dates its foundation from 61AD by Joseph of Arimathea, although archeology puts the date nearer 700AD. The remains of the original wattle and daub church can still be seen, along with the famous flowering thorn tree nearby. More substantial ruins date from the 12th and 13th centuries, including the Lady Chapel, with its sculptured doorways and late Norman decoration. Pilgrimage last Saturday in June; miracle plays twice weekly in July and August. *June to August: daily 0900-1930. Rest of year: daily from 0930.* 📷 ⬇T

St John the Baptist: Perpendicular church with a fine 15th century tower and a 16th century altar tomb.

67f Wells Cathedral. In 909AD Wells became the see of a bishop; the present cathedral dates from two main periods—1180-1240 and 1290-1340—the east end of the nave being the earliest part. The two western towers were the last additions, the south one dated 1384, that to the north 1424. On the west front is the most extensive array of mediaeval sculpture to survive in Britain. Also of note: the inverted arches under the crossings that support the massive weight of the central tower; the 13th century octagonal Chapter House with its fine vaulting and canopied seats for the canons; a remarkable 14th century astronomical clock with knights that joust every hour; 14th century glass and vaulting in the Lady Chapel; and the gold Jesse window in the choir. A glorious building well worth a visit.

St Cuthbert. 15th century church with magnificent pinnacled and embattled west tower. Remains of the original rood screen and a 17th century pulpit.

68a Downside Abbey: set amongst Victorian monastic buildings (now a school), this Victorian/20th century church has a 166 ft high tower and cathedral-sized dimensions. Notable 18th century monuments. *Monastic buildings open to male visitors only, by appointment.*

68b Mells: St Andrew. 15th century church with 104 ft high pinnacled tower. Of note are the 16th

Wells Cathedral (67e)

century benches, mediaeval stained glass and monuments to Burne-Jones and Sir Alfred Munnings.

68c Beckington: church with Norman tower and many good monuments dating back to 1370.

68d Shepton Mallet: SS Peter and Paul. Notable church with a magnificent panelled roof.

68e Witham Friary: remains of a Carthusian monastery founded by Henry II. Only part of the church and dovecote remain, the latter converted into a reading-room.

68g Wyke Champflower: church, built in 1623 by Henry Southworth, containing box pews with their own hat pegs.

68h Bruton: 18th century parish church with a 13th century crypt.

68f Horningsham: the thatched Nonconformist chapel, built by Scotsmen, in 1568, is one of the oldest in Britain.

69f Codford St Peter: church contains an unusually beautiful piece of stone carving on a 9th century cross.

68i Mere: St Michael. Mainly Perpendicular church with tower built about 1450. Also a 15th century octagonal font; fine rood and chapel screens and brasses; good 19th century stained glass.

70e Woodspring Priory: remains of a 13th century Augustinian priory; the church is being restored by the National Trust.

70f Yatton: St Mary. Impressive 14th/15th century church with an elaborate, highly decorated south porch. Other features include a fine west front and 15th century central tower.

70g Uphill: St Nicholas. Interesting ruined Norman church (roofless since 1864).

70i Banwell: St Andrew. Perpendicular church with imposing west tower. Features a Norman font, 16th century rood screen, some 15th century Flemish stained glass and interesting brasses.

71 Bristol: Cathedral. Originally built as an Augustinian monastery in 1140, little remains from that time except the chapter house, which has rich Romanesque decoration. The abbey church was started in 1298 and developed constantly thereafter, receiving cathedral status from Henry VIII. Its many interesting features include complex aisle vaulting, stalls with misericords and many monuments. The anteroom to the Berkerley Chapel includes an early 14th century skeleton vault.

Clifton Roman Catholic Cathedral, off Pembroke Road. Completed in 1973, this stark modern design is intended to provide space for the entire congregation near the altar.

St Mark, College Green, off Park Street. The Lord Mayor's Chapel, it was founded in 1220 as part of St Mark's Hospital, but passed into the hands of the City Corporation after the Dissolution, thus becoming the only municipally-owned church in Britain. Restored in 1889, its features include a 15th century tower, a 16th century fan-vaulted chapel and a wealth of stained glass.

All Saints: originally Norman, this church was much modified in the 15th century and was topped by a cupola on the north tower during the 18th century. Contains many fine monuments.

St Mary Redcliffe, off Redcliffe Hill. This magnificent 13th to 15th century church is one of the largest in England. Its hexagonal north porch is lavishly decorated; there are many monuments and brasses inside, plus candlesticks, a sword rest, lectern and wrought iron screens; the spire is 285 ft high.

John Wesley's Chapel, Broadmead (tel. 0272 24740). The oldest Methodist chapel in the world, it was built in 1739 and rebuilt 9 years later. The chapel and Wesley's living rooms are preserved. Wesley Day celebrations on 24 May. *Mondays, Tuesdays and Thursday to Saturday (not Bank Holidays): 1000-1600. Free.*

St John: a small 14th century church built above the Old City Gate.

St Nicholas, St Nicholas Street, off Baldwin Street (tel. 0272 299771). Church with 18th century Gothic exterior and a complete 16th century crypt, although the majority of the interior has been rebuilt as a museum. *Monday to Saturday 1000-1700. Free.* 📷

71e Dundry: church erected in 1484 as a landmark by the Merchant Venturers of Bristol. Churchyard contains a stone block used as a table for dispensing charity.

71h Compton Martin: St Michael. Norman church with a Perpendicular west tower. Vaulted chancel, nave and font are good examples of Norman craftsmanship.

72c Castle Combe: mainly Perpendicular church restored in 1851; the turreted tower is original. Notable fan vaulting and 13th century font.

72 Bath: Abbey Church. The church, founded in 1495, is built in a restrained and uniform Perpendicular style—the last great example of the type—on the site of a Saxon and Norman Abbey. Its most notable features are its fine tower and west facade, portraying the ladder dream of Bishop Oliver King which led to the rebuilding of the abbey. After suffering much damage during the 1539 Dissolution the church was restored in the 16th and 17th centuries and again under Sir Gilbert Scott from 1864 to 1874. Other features include a heavily carved west door set in a triple arch; elaborate and striking fan vaulting in the chancel; Prior Byrde's Chantry with its richly carved and canopied niches and a delightful fan-vaulted roof; and the enormous clerestory windows.

72h Hinton Priory (tel. Limpley Stoke 022 122 3596). Remains of a Carthusian priory founded in 1232. Most notable are the chapter house ruins; a 15th century gatehouse forms part of the present house. *April to 1 October: Wednesdays, Saturdays and Bank Holidays 1400-1800.*

72i Bradford-on-Avon: St Laurence. One of the few pre-Conquest Anglo-Saxon churches to survive intact. Possibly dating from the 7th century the church was hidden among houses and stables until the late 19th century. This little church with its stone roof, narrow arched porches and two sculptured angels is well worth visiting.

Holy Trinity. 14th century church with visible Norman remains such as the chancel windows. Note the mediaeval wall painting of the Virgin, the short spire of the west tower and some fine monuments and brasses.

73a Hardenhuish: elegant Georgian church with Venetian windows.

73d Lacock Abbey. Founded as a nunnery in 1232, the original cloisters, sacristy, warming rooms and chapter house survive, although the rest of the building was converted to a country house after the Reformation. *June to end September daily; April, May and October Wednesday to Sunday and Bank Holiday Mondays; 1400-1730.* 📷 ⬛

73e Sandy Lane: St Nicholas. Timber-framed church built in 1842 with thatched roof—rare in Wiltshire.

73f Calne: impressive parish church dates from 12th century with 15th century additions paid for by local wool merchants.

Bird Watching

These pages list the most popular bird watching sites and those of ornithological significance. Birds in captivity are included in the section on Wildlife in Captivity (pages 100-101).

19c The Island. One of the best places on the Cornish coast for seabird passage. Numerous shearwaters; storm petrels in autumn. *Free access.*

19f Penzance. Good area for seabirds and winter wildfowl; divers and grebes appear in autumn. Best viewpoints from harbour walls and monument.

19f Marazion Marshes. Rich habitat, with reeds and shallow pools, which attract passage waders in spring and autumn and numerous divers and grebes in winter.

20a Hayle Estuary. Good selection of winter and autumn waders, like godwits and curlew, and winter wildfowl.

20b Crowan Reservoirs. 3 small lakes where autumn waders are regular as well as duck and terns.

20c Stithians Reservoir. 274 acre lake visited by a wide variety of passage waders and wildfowl. Permits from Argal Reservoir (see 🔦).

20e Loe Pool. 150 acre lake with marshy, reedy area that holds many species of birds. Main attraction is duck in winter, including teal, wigeon, goldeneye. *Limited access.*

21d Helford. Frequently visited by swans which can often be fed by hand.

22b Tresco: Great Pool. Attracts waders trans-Atlantic migrants and numerous widlfowl.

22b St Mary's: Hugh Town. Best for passage birds; rare herons are annual whilst most beaches hold waders.

22d Western Rocks/Gorregan. Breeding auks and kittiwake colony; birds on passage. Access by boat from St Agnes.

22e Annet: Bird Sanctuary. Outstanding for Manx shearwaters, storm petrels, puffins and terns. Access by boat from St Agnes.

22i The Island. See 19c.

23c Gull Rocks. Mainly noted for mixed colony of auks in summer including puffin, guillemot and razorbill.

23f St Agnes Head. Main attraction is breeding seabirds in summer, like kittiwake and guillemot. Access on foot.

23g Hell's Mouth. View gulls, cormorants and countless other seabirds from the cliff path to Godrevy Point. Best viewpoint is Navax Point.

24a Gull Rocks. See 23c.

24b Porth Reservoir. 40 acre lake with numerous wildfowl. Permits from Warden at site.

24g Devoran Creek. Frequent passage waders (spring) and some wildfowl.

24h Merther: Tressillian River. Waders in spring whilst godwits and greenshank winter here.

24h Truro River. Wildfowl such as pintail, teal and wigeon in winter; waders in spring; and sandpipers and redshank in autumn.

24i Ardevora: Fal River. Wildfowl are not frequent but brent geese are occasionally present; abundance of waders in spring.

27a St Germans River. Mainly wildfowl, including wigeon and teal.

27a St John's Lake. Main attraction is the winter wildfowl.

27c Plym River. The small estuary attracts golden plover, redshank, knot and black-tailed godwit in autumn and winter.

27f Yealm River Estuary. The main mud flats in the upper estuary hold numerous waders (autumn); wildfowl in winter.

27f Wembury Point. Large area of intertidal rocks and foreshore, the haunt of fulmars, large flocks of turnstones, sandpipers and passage migrants.

28f Newquay: Kingsbridge Estuary. Numerous wildfowl, including teal, shelduck and goldeneye (winter); many species of waders (autumn).

29c Berry Head. Good summer spot for observing seabirds like fulmar and razorbill.

29c Scabbacombe Head. Relatively unspoilt area which holds a small colony of breeding seabirds. Access by foot from the beach.

29d Frogmore Creek. Winter wildfowl and waders in autumn.

29e Slapton Ley Nature Reserve. The two lakes, rimmed by reeds, attract great numbers of winter wildfowl; rare birds often seen. Bird observatory Permits from Slapton Field Centre (tel. Kingsbridge 0548 580466) which also hosts residential one week bird study courses. ♣

29g Prawle Point. Good viewpoint for large variety of migrants (spring and autumn); seabirds also abound in autumn.

29h Start Point. Headland nature reserve attracts many birds, particularly migrants; seabirds inhabit the area in autumn. The lighthouse attracts nocturnal migrants. ☆

30f Padstow: Camel Estuary. At low tide wide areas of sandflats are visited by large numbers of waders in spring (see also 31d).

30h Porth Reservoir. 40 acre lake with numerous wildfowl. Permits from warden at site.

31c Crowdy Reservoir. 115 acres of water which mainly attracts winter wildfowl. Hide available; permits from Information Office at site. ♣

31d Camel River. This area of the estuary holds large numbers of waders throughout the year, as well as grebes, divers and winter wildfowl.

32e Siblyback Lake. A great variety of birds visit all year round. Holders of SWWA permit (available from Warden at site) may use a bird hide with identification charts.

33h Weir Quay: Tamar River. Good vantage point for white-fronted geese and avocets in winter as well as large numbers of wildfowl.

33h Cargreen: Tamar River. Numerous waders (autumn) and wildfowl (winter).

33h Bere Ferrers: Tavy River. Wintering species include white-fronted geese, black-tailed godwit and avocet; waders in autumn.

33i Burrator Reservoir. Holds a small number of winter wildfowl; the plantations around it carry a mixture of heath and woodland birds. Permit from Information Office.

34a Wistmans Wood. Redstart and wood warbler, amongst many woodland species, as well as large numbers of buzzards.

34b Fernworthy Reservoir. Small amount of winter wildfowl; mixture of heath and woodland birds in surrounding plantations. ♣

34e Bellever. The Forestry Commission plantation abounds with a large mixture of woodland and heath birds. ♣

34f Holne Chase. Oakwoods, with a number of

streams running through them, holding ring ouzel, dipper and wagtail.

34g Burrator Reservoir. See 33i.

35i Hopes Nose. Popular area in summer holding a large kittiwake colony as well as huge numbers of other seabirds offshore.

36a Lye Rock. An area of high cliffs with breeding colonies of auks including puffins.

36f Crowdy Reservoir. See 31c.

37g Siblyback Lake. See 32e.

39d Fernworthy Reservoir. See 34b.

39d Wistmans Wood. See 34a.

39g Bellever. See 34e.

39h Holne Chase. See 34f.

40f Exe River. 5 mile estuary provides several square miles of mud flats at low tide. Winter wildfowl dominate, especially ducks; brent geese and Slavonian grebes are also present. Waders appear in all seasons and include godwits, sanderling, greenshank and spotted redshank. Terns are numerous in autumn. Best viewpoints are marked at **Powderham, Lympstone, Starcross** and **Dawlish Warren.**

41a Woodbury Common. Large area of heath and scrub provides habitats for heathland species, including stonechat, nightjar, tree pipit, redstart and buzzard.

41e The Warren. Salt marshes that provide a feeding place for a great variety of birds, including large numbers of swans.

42d Axmouth: Axe River Estuary. Small numbers of winter wildfowl and waders; godwits, ruff and redshank appear in autumn.

42g Beer Head. A colony of cormorants live on this 426 ft high headland.

43h Burton Mere. The tangle of trees and bushes behind the now overgrown mere is an excellent place to watch migration birds—finches, skylarks and thrushes (October).

44c Puddletown Heath. Typical mixture of birds found in woodland. Access from nature trail. ♣

44e Lodmoor. Low area of rough grazing intersected by dykes with large numbers of winter wildfowl, waders and passage migrants. ☆

44e Radipole Lake Reserve. Fine area of lake and reed-bed, with breeding reed warblers and bearded tits; wide selection of passage migrants and winter wildfowl.

44e Ferry Bridge/Portland Harbour. Small intertidal area of sand and mud regularly attracts waders, terns and gulls; the harbour is the haunt of seaduck, divers and grebe.

44h Portland Bill Bird Observatory and Field Centre (tel. 0305 820553). Large numbers of migrants of all types pass the observatory. The obelisk is a good shelter for sea-watching; regular species include shearwaters, fulmar and gannet. *1st March to 31st October; other dates by appointment.*

45c Hamworthy: Rockley Sands. Overlooks the vast Poole Harbour where large numbers of duck concentrate in winter, as well as divers, grebes and a variety of waders.

45c Arne Bay/Shipstal Point. Winter wildfowl and waders; stonechat and night jar (autumn). ♣

45c Arne Heath. RSPB nature reserve in Dorset heathland, with breeding nightjar, stonechat and

Dartford warbler; good selection of wildfowl and waders in autumn and winter. *Access by permit only from RSPB.* ♣

45i St Albans Head. Good area for breeding seabirds, like puffin, guillemot and cormorant; abundance of black redstarts in autumn and winter.

46f Tamar Lakes. Two reservoirs that attract winter wildfowl, including geese, wild swans, unusual duck, and waders.

52f Sutton Bingham Reservoir. 145 acres of water attractive to duck, especially pintails; passage waders and black terns. ☞

53i Puddletown Heath. See 44c.

54h Tamar Lakes. See 46f.

55i Horsey Island: Torridge/Taw Estuary. Excellent viewing point for winter wildfowl; waders and seabirds also numerous in autumn.

55b Northam Burrows: Torridge/Taw Estuary. Same species as at Horsey Island (above).

57c Wimbleball Reservoir. Winter wildfowl and passage waders. Permits from the warden at the reservoir.

58a Wimbleball Reservoir. See 57c.

60i Sutton Bingham Reservoir. See 52f.

62a Lundy Island Field Centre/Bird Observatory (tel. Barnstaple 0271 73333). Breeding seabirds, raven, buzzard and a wide variety of migrants. Boats from Ilfracombe. *Daily.*

62e Spreacombe: Chapel Wood. RSPB-owned valley containing common woodland birds. Permits from C. G. Manning, Sherracombe, Raleigh Park, Barnstaple, Devon. *Free.*

62h Horsey Island. See 55b.

63d Arlington Court (tel. Shirwell 027 182 296). Heronry and wild-duck sanctuary on a lake in a wooded setting. *Daily during daylight hours.* ☞ ♣ ❉ ▣ ⊞ ✝ ♠

63d Wistlandpound Reservoir. Permit for bird watching from the information office at site. *1 April to 31 March.* ☞

64e West Porlock: Porlock Marsh. Area of gorse, reed beds and shallow pools supports winter duck and waders; frequent passage waders.

64i Wimbleball Reservoir. See 57c.

65d Marsh Street: Minehead/Dunster Beaches. Sand, mud and shingle backed by sand dunes support winter duck and waders.

65g Nettlecombe Court: Leonard Wills Field Centre (Washford 098 44 320). One week residential birdwatching courses. *February to November.* ♣ ⊞

66e Bridgwater Bay National Nature Reserve. Excellent for waders and winter wildfowl, including white-fronted geese; unique moulting shelduck flock (late summer/autumn). *Access by foot.*

66h Durleigh Reservoir. Shallow lake attracts dabbling duck and passage waders in autumn; mute swans gather in July-August.

Lesser Spotted
Woodpecker

67a Cheddar Reservoir. Wide variety of winter wildfowl.

67d Shapwick Heath. National nature reserve in ancient peat works with breeding nightjar, curlew and nightingale. *Limited access — view from footpaths on western side.*

69d Longleat Park. (tel. Maiden Bradley 098 53 55). Chain of lakes with a large number of winter wildfowl, including teal and tufted duck. *Daily.* ☞ ❉ ♠ ☆

69d Shear Water. Large variety of wildfowl and numerous winter finches.

70g Brean Down. 300 ft high limestone headland with variety of birds — gulls, kestrels, chats and redshanks; ideal migration watch point — heavy in October. ♠

70g Steep Holme. Breeding colony for gulls and cormorants. Access details from Steep Holme Trust, 11 Kendon Drive, Westbury-on-Trym, Bristol. ♣

71b Leigh Woods. Mixed broadleaf woods provide habitat for woodpeckers, nightingale, redstart and hawfinch in summer. ♣

71e Barrow Gurney Reservoirs. Attract moderate numbers of wildfowl and waders.

71g Blagdon Lake. Good for winter wildfowl such as wigeon, teal and pochard; waders appear in autumn in moderate numbers.

71h Chew Valley Lake. One of the best areas of winter wildfowl in Britain; the autumn is outstanding for waders, divers and grebes. Large gull roost in winter.

72c Long Barrow: By Brook. Wooded valley with stream where a wide variety of woodland birds breed, such as dipper and redstart.

73d Corsham Park (tel. 0249 712214). Lake which holds winter wildfowl and terns on passage. *July to mid September: Tuesday to Thursday and weekends 1100-1800. Rest of year: Sundays, Wednesdays and Thursdays 1100-1630.* ❉ ⊞

Wildlife in Captivity

Including zoos, aviaries, aquaria and outdoor safari parks. Animals in the wild are included in the sections on Countryside (pages 74-76). and Bird Watching (pages 100-101).

19i Mousehole: Bird Sanctuary, on the hill above the village, is a hospital for seabirds of every kind. It is open to the public.

20a Hayle Bird Paradise (tel. 0736 753365). Birds from all over the world, including several endangered species; breeding colony of penguins (feeding time 1500 daily); children's zoo; craft village; miniature steam railway; donkey rides, etc. *Daily 1000 to dusk.* ☞ ⌂

20f Gweek: Cornish Seal Sanctuary (tel. Mawgan 032 622 361). Hospital caring for all sea creatures, including seals (usually babies), dolphins, porpoises, turtles and birds, all washed up on the Cornish coast. Always plenty of animals. *Daily 0930 to sunset.*

24b Newquay: Marine Aquarium, with live fish and crustacea caught locally.
Zoo, Trenance Park on A3075 (tel. 063 73 3342). Good selection of wild animals, including chimpanzees, lions and leopards; large bear pit; walk-through aviary with tropical birds; large walking birds; reptiles, seals, penguins, pet's corner, pony rides. *Daily.* ☞

25d Mevagissey: small aquarium in the former lifeboat station.

26b Looe: Marine Aquarium (tel. 050 36 2423). Exhibits limited to specimens which have been caught within one mile of the local pier. Also shark museum. *June to September 1000-2100.*

26c Murrayton: The Monkey Sanctuary (tel. Looe 050 36 2532). The world's first protected breeding colony of rare Humboldt's woolly monkeys from the Amazon. They live in a giant cage with trees, ladders, ropes, etc., but can wander among the visitors. Take care — they bite! Talks AM and PM; indoor facilities in rain. *First two weeks of April; then mid-May to October 1030-1730.* ☞

27b Plymouth: Zoological Gardens, Central Park. Mixed collection of mainly African animals, including lions, giraffes and antelopes. *Daily 1000 to sunset.*
Marine Biological Association Aquarium, The Hoe. One of the finest in Europe with wide range of species. *Daily 1000-2000 (closed Sundays).*

28a Sparkwell: Dartmoor Wildlife Park (tel. Cornwood 075 537 209). Mainly British and European animals in natural surroundings. Six deer species; badgers, polecats, foxes and squirrels; free-flying waterfowl; monkey pen, donkeys for children. *Daily 1000 to dusk.* ☞

29c Paignton: Zoological and Botanical Gardens, Totnes Road (tel. 0803 557479). Major zoo in 100 acres with large selection of species, including elephants, lions, tigers, rhinos, hippos and giraffes. Many apes, including rare colony of Lar gibbons on an island. Also a monkey house, tropical house, reptiles, birds (including the Cornish chough) and fish (including piranha). Children's play area; miniature railway. *Daily 1000-1930 (1730 in winter).*

Seashore Aquarium, The Harbour. Fine collection of living creatures and static displays. *End May to September daily.*

29c Brixham: Marine Aquarium. The largest tank in Britain containing only fish caught within 40 miles of the town by the local trawler fleet. Despite this limitation, there are jellyfish, crutacea, squid, octopus, rays and a wide variety of fish. Display of model trawlers.

30f Padstow: Bird & Butterfly Garden Fentonluna Lane (tel. 0841 532262). Over 200 bird species, especially softbilled ones, with heated Tropical House containing free-flying birds; over 400 butterflies include live examples on their favourite plants (best seen on sunny summer days). *Daily 1030 to 1 hour before dusk.* ☞

30h Newquay. See 24b.

31i Fletchersbridge: Bodmin Farm Park (tel. Bodmin 0208 2074). Farm animals; pony and donkey rides; collection of farm tools, etc. *Sunday to Friday 1000-1800.* ☞

35f Teignmouth: Aqualand Aquarium, The Den (tel. 062 67 3383). Local fish, including sharks, rays and eels; tropical display including crocodiles and turtles. *Easter to October 1000-1800.* Model railway exhibition downstairs.

35f Shaldon: Children's Zoo (tel. 062 687 2234) with monkeys, goats, chipmunks, wallabies, birds

and donkeys; pet's corner. *Daily after Easter; winter weekends; 1000 to dusk.*

35h Paignton. See 29c.

35i Torquay: **Aqualand Aquarium**, Beacon Quay (tel. 0803 24439). One of the largest collections of tropical sea fish in Britain; also penguins, rare turtles, otters and local sea and freshwater species. *April to October 1000 to dusk (2200 in summer).*

40i Teignmouth. See 35f.

40i Shaldon. See 35f.

41c Farway Countryside Park (tel. 040 487 224). Collection of rare British farm breeds, past and present; also pony rides, donkey carts, pets' enclosure. *April to end September (closed Saturdays but open Bank Holiday Saturdays); 1000-1700.* ♣ ⌐

41d Exmouth: **Aquarium.** Local and tropical species, plus terrapins and turtles—one Giant Loggerhead turtle is over 60 years old. *Easter to October daily; rest of year Tuesday, Fridays and weekends.*

   Zoo. Extensive collection of mainly small species, including unusual mammals (Saki monkeys, Slender Loris, etc.), birds, reptiles and lizards. *Daily 1000 to dusk.*

41d Sandy Bay: **Countryside Museum** (tel. Exmouth 039 52 74533). One of the largest open-air museums in Britain, with shire horses, ponies and other animals. *Early April to late September daily from 1030.* ↓T

42f Lyme Regis: **Marine Aquarium.** Local sea species which are returned to the sea at the end of every summer.

43i Abbotsbury Swannery, New Barn Road (tel. 030 587 228). Famous breeding ground for swans, established in the 15th century by Benedictine monks as a source of meat for their tables. Also visited by many other species of wild birds. *May to mid September daily 1000-1700.* ❉

45c Poole: **Park Zoo** (tel. Parkstone 0202 745296). Small, but with many species, including big cats, bears, monkeys, otters, porcupines, penguins, parrots and other birds. Also a monkey house, tropical house and children's corner. *March to October daily; November to February weekends, Bank Holidays and daily during school holidays; 1000-1800 (or sunset if earlier).*

   Merley Tropical Bird Gardens, Wimborne Road. Walled garden of 3½ acres with over 100 species of bird. *April to October daily 1000-1900 (or sunset).*

45e Church Knowle: **Margaret Green Animal Sanctuary.** Abandoned birds and animals cared for. *Daily.*

46i Furze Farm Park, Bridgerule (tel. 028 881 342). Working farm museum with 22 breeds of British sheep, 8 of cattle, together with deer, rabbits, hamsters, pheasants, goats and donkeys. Commando play area and slideshows. Indoor activities for wet days. *March to September daily 1030-2000.* ⬤ ⌐ ↓T

48e Wembworthy: Ashley Countryside Collection, Ashley House (tel. Ashreigney 076 93 226). Unique collection of 45 breeds of British sheep, including many rare old domestic species. Farming exhibits under cover. *Easter to October: Mondays, Wednesdays, weekends and Bank Holidays; Friday to Wednesday in August; 1000-1300, 1400-1800.* ⌐ ↓T

48g Follygate: **Pinevalley Wildlife Park** (tel. Okehampton 0837 2595). Small collection of birds and

mammals, including Himalayan bears, living in natural surroundings. *Daily 1000 to dusk.*

50d Bickleigh Mill Heritage Farm (tel. 088 45 419). Rare breeds of poultry; cows and goats milked by hand; working shire horses. *Early January to mid March 1400-1700; March to end December 1000-1800.* ↓T

51a Widcombe Bird Gardens, Culmhead. Wildfowl, peafowl and ornamental bantams. *March to October 1030-1800.* ⬤ ⌐

51f Farway Countryside Park. See 41c.

52d Cricket St Thomas Wildlife Park (tel. Winsham 046 030 396). Beautiful 80-acre park with deer, zebras, llamas and wallabies; also wild birds, small mammals, and penguin enclosure. National Heavy Horse Centre; children's fort; countryside museum. *Daily 1000-1800.* ⬤ ⌐ ▒

53a Compton House: Worldwide Butterflies and Lullingstone Silk Farm (tel. Yeovil 0935 4608 or 4609). 16th century manor house with butterfly breeding centre: all stages of development can be seen, also live specimens in Tropical Jungle, Palm House, etc. The silk farm produced the silk for the Queen's wedding dress and the last two Coronations. *April to October 1000-1700.* ⬤ ❉

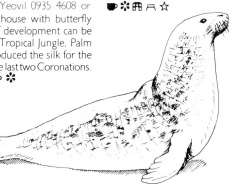

Grey Seal, Gweek (20f)

55e Bideford: small but well-kept zoo with range of animals and pet's corner.

57a Molland: London Inn. Thatched building with miniature zoo in garden.

59g Widcombe Bird Gardens. See 51a.

59i Cricket St Thomas. See 52d.

61d Compton House. See 53a.

62e Ilfracombe: Tropical Wildlife Garden, Bicclescombe Park. Birds, monkeys, racoons, penguins, macaws, ocelots, wild cats, pumas, wallabies and other species in small enclosures. Pet's corner; children's play area; boating pool; water garden. *Easter to Spring Bank Holiday: daily 1100-1700. June to mid September: daily 1000 to dusk.* ↓T

63d Arlington Court (tel. Shirwell 027 182 296). Shetland ponies and rare Jacob's sheep grazing in attractive grounds containing many other activities. *Daily.* ⬤ ♣ ❉ ▣ ⌗ ✛ ❧

66c Lower Weare: Ambleside Water Gardens and Aviaries. Over 250 species of birds, including parrots, mynahs, budgerigars, pigeons and waterfowl; also gerbils, rabbits, guinea pigs, etc. and fish lake. *Easter to mid October daily except Mondays.*

67a Cheddar: Marineland (tel. 0934 742854). Impressive range of tropical and domestic fish, both sea and freshwater, plus baby seal pool and shark pool. *Daily 0930-2100.*

68c Rode Tropical Bird Gardens (tel. Beckington 037 383 326). Brilliant collection of almost 200 species of colourful birds in 17 acres of gardens, with aviaries designed to blend into their surroundings. Larger birds include penguins, vultures, owls, macaws and flamingoes. During summer, there are also domestic animals—rabbits, pigs, goats and donkeys—plus pets' corner and donkey rides. *Daily 1030-1900 (sunset in winter).* ⬤ ❉ ❧

69d Longleat (tel. Maiden Bradley 098 53 328). Europe's first Safari Park, with the famous lions, plus tigers, rhinos, gnus, zebras, camels, hippos, sealions, a chimpanzee island and a pet's corner. All part of a complex with many other attractions. *March to October daily 1000-1800 (or sunset).* ⬤ ❉ ▣ ⌐ ☆

70g Weston-super-Mare: Aquarium and Miniature Zoo. Monkeys, parrots, tropical birds, insects and domestic animals, plus sea and freshwater fish, small alligators, snakes, lizards and other reptiles. *Easter to September daily.*

70g Brean Down Bird Gardens (tel. 027 875 209). Collection of some 300 birds from all over the world in large aviaries. *April to October 1000-1800.* National Trust reserve nearby. ❧

71 Bristol: Zoological Gardens, Clifton Down (tel. 0272 38951). The second oldest in Britain, dating from 1836, with one of the biggest collections in the West Country. Among many famous animals are its white tigers, okapis and breeding apes—Bristol was the first to breed a gorilla in Britain in 1971. Also black rhinos, polar bears, monkeys, reptiles and fish. *Daily from 0900 (1000 Sundays).* ⬤ ❉

71b Westbury on Trym Wildlife Park (tel. 0272 625112). British animals, such as badgers, foxes, deer, seals, magpies, eagles, barn owls, etc. *Daily 0900 to dusk.*

72b Dodington (tel. Chipping Sodbury 0454 312232). Children's farm and horses in park with much else of interest. *April to September daily 1100-1700.* ⬤ ❉ ▣ ⌗ ↓T

Bristol Zoo (71)

Industry Past and Present

From industrial archeology to the latest nuclear power stations, including open-air museums, craft workshops, modern factories and collieries. Preserved railways offering rides to the public are, however, detailed in the section on Tourist Railways (page 106).

19d Levant Mine. Remains of an 1840 tin mine closed in 1919 when its unusual man engine collapsed and killed 31 men; the man engine consisted of a huge wooden beam which moved 12 ft up and down, the miners stepping from one platform to another to descend over 1600 ft in half an hour. Botallack Head is riddled with the remains of both copper and tin mines and visitors should beware of many unmarked shaft holes.

Geevor Mine (tel. St Just 0736 788662), adjacent to the Levant Mine, is a working pit with a preserved beam engine which can be viewed. *By arrangement only:* the manager.

19f Ordnance Survey Tidal Observatory, South Pier, Newlyn. Point at which mean sea level (and, therefore, all heights) is calculated for maps of Britain.

20c Wendron: The Poldark Mine (tel. Helston 032 65 3173 or 3531). Partly restored tin mine converted into a 3 acre industrial museum, much of which is underground. Nine chambers, including the Great Chlorite Chamber, which remained closed for 200 years; Britain's only working underground waterwheel; underground rivers and waterfalls. Above ground is an impressive collection of working stationary steam engines of many kinds, including a 40 ft beam engine; also craft shops with wheelwrights, artists, printers, blacksmiths and woodcarvers at work. "Penmarric" was filmed here. Children's amusements. Allow at least 3 hours. *April to early November daily 1000-1715.* 🍽 🚻

20e Trewavas Head. Remains of tin mine engine houses perched on the edge of the steep granite cliffs.

Rinsey Head, to the west, has the roofless engine house of Wheal Prosper, an 18th century copper mine.

20f Gweek: overgrown remains of quays for what was once an important port, handling timber and tin. The harbour closed in 1880 and the river is badly silted-up. Gweek was Alef's Town in "Hereward the Wake". 🐎

20i Poldhu Point: Marconi Monument. Marks the spot from which the first wireless signals were transmitted across the Atlantic.

21b Falmouth: The Docks. Once the second busiest port in England (with up to 8000 vessels each year), Falmouth was from 1688 to 1850 the country's main mailboat harbour. The current docks were built in 1860 and much enlarged during World War II, when convoys assembled here. Dry docks can handle ships of up to 90,000 tons. No admittance to docks, but good views from Castle Drive, on the cliffs leading to Pendennis Point.

23f St Agnes: one of the great mining areas of the 18th and 19th centuries, during which the 350 ft hills were covered in tin and copper workings. Seal Hole was said to have earned a guinea a minute for the man who built Trelissick House (🏠 Six of the more interesting disused mines are marked.

23h Pool: Winding and Pump Engines. A 30 inch rotative beam winding engine of 1887 and a 90 inch beam pumping engine of 1892, both in complete buildings on either side of A30. Good examples of early high pressure steam technology. *April to end October daily 1100-1230, 1400-1730 (sunset if earlier).*

South Crofty Mine (tel. Camborne 0209 714821) is a working pit whose preserved steam beam engine can also be viewed. *By arrangement only:* the manager.

23h Camborne: Holman Museum of Engineering and Industry, near Camborne Station (tel. 0209 712750). Large collection of photographs, models, rocks, mineral samples, and working and stationary exhibits depicting the history of local mining and engineering from the 17th to 20th centuries. Includes the giant Rostowrack beam engine. *Monday to Saturday (not Bank Holidays).*

23i Tolgus Tin (tel. Redruth 0209 215171), on B3300 to Portreath. The only surviving Cornish streaming mill, in which tin ore is crushed, soaked, vibrated and sifted to produce tin concentrate. The mill has been in use since about 1800 and the whole process can be viewed, with finished produce for sale on the site, most of which is under cover. Guided tours; audio-visual shows; exhibition; children's maze. *Late March to mid October daily from 1000; mid October to late March weekdays 1000-1800.* 🍽 🚻

23i Redruth: Foster's Pottery (tel. 0209 5754), on the old by-pass at Tolgus Hill. Every stage of the potter's art can be seen and explained. Guided tours of the factory. *Weekdays 1000-1545.*

Cauldron Bristol Potteries. Makers of tableware and advertising materials. Factory tours. *Weekdays.*

24b Newquay: Yonder Towan Field Holiday Centre, Beechfield Avenue (tel. 063 73 2756). Industrial archeology holidays arranged; equipment supplied. Minimum age 14. *March to June; August to November.*

24b Dairyland, on A3058 south east of Newquay (tel. Mitchell 087 251 246). Working farm with ultra-modern 'merry-go-round' milking machine where 160 cows are milked to music every afternoon. Also a Country Life Museum with 19th century farming equipment and many working exhibits. Farm animals; pets; electric dog; adventure playground. *April to October daily 1000-1730 (milking 1515-1630).* 🍽 🚻

24b Newlyn East: East Wheal Rose Halt on the Lappa Valley Railway (tel. Mitchell 087 251 317). Engine house and chimney stack of a disused silver lead mine. Part of a 5 acre pleasure park reached only by the railway. Children's play area; boating lake; nature walk. *Good Friday to late May Wednesday to Sunday 1100-1700; late May to 30 September daily 1000-1800; also October Sundays.* 🍽 🚻 🛶

24h Truro: Mount Hawke Weavers. Small firm producing clothes, rugs and bedspreads. *Weekdays AM.*

Railway Viaduct. Splendid 1908 viaduct with 28 granite arches.

Chapel Hill Pottery, on the site of a 1670 kiln. Guided tours. *Weekdays.*

25a Carthew: Wheal Martyn Museum (tel. Stenalees 0726 850362). Fascinating restored china clay works of 1880, with water wheels, pumps, horse-drawn wagons, steam locomotives, huge granite settling tanks, etc. all in working order to demonstrate every stage in the production of kaolin, which is still used to make porcelain, glossy paper, stomach powders and cosmetics. Indoor exhibition areas; audio-visual shows. *Easter (or 1 April) to 31 October daily 1000-1700.* 🍽 🚻

Wheal Martyn Craft Pottery, at the museum (above) produces and sells porcelain and stoneware. *Open as above.*

25b Treffry Viaduct. Built in 1839 to carry a mineral railway and a canal over the valley, it is 660 ft long and 100 ft high. Now disused.

26a Lanreath: Trevollard Farm Museum and Mill.

Tractors, steam and oil engines and a restored farmhouse kitchen, plus many working models. Pets' corner. *May to September daily 1000-1800.*

27b Saltash: Tamar bridges. The river is spanned by Brunel's 1859 railway bridge, built for the Great Western Railway and still in use; and by the magnificent 1962 suspension bridge carrying A38.

27c Plym Bridge Woods: remains of a slate quarry, granite railway and other industrial relics in National Trust woodlands. ♣ 🐾

27f Wembury Beach: The Old Mill. Mediaeval mill house now housing a cafe and National Trust shop. *April to end October daily 1100-1800.* 🍽

29b Dartmouth: Newcomen Engine, Royal Avenue Gardens (tel. 080 43 2923). One of Thomas Newcomen's original atmospheric pressure steam engines dating from 1725 and still in working order. Probably the oldest in the world. Housed in a glass-fronted building built as a memorial to the great engineer. *Easter to October: Monday to Saturday 1100-1700; Sundays 1400-1700.*

30c Pentire: remains of an 18th/19th century silver lead mine above Pentireglaze Farm.

30h Newquay. See 24b.

31b Delabole Slate Quarry (tel. Camelford 084 02 2242). Probably the largest man made hole in Europe, it is over 1¾ miles round and 500 ft deep. It has been worked since 1555 and can be seen in action from an observation platform. Also slate-splitting demonstrations. *Easter, then May to September weekdays; 1000-1800.* 📷

31b Camelford: North Cornwall Museum, The Cleese (tel. 084 02 3229). Restored Cornish cottage, plus displays about slate and granite quarrying, tradesman's tools, etc. *1 April to 30 September: Monday to Saturday 1030-1700.* 📷

31h Bodmin: Great Western Society. Two ex-GWR steam locomotives and some rolling stock are on display. *Sundays.*

32g Carnglaze Slate Caverns, off the A38 (tel. Dobwalls 0579 20251). Beautifully situated disused quarry, from which half a million tons of slate were taken. Huge underground chambers include one 300 ft long and a turquoise lake. Guided tours take 45 minutes. Temperature in caves only 52°F. *Easter to 30 September: July and August weekdays and all Bank Holidays 1000-1730; May, June and September weekdays and all Sundays 1400-1700.*

32h Liskeard: Liskeard Glass Ltd. Small factory making glasses, candle holders and paperweights by traditional methods of blowing and hand shaping. *Weekdays.*

33e Morwellam Open Air Museum (tel. Gunnislake 0822 832 766). In the 19th century, this small hamlet was one of the busiest ports in England, shipping copper, manganese and arsenic down the Tamar to Plymouth. The whole place is now an industrial museum: on arrival, visitors are given a printed guide and directed to a slide show describing two well marked trails. The Port and Mine Trail includes the George and Charlotte copper mine, into which one rides 200 yds by tram, the port facilities, a hydro-electric station and 3 museums. The Canal and Woodland Trail takes in old farm buildings, the remains of a 250 ft inclined plane railway, and the Tavistock Canal, with its 2 mile tunnel through Morwell Down built by French prisoners of war in 1817. Old Ship Inn still open. *Daily 1000-1800 (dusk in winter).* 🍽 🚻

104

33g Cotehele (tel. St Dominick 0579 50434). Restored 18th century hamlet including a blacksmith's forge, cider press, saddlery and a watermill whose wheel both grinds flour and drives a sawmill. The site has many other attractions and requires a full day. *April (or Easter) to October daily 1100-1300, 1400-1730.*

33h Calstock: Tamar Valley Museum. Old bakery, exhibits connected with shipbuilding on the River Tamar and other industrial items.

35e Newton Abbot: New Devon Pottery and Devon Leathercrafts, Forde Road (tel. 0626 4262). Two factories making tableware and vases and fancy leather goods. Guided tours. Joint ticket saves money. *Easter to October weekdays 0930-1200, 1330-1630.*

35g Riverford Farm (tel. Staverton 080 426 636). 500 acre working farm with waggon tours showing three stages of farming from Tudor to modern. Machine milking seen on afternoon tours (1430); barn dance and barbecue on evening tours. *April to September: telephone first.*

35g Dartington Hall (tel. Totnes 0803 864171). Restored 14th century house which is the headquarters of the Dartington Hall Trust, whose extensive activities include an adult educational centre, a co-educational school and a college of art, plus several industrial enterprises such as a dairy farm (on this estate), the Dartington Glassworks at Great Torrington (47c) and those described below.

Tweed Mill. A working factory where every stage of turning raw wool into tweed cloth can be seen. *Monday to Thursday 0900-1200, 1330-1700; Fridays 0900-1530.*

Cider Press Centre. Actually a complete craft centre, with exhibitions and shops arranged as a village. *Monday to Saturday 0930-1730.*

35h Cockington Forge (tel. Torquay 0803 67162). Working forge in a 19th century thatched cottage.

36e Delabole Slate Quarry. See 31b.

36e Camelford. See 31b.

38g Morwellam Open Air Museum. See 33e.

39a Sticklepath: Museum of Rural Industry (tel. 083 784 286 or 352). A 19th century forge, edge-tool factory and grinding house, plus other machinery, all driven by 3 waterwheels. Exhibits of farming tools. *Daily 1000-1730 (machinery works weekends).*

40b Exeter Ship Canal. One of the oldest canals in Britain, dating from the 16th century, it runs 5½ miles from Exeter Maritime Museum to the Exe Estuary near Barton (40f). There are locks with circular balance beams, lift and swing bridges, all working, as the canal is still used by small vessels. Towpath walk to opposite Topsham, where there is a ferry across the river.

40f Starcross: Atmospheric Pumping House, next to the signal box. The only survivor of 10 such stations, which sucked air from a cylinder between the rails of Brunel's unique Atmospheric Railway. The pumping created a vacuum, which was used to pull trains from Exeter to Teignmouth. These trains ran reliably—and silently—at up to 80 mph until rats ate the grease of the all-important leather seats, forcing abandonment of the scheme in 1848. This red sandstone building is one of very few relics of the system. (See also Dawlish Warren, below.)

40f Dawlish Warren Station: South Devon Railway Museum (tel. Dawlish 0626 862131). Nameplates, tickets, photographs and other railway memorabilia, plus a few items from Brunel's Atmospheric (see Starcross, above). Model railways. *Easter, then April to end September daily 1100-1700.*

40g Newton Abbot. See 35e.

41d Sandy Bay: Steam and Countryside Museum (tel. Exmouth 039 52 74533). One of the largest open-air museums in Britain, with hundreds of exhibits. *Early April to late September daily.*

41e Otterton Mill (tel. Colaton Raleigh 0395 68521). Restored Devon corn mill, first mentioned in the Doomesday Book, now once again producing wholemeal flour by water power. Also exhibition gallery and workshops making pottery, furniture, lace, glass and leather goods. *Daily 1100-1730.*

42b Axminster Carpet Factory. The original factory, where every stage of the manufacturing process can be seen. *Weekdays.*

42d Seaton: River Axe Bridge. Built in 1877, it was one of the first concrete structures in Britain. Concrete houses on the eastern bank were also among the first of their kind.

42f Morcombelake: Golden Cap Biscuit Factory Home of famous Dorset Knob. *Weekdays.*

43b Parnham House (tel. Beaminster 0308 862204). Home of famous John Makepeace furniture. As well as the Workshops, there is a Museum of Woodcraft and the house itself. *April to October Wednesdays, Sundays and Bank Holidays 1000-1700 (but closed on Sunday in June).*

45a Nuclear Power Station, Winfrith Heath, operated by the Atomic Energy Authority.

45c Poole: Poole Pottery, The Quay (tel. 020 13 2866). Famous centre founded in 1873 and occupying several floors. Individual skills are emphasised. Guided tours. *Weekdays 1000-1230, 1350-1615.*

Scalpen's Court, High Street (tel. 020 13 5323). Small museum which includes industrial exhibits. *Monday to Saturday 1000-1700; Sundays 1400-1700*

46e Coombe: small watermill in charming National Trust village.

46h Marhamchurch: remains of an unusual inclined plane, on which barges on the old Bude Canal were raised and lowered by a continuous chain.

46i Furze Farm Park, Bridgerule (tel. 028 881 342). Working farm museum covering 26 acres and including a display of farming history, blacksmith's and wheelwright's shops, steam engines, waggon rides, etc. Clay pigeon shooting, commando play area, slideshows and indoor displays for wet days. *March to September daily 1030-2000.*

47c Great Torrington: Dartington Glassworks (tel. 080 52 2321). Tours of the factory, famous for its hand blown glass. It was built in 1967 by the Dartington Hall Trust (see 35g). *Weekdays 0900-1030, 1200-1530.*

47e Alscott Farm Museum (tel. Shebbear 040 928 206). Extensive collection of old agricultural equipment, including vintage farm tractors, ploughs, carts, cider and cheese presses, dairy and household implements. Also photographs and a fascinating scale model of an Edwardian travelling fair. *Easter to 30 September daily 1200 to dusk.*

48e Wembworthy: Ashley Countryside Collection, Ashley House (tel. Ashreigney 076 93 226). Old farm and farmhouse equipment, plus the tools and workshops of wheelwright, blacksmith, cooper and other country craftsmen. Most exhibits under cover. *Easter to October: Mondays, Wednesdays, weekends and Bank Holidays; also Friday to Wednesday in August; 1000-1300, 1400-1800.*

49c Chain Bridge: interesting old iron bridge over the River Exe.

50d Tiverton: Town Museum, St Andrew Street (tel. 088 42 56295 or 2446). Restored 19th century school housing an outstanding collection of exhibits, including two water wheels, a gallery devoted to the Grand Western Canal (see below), a complete blacksmith's shop, farm waggons and agricultural implements and a large railway gallery with Great Western steam loco No. 1442 and other relics. *Monday to Saturday (not Bank Holidays): 1030-1300, 1400-1630. Free.*

Grand Western Canal. Opened in 1814, the canal runs for 11 miles north east to the Somerset border. It closed in 1924, but has now been converted into a country park, with horse drawn barges, etc.

50d Bickleigh Mill Craft Centre (tel. 088 45 419). Restored watermill and stone farm buildings with displays of horse drawn equipment and tools used in cider and lace making and thatching; also an extensive crafts area where visitors can watch skilled craftsman at work on pottery, glass, wood and jewellery. *Daily: early January to mid March 1400-1700; March to end December 1000-1800.*

51f Hornsbury Mills. Restored 19th century corn mill on 4 floors, with displays of equipment, some very old. *March to December Tuesday to Sunday and Bank Holidays.*

51g Honiton Pottery, High Street. Visitors welcome to walk round and see all processes. *Weekdays 0930-1200, 1400-1630 (1600 Fridays). Free.*

51i Axminster. See 42b.

52a Dowlish Wake. The local cidermaker has a collection of Somerset bric-a-brac, including farm machinery and, of course, items connected with cider, notably old firkins—small barrels (up to 1 gallon) of cider issued daily to farmhands from the 16th century until about 1950.

52c Brympton d'Evercy: Priest House Country Life Museum (tel. West Coker 093 586 2528). Illustrates the role of agriculture in supporting a large country house, with displays of cider and wine making, tools, etc. *1 May to late September: Saturday to Wednesday 1400-1800.*

52g Morcombelake. See 42f.

52h Parnham House. See 43b.

54g Coombe: small watermill in charming National Trust village.

55b Appledore: Britain's largest covered shipbuilding yard, opened in 1970.

55c Barnstaple: Craft Market and Workshop, Church Lane (tel. 0271 75171). Workers' co-operative including printer, weaver and workers of pottery, wood, leather and cane. *Monday to Saturday 0930-1730. Free.*

Barnstaple Potteries, Litchdon Street (tel. 0271 3035). Conducted tours of the factory where Barum Ware is made. *Mid May to mid September (but closed 2 weeks late July); weekdays 1015-1545.*

S Sanders & Son, Pilton Bridge, A39 (tel. 0271 2335). Tannery making sheepskin rugs and clothing. *Weekdays 0800-1700. Free.*

55e Great Torrington. See 47c.

55h Alscott Farm Museum. See 47e.

Carriage Museum, Dodington (72b)

56c Heasley Mill: overgrown remains of the buildings and shafts of copper and iron mines closed in the late 19th century.

57f Chain Bridge: interesting old iron bridge over the River Exe.

57i Tiverton. See 50d.

58f Bradford: Sheppy's Farm, A38. Small cider farm with its own orchards, so that visitors can see every stage of the cidermaking process and purchase the results. Also a cider museum. *1 April to mid October daily.*

59c Burrow Bridge Pumping Station (tel. Bridgwater 0278 57333 or Burrow Bridge 082 369 324). Small museum beside the River Parrett, containing steam pumping engines dating from 1864 and 1869, plus hand pumps and other equipment. *Weekdays 0900-1700 when attendant is present. Free.*

59d Taunton: Post Office Museum, 38 North Street (tel. 0823 3391). Displays the history of postal telecommunications, with fascinating exhibits including a 1900 manual exchange and a 1929 automatic exchange; also telephones from 1877, part of the first transatlantic cable of 1857, etc. *Saturdays 1330-1700; other times by arrangement. Free.*

59e Creech St Michael: Chard Canal. One of the shortest-lived canals ever built, the Chard was opened in 1835 and closed in 1860, having never made money. It ran from Taunton, via Wrantage (see below) and Ilminster, to Chard (59i). Its route included 4 inclined planes and 3 tunnels. At Creech is the aqueduct and embankment which carried the canal over the River Tone.

59e Wrantage: Chard Canal. The entrance to a 1 mile tunnel which carried the canal under Crimson Hill to a point near Beer Crocombe. See also Creech St Michael, above.

59i Dowlish Wake. See 52a.

59i Hornsbury Mills. See 51f.

60a Sedgemoor Hill: High Ham Windmill (tel. Langport 0458 250818). Last survivor of many such mills in the area, this stone building has an unusual thatched roof. Built in 1822, it was used until 1910. *By appointment only.*

60b Somerton: Maurice Leach Furniture, Market Place (tel. 0458 73089). Hand-made tables, chairs and dressers made to high standards. *Tuesday to Saturday 1030-1300, 1430-1700.*

60i Brympton d'Evercy. See 52c.

61i Sturminster Newton: working 17th century water mill and wooden-fronted Mill House on the Blandford Forum road.

62e 62f Ilfracombe: Hele Mill, Hele Bay (tel. 0271 63162). Complete, working water mill dating from 1525, with 18 ft overshot wheel and interesting machinery, producing wholemeal flour. *Easter to end September: weekdays 1000-1700; Sundays 1400-1700.*

Bicclescombe Mill, Bicclescombe Park, Ilfracombe. Restored 18th century corn mill with water powered machinery. *Late May to end September daily 1030-1245, 1400-1730.* 🍺

62f Combe Martin: New Forge, Rows Lane (tel. 027 188 3292). Working rural blacksmith's forge. Items made to order. *Weekdays 1400-1800.*

62i Muddiford: Plaistow Mill, on B3230 south of village (tel. Shirwell 027 182 224). Restored mill and water wheel. *Any time. Free.* 🍺

62i Barnstaple. See 55c.

63b Lynton: Woodpecker Toys, Jubilee Hall, Burvill Street (tel. 059 85 2375). Skilled workmen creating hand crafted wooden toys. Guided tours by arrangement. *Monday to Saturday 0900-1300, 1345-1730. Free.*

The Smithy. Was in daily use until 1975, when it was the oldest working blacksmith's in Britain. Forge, bellows and all tools on show. *Easter, then May to end September Sunday to Friday.*

63i Heasley Mill. See 56c.

65d Old Cleeve: John Wood Tannery (tel. Washford 098 44 291). Makers of the famous "Exmoor" sheepskin moccasins and other products. Seconds shop open all year. *Factory tours: April to October weekdays open at 1100; Thursdays also at 1500.*

65d Washford Station: Somerset and Dorset Railway Museum. Main storage depot for the West Somerset Railway (see page 106), with locomotives and rolling stock undergoing repairs and/or restoration. Also a small museum devoted to relics of the Somerset & Dorset Joint Railway. Occasional engines in steam. *Weekends and Bank Holidays.* 🍺 🐦

66d Hinkley Point Nuclear Power Station.

66i Burrow Bridge. See 59c.

67b Wookey Hole Paper Mill (tel. Wells 0749 72243). Old machinery restored to demonstrate hand made papermaking. *Daily: April to September 1000-1800; October to March 1000-1630.* 🍺 📷 ☆

67e Glastonbury: Somerset Rural Life Museum, Abbey Farm, Chilkwell Street (tel. 0458 32903). Restored Victorian farmhouse and 14th century Abbey Barn, with horse drawn agricultural machinery, farmhouse kitchen, displays of cider and cheese making, wheelwrights shop etc. *Easter to 31 October: weekdays 1000-1700 (2000 Thursdays); weekends 1400-1900. 1 November to Easter: weekdays 1000-1700; weekends 1430-1700.* 📷 ✝

67f North Wootton: Wootton Vines, North Town House (tel. 074 989 359). 4 acre vineyard with 8500 vines from Alsace and the Rhine, making dry white wine by traditional methods. *Wednesday to Monday 1400-1700.*

Pilton Manor Vineyards, about 1½ miles south east at Pilton, produce English wines which can be tasted. *End August to early October Sundays and Bank Holidays.*

67g Sedgemoor Hill. See 60a.

67h Street: Clark's Shoe Museum, High Street (tel. 0458 43131). Housed in the oldest part of the factory, it contains shoes and items connected with shoemaking from Roman times to about 1950. *May to October Monday to Saturday 1000-1300, 1400-1645. Free.*

70f Nailsea Moor: Clevedon Craft Centre, Moor Lane (tel. 0272 872867). Working centre with 10 studios offering carving, wood turning, etc.; experts available for discussion. *May to December: Tuesday to Sunday and Bank Holiday Mondays: 1000-1730. Free.* 🍺 📷

70g Weston-Super-Mare: Woodspring Museum, Burlington Street (tel. 0934 21028). Located in the old workshops of the Edwardian Gaslight Company, it includes a reconstructed chemist's shop, a display of lead mining history, a dairy and a transport section. *Monday to Saturday 1000-1300, 1400-1700. Free.* 🍺 📷

70h Bleadon and Uphill Station: Somerset Railway Museum. Privately owned collection of relics indoors, plus several industrial engines and a 1958 British Rail railbus outside. Main line trains still pass through the station, but no longer stop. *Open on request.*

71 Bristol: Harvey's Wine Museum, 12 Denmark Street (tel. 0272 298011). Vaulted cellars dating from the 12th century, when they were storerooms for an Augustine Monastery, now house a display dominated by sherry, with giant butts stacked to demonstrate maturing and blending. Also a magnificent display of glassware. *By appointment only.*

W D & H O Wills (tel. 0272 641111) have several cigarette factories in the town, all of which offer guided tours. *By appointment only.*

Clifton Suspension Bridge. Designed by Isambard Kingdom Brunel and completed in 1864, this famous bridge soars 245 ft above the River Avon and is 702 ft long.

Industrial Museum, Prince's Wharf (tel. 0272 299771 ext 290). Converted dockside warehouse now housing an extensive collection, most of which is connected with transport by land, sea and air. Star items include the 1875 Grenville Steam Carriage —the oldest self-propelled passenger carrying vehicle still in working order; also an 1880 caravan, the industrial tank loco *Henbury* (steamed once a month), a working steam crane and the definitive collection of Bristol-built aero engines (which have included the Olympus jets used on Concorde). Impressive model railway. *Saturday to Wednesday 1000-1200, 1300-1700. Free.*

Floating Harbour. A large tide-free dock created by diverting the Avon during the early 19th century. At high tide, a 270 ft section of dual carriageway at the western end is raised ¼ inch and swung out of the way to allow ships in and out, an impressive operation which can be watched from the north bank recreation area. ☆

71b Blaise Castle Folk Museum, Henbury (tel. Bristol 0272 506789). Reconstructed 18th/19th century farmhouse kitchen and dairy, plus many domestic and agricultural implements of the time. *Monday to Saturday 1400-1700. Free.* 🍺 🏠

71i Pensford Railway Viaduct. Dramatic 16 arch stone and brick span built in 1873 to carry coal from mines near Radstock to Bristol.

72b Dodington House (tel. Chipping Sodbury 0454 318899). Carriage Museum contains horses and over 30 carriages; Family Museum includes display of antique agricultural implements. Much else on site. *Easter to last Sunday in September daily 1100-1700.* 🍺 🍴 📷 🏠 🐦

72e Bath: Camden Works Industrial Museum (tel. 0225 318348). J B Fowler was a Victorian entrepreneur who ran a brass foundry, general engineering shop and made aerated water from 1872 onwards. His entire stock-in-trade is displayed here, all placed in appropriate contemporary settings. *Saturday to Thursday 1400-1700.*

Postal Museum, 51 Great Pulteney Street (tel. 0225 63073). The first stamp posted in the world, a Penny Black on a letter dated 2 May 1840, sent accidentally 4 days before the stamp became official; also many old magazines, letters, postal scales and a replica 1870 travelling post office. All contained in a small basement museum. *Monday to Saturday 1100-1700.*

72f Box Tunnel. Another of Brunel's achievements, this Victorian railway tunnel is almost 2 miles long, linking Box and Corsham (73d).

72g Priston Mill, 1 mile north of the village (tel. Bath 0225 23894). Flour mill founded over 1000 years ago and mentioned in the Doomesday Book. The present building dates from 1700, with a working waterwheel renewed in 1850. Flour is still ground to make "Priston Mill Whole Wheat Bread". *Late March to 31 October: weekdays 1415-1700; weekends and Bank Holidays 1100-1245, 1415-1800. Free.* 🍺 🍴

72i Claverton Pump. Designed by the engineer of the Kennet and Avon Canal, this waterwheel pump was built in 1813. 🍺 ❄ 📷 🏠

72i Conkwell: Dundas Aqueduct, beside A36. Built in 1810, this impressive structure carried the Kennet and Avon Canal over the River Avon and the railway line.

73e Lackham College of Agriculture (tel. Chippenham 0249 3251). Includes a display of agricultural implements and tools. *April to October: 1st Sunday of each month.*

73f Calne: Lansdowne Arms. Public house rebuilt in the 18th century on the site of a Middle Ages Inn, whose original brew house survives.

73h Canal Locks. Still-impressive flight of 29 disused locks built to carry the Kennet and Avon Canal up this single hillside on the way into Devizes.

Tourist Railways

These are railways on which the public can ride and include both standard and narrow gauge lines, together with some of the most impressive miniature systems. Where trains can only be watched, they are listed under Industry (pages 103-105).

19f Crowlas: Age of Steam (tel. Cockwells 073 674 631). 1¼ mile miniature (10¼ inch gauge) steam railway in an 18 acre steam park. Unlimited free rides after paying admission. Also self drive model paddle steamers and trains; children's boating lake with island; model railways; occasional traction engines. *Easter to October daily from 1030.* 🍵 🎦 🍴

20a Towans Miniature Railway. Runs through landscaped sand dunes and includes stations, embankments and a 40 ft tunnel. *Easter to October daily; winter Sundays in fine weather.*

20a Crowlas: Age of Steam. See 19f.

21b Falmouth: The Dell. British Rail standard gauge line covering the ½ mile between Penmere Station and Falmouth Station; steam traction.

23g Towans Miniature Railway. See 20a.

24b Newquay: Little Western Railway, Trenance Park on A3075. Miniature railway, with stations, bridges and embankments. Steam and diesel traction. 🍵 ❋ 🎦 🐾 ✏

24b Benny Mill: Lappa Valley Railway (tel. Mitchell 087 251 317). Steam-hauled 15 inch gauge line over 2 miles of the old Great Western line from Newquay to Chasewater, stopping at East Wheal Rose Halt, where the facilities include a children's railway and play area; boating lake; nature walk, etc. *Good Friday to late May: Wednesday to Sunday 1100-1700; late May to 30 September daily 1000-1800; also October Sundays.* 🍵 🍴 🍵T

28f Kingsbridge Miniature Railway, The Quay. 7¼ inch gauge line covering ½ mile. *Easter, then mid May to mid September daily 1100-1700.* 🎦

29b→29e Torbay and Dartmouth Railway (tel. Paignton 0803 555872). Standard gauge line running 6¾ miles from Queens Park Station, Paignton (next to the British Rail terminus) to Kingswear (where a chain ferry connects with Dartmouth). The journey takes 35 minutes each way, including stops at Goodrington Sands and Churston, a ¼ mile tunnel at Higher Greenway and a testing 1 in 60 bank. Steam traction includes the magnificent 1950 British Rail 4-6-0 loco *Lydham Manor*, while some trains are hauled by diesels, including an ex-BR Western Class diesel-hydraulic. The line is popular with visiting 'specials' from all over Britain, which have included *Flying Scotsman*. Interesting rolling stock and model railway display at Paignton. *Mid May to mid October daily from 1015.*

30h Newquay: Little Western. See 24b.

32g Dobwalls: Forest Railroad Park (tel. 0579 20325). Probably the finest miniature railway in the world, with over 2 miles of 7¼ inch gauge track built to represent the arduous operating conditions of the Rio Grande and Union Pacific railroads in North America, the latter including a scale model of the 7,700 ft Sherman Hill pass in the Rocky Mountains, which causes the miniature engines to climb 1 in 66. All steam traction, including a fantastic 13 ft long, 1/6 scale model of the world's largest steam loco, the Union Pacific Big Boy articulated 4-8-8-4 Mallet *William Jeffers*. Indoor model layouts; children's play area; radio-control boats; ½-price admission to next door Thorburn Museum (see page 84). *Good Friday for 10 days, then Wednesdays and Sundays to 1 May; then May to early October daily; 1030-1730.* 🍵 🎦 🍴

34i→35g Dart Valley Railway (tel. Buckfastleigh 036 44 2338). Standard gauge ex-Great Western line covering 7 miles from Buckfastleigh to Totnes, although access at the latter end must await com-

pletion of the new Riverside Station. The whole line has been restored to GWR appearance, with no fewer than 15 steam locomotives, the star being the 1929 GWR 4-6-0 *Dumbleton Hall*. The round trip takes 55 minutes, including stops at Staverton Bridge, where rolling stock is often stored. Railway museum at Buckfastleigh. *Easter, then late May to mid September daily from 1130.* 🍵 🍴

Riverside Miniature Steam Railway carries passengers ½ mile around the Dart Valley station area at Buckfastleigh. *Open as Dart Valley (above).*

41a Bicton Woodland Railway (tel. Colaton Raleigh 0395 68465 or Budleigh Salterton 039 54 3881). A 1 ft 6 in gauge line running through the attractive gardens with steam haulage, including an 0-4-4-0 Hunslet, and some diesels. Closed carriages in poor weather. *1 April to 31 October daily 1000-1800.* 🍵 ❋ 🎦 🍴

42d Seaton and Colyford Electric Tramway. Open top tramcars running for 2½ miles on 2 ft 9 in gauge track along the abandoned Southern Region railway route between Seaton and Colyton. The trams came from Eastbourne seafront. *Limited service in Easter week, then late May to 30 September daily. Every ½ hour when busy.*

Torbay and Dartmouth Railway (29b)

42d Beer Heights Miniature Railway (tel. Seaton 0297 21542 ext 36). Steam operated line running for ¼ mile through the Peco Pleasure Park and Modelrama. Trains can be driven. Pullman car restaurant and station buffet. Model railway exhibition. *After Spring Bank Holiday to mid October: weekdays 1000-1700; Saturdays 1000-1230. Closed Bank Holidays.* 🍵

51h Seaton and Colyford. See 42d.

58c West Somerset Railway (tel. Minehead 0643 4996). Britain's longest private railway, covering 20 miles between Minehead (64f) and Bishop's Lydeard (58c) with track running to Norton Fitzwarren (59d) and plans to eventually extend the line into the British Rail station at Taunton. Run as a commercial railway, it offers services all year, mostly by diesel railcars, which take one hour to complete a one-way journey. There are several steam locos, including an impressive Great Western 2-6-2 Prairie tank and TV's *Flockton Flyer*, a GWR 0-6-0 pannier tank. Steam hauled trains start from Minehead, some

terminating at Williton (65e). Coach service connects Taunton BR station with Bishop's Lydeard. *March to mid October daily from 0900; October to March Monday to Saturday from 0900. Steam trains early June to mid September; also winter Sundays.*

63e Lynton: Cliff Railway. This 900 ft long line was opened in 1890 and links the town with Lynmouth via a 30-degree slope, the steepest of its kind in the world when built. The system is water powered, each car taking on 700 gallons at the top to pull up a car from the bottom. Very busy in season—it carries almost ½ million passengers each year.

64d Minehead: West Somerset Railway. Headquarters of the line are here. See 58c. 🍵

65d Washford Station: West Somerset Railway. Locomotives and rolling stock are stored, repaired and restored here. Occasional short steam rides in the station area. *Depot: weekends and Bank Holidays.* For railway, see 58c. 🍵 🍵T

68d West Cranmore: East Somerset Railway (tel. Cranmore 074 988 417). Short standard gauge line using ½ mile of the old Great Western Cheddar Valley line. Owned by the well-known railway artist and chairman of the Return to Steam Movement, David Shepherd, whose work is on display in the Signal Box Art Gallery. Engines include the giant 9F class 2-10-0 *Black Prince*, built in 1959. Restored station, engine shed and workshops. Model trains. Brake van rides on steam days. *April to October daily 0900-1730; November to March weekends 0900-1600; steam on Sundays and Bank Holidays in summer.*

70f Clevedon Miniature Railway. 9½ inch gauge line covering ½ mile, with steam and electric locos. Also swimming pools and boating lake. *Easter, then Spring Bank Holiday to late September daily.*

72d Bitton: Bristol Suburban Railway Society. Based at the old Midland Railway Station, once a stop on the Bristol-Mangotsfield-Bath suburban line, this organisation has 1 mile of standard gauge track. Several preserved steam locos include a 1937 Stannier Black Five 4-6-0 and interesting industrial engines. Brake van rides on steam days. *Weekends. Steam days March to July and September, October, December.* 🍵

Cruising by Boat

Includes all kinds of boat trips: sea cruises, island visits, river and canal boats, on all of which you can relax while someone else does the driving. Self-drive boating is dealt with on page 109

19c St Ives: boat trips in and around St Ives Bay.

19f Penzance: RMV *Scillonian* sails to St Mary's, Isles of Scilly (22b) on a regular scheduled service, taking about 2½ hours. Run by the Isles of Scilly Steamship Company, 16 Quay Street, Penzance (tel. 0736 2009), the vessel has room for 600 passengers and a few cars. The crossing can often be rough. *Daily.*

21b Falmouth: steamer trips along the coast; also up the Porthcuel, Helford and Fal Rivers, the latter as far as Truro (24h).

22b Hugh Town: a fleet of small boats based in the harbour provide daily services (except in very bad weather) to the five other inhabited islands — Bryher, Tresco, St Martin's and St Agnes. They also offer tourist trips to the uninhabited islands, where you can be left behind and collected by arrangement, and to sights such as the Bishop Rock light (☆ 22d).

22i St Ives: boat trips in and around St Ives Bay.

24h Truro: cruises down the estuary to St Mawes and Falmouth (21b) leave from Worth's Quay.

25c Lostwithiel: cruises down the River Fowey in season.

25d Mevagissey: trips around the bay in small boats.

25f Fowey: boat trips up the River Fowey to Losthwithion.

26b Looe: river trips on the West Looe (to Watergate 🚤) and East Looe (to Sandplace); also coastal steamers and speedboat trips in the bay; boat trips to St George's Island, a bird sanctuary.

26d Polperro: steamer trips along the attractive coast and into Looe Bay.

27b Plymouth: pleasure cruises to sea and up the extensive local river systems leave from the west side of Sutton Harbour (south of Exeter Street on the town plan).

27b Saltash: cruises by launch up the River Tamar to Calstock (33e).

28i Salcombe: cruises in the many creeks of the estuary.

29a Totnes: the pier marks the navigable limit of the River Dart. Launches from here offer the only access to the upper reaches of the estuary; also trips to Dartmouth.

29b Dartmouth: pleasure cruises up the River Dart to Totnes (29a).

Ferries over Dartmouth Harbour run throughout the year. Higher Ferry: *Monday to Saturday 0630-2300, Sundays 0900-2100;* Lower Ferry: *Monday to Saturday 0700-2300, Sundays 0800-2300.*

29c Brixham: cruises north into Tor Bay; also round the coast and up the River Dart; speedboat trips in the bay.

33g Cotehele (tel. St Dominick 0579 50434): steamer trips up the River Tamar, occasionally as far north as Wear Head (33e). *April to October.* 🚤 ✳ 🏠 ⬇T

35c Dawlish: sea cruises in season.

35f Teignmouth: sea cruises in season.

35g Totnes. See 29a.

35i Anstey's Cove: launch trips to Torquay.

35i Torquay: steamer trips, cruises and speedboat rides all leave from the harbour; also launches to some of the nearby beaches.

40b Exeter: trips by steam launch on the Exeter Canal from the Maritime Museum (tel. 0392 58075). *Summer: daily 1000-1800.* 🚤 📷 ⬇T

40f Dawlish: sea cruises in season.

40i Teignmouth: sea cruises in season.

41b Sidmouth: pleasure cruises along the coast in season.

41d Exmouth: pleasure trips from the harbour along the coast as far as Torbay in the west (35i) and Lyme Regis in the east (42f); also launches up the River Exe.

41e Ladram Bay: departure point for pleasure trips along the coast.

42d Seaton: cruises to Lyme Regis (42f), Sidmouth (41b) and other ports in the area.

42f Lyme Regis: cruises to towns as far away as Sidmouth (41b); also coastal pleasure trips.

43d West Bay: cruises to Lyme Regis (42f) and other ports in Lyme Bay.

44e Weymouth: sea cruises by steamer and motor boat; launch trips around the Royal Navy ships and facilities in Portland Harbour. ☆

45b Wareham: boat trips via the River Frome and Wareham Channel to Poole.

45c Poole: wide choice of sea and river cruises; also trips round the huge harbour, berthing place for thousands of yachts of every shape and size.

45d Lulworth Cove: boat trips to Durdle Door and other attractive spots on this coast.

50d Tiverton: Grand Western Canal. Trips by horse-drawn barge over 2 miles of the restored canal to East Manley· viaduct. Operated by The Grand Western Horseboat Company, The Wharf, Canal Hill, Tiverton (tel. 088 42 3345). *Easter and Spring Bank Holiday weekends; then late May to end September daily; usually at 1100 and 1430.* 🚤 ⬇T

54f Clovelly: boat trips around the bay leave from the quay (high tide) or the beach (low tide). No cars in the area.

55e Bideford: steamer trips into Barnstaple Bay; also launches travel up the River Torridge to Wear Giffard.

57i Tiverton. See 50d.

62e Lee Bay: boat trips to some of the remote bays of the north Devon coast.

62e Ilfracombe: trips to Lundy Island by the steamer *Polar Bear*, a 200 ton vessel carrying 12 passengers. Some day trips available, but advance booking always essential (apply to The Administrator, Lundy Island; tel. 0271 73333 during office hours). *All year.*

Day trips to Lundy by P & A Campbell White Funnel steamer; no booking required. Times from P & A Campbell, 10 The Quay, (tel. 0271 62687). Trip takes about 2 hours. No landing in bad weather. *Easter to mid October: daily.*

A whole range of other steamer trips are also run by the White Funnel fleet (tel. Weston-Super-Mare 0934 32472). These include cruises to Clovelly (54f) and Lynmouth (63e), with optional return by bus; trips to Lundy Island; and cruises to Swansea and Mumbles in South Wales. Also afternoon excursions to Barnstaple Bay (62i) and Porlock Bay (64e) and occasional trips to other places on both sides of the Bristol Channel. *April to September: daily.*

Motor launches operate from the harbour for short trips along the coast in both directions.

62f Watermouth: motor boat cruises along the coast. 🚤 ☆ ⊕

63e Lynton: motor boat and steamer trips available (see also 62e Ilfracombe).

64e Porlock Bay: boat trips from Porlock Weir. *High tide only.*

64f Minehead: sea cruises, coastal steamer trips and tours of the harbour by motor launch.

70f Clevedon: pleasure trips along the coast in season.

70g Weston-Super-Mare: sea trips to Lundy Island (62a), Ilfracombe (62e), Lynmouth (63a) and to Cardiff in Wales. Operated by the White Funnel fleet (tel. 0934 32472). *April to September: daily.*

71 Bristol: steamer cruises of the Bristol Channel depart from Hotwell Wharf, at the western end of the Floating Harbour. ⬇T ☆

72e Bathampton: cruises by paddleboat on the Kennet & Avon Canal. *Weekends.*

Exeter Maritime Museum (40b)

Water Sports

Swimming pools; waterskiing clubs and tuition centres; sub-aqua/diving clubs. Any sea area outside bays can be used for waterskiing but in bays, harbours, estuaries and creeks the local by-laws and speed restrictions (up to 6-8 nautical mph) must be adhered to.

DO Swim between the red and yellow flags where these are flying. These indicate that the area is patrolled by lifeguards.

DO Check the water before allowing children to bathe. Look for dangerous ledges, etc. and make sure any currents are not too strong for them.

DO Keep an eye on children in the water at all times, even if lifeguards are on duty. Swimming accidents tend to happen very quickly.

DO NOT Swim when red flags are flying, however tempting the beach may appear.

DO NOT Swim on an empty stomach or for one hour after a meal - both these states can cause cramps.

DO NOT Swim alone. Always swim near others or at least where you can be seen by others.

DO NOT Let small children go too far in. Unless they are proficient swimmers, they should not go past the point at which the water comes to their waist.

DO NOT Use inflatable airbeds, rings or other such toys in the sea, especially if there is an offshore wind or the tide is ebbing. Not only are these inflatables easily carried out to sea, but most of them are easily overturned by wind or swell.

In an Emergency

Do not panic. If you are in difficulty, tread water gently and raise one arm vertically as a signal for help. If you see someone else in difficulty, it is usually best to shout for help and/or to telephone 999 and ask for the coastguard, whose duties include alerting the appropriate rescue forces.

19f Penzance. Good waterskiing area; swimming pool on the sea-front.

19g Sennen Cove: Skewjack Surf Village (tel. Sennen 073 687287). Surfing holidays with expert tuition; boards provided; minimum age 16 years. *May to October.*

19i Mousehole. Swimming pool.

20c Stithians Reservoir. Waterskiing available but short term membership must be sought from I. Doble, Wickham, 1 Quay Road, St Agnes.

21b Falmouth. Waterskiing off Swanpool Beach and in Carrick Roads; facilities for air bottle recharging.

22b Hugh Town: Isles of Scilly Underwater Centre, Warleggan (tel. Scillonia 0720 22563). One week sub-aqua diving holidays. *Easter to October.*

24b Newquay: Great Western Hotel (tel. 063 73 2010). Malibu surfing holidays; must be able to swim. *April to September.* Swimming pool at Trenance Park ( ) which also has golf driving range, amusement park and pitch and putt course.

25e Carlyon Bay: Riviera Lido (tel. Par 072 681 4261). Olympic-size swimming pool; waterskiing.

25e Charlestown. Diving school with aqualung training tank.

26b Millendreah Beach. Swimming pool on the beach is filled by the tide.

27b Plymouth: Fort Bovisand Underwater Centre (tel. 0752 42570). Diving holidays for 2 or 5 nights; minimum age 11 years. The town has four swimming pools, including the Tinside open-air pool in Hoe Road.

28f Courtlands: Outdoor Pursuits Centre (tel. Loddiswell 054 855 227). Holidays organised include surfing and waterskiing. No experience needed; minimum age 6 years, 9 years if unaccompanied. *March to October.*

28i Salcombe. Good waterskiing to seaward of the bar in settled weather.

29b Dartmouth: Aquadivers, 5 Swan Court (tel. 080 43 3639). Diving holidays on board a 70 ft boat.

30f Padstow. Heated swimming pool at the re-creation ground. Good waterskiing in marked area of the estuary between Padstow and Rock (as tide permits).

30h Newquay. See 24b.

32c Launceston. Swimming baths in Coronation Park.

32e Siblyback Reservoir. Waterskiing permits (short term membership) from the warden at the lake or in advance from Siblyback Lake Recreational Centre, Tregarrick, Common Moor, Liskeard.

34i Buckfastleigh. Swimming pool.

35e Newton Abbot. Open-air swimming pool.

35i Torquay: Nethway Hotel, Falkland Road, Belgravia (tel. 0803 27630). Waterskiing tuition. *Easter to end October.* Waterskiing competitions and long distance swimming races held throughout summer.

37e Launceston. See 32c.

37g Siblyback Reservoir. See 32e.

40h Newton Abbot. Open-air swimming pool.

41d Exmouth. Open-air swimming pool.

42f Lyme Regis. Waterskiing west of Cobb only (when red flag flies).

43d West Bay. Good waterskiing area.

44e Weymouth. Sub-aqua club with air-bottle recharging facilities; waterskiing.

44h Fortuneswell: Chesil Cove. Good facilities for scuba-divers at Ron Parry's dive shop; good diving area.

45c Hamworthy: Rockley Sands. Waterski school; swimming pool at caravan site.

Surfing Beaches

Surfing beaches indicated are good for both malibu and belly-board surfing; where the use of malibu boards is restricted, surfing lanes are denoted by flags on the beach. Good surf depends on the weather and the direction the beach faces; it will be best two or three tides after a major blow, on an incoming tide with an offshore wind. Most of the larger beaches are patrolled by life-guards in summer and most will have malibu boards for hire. Surfing in winter is possible but dangerous (for general notes about safety on the beach, see above).

45c Poole. Indoor heated swimming pool.

46e Bude. Outdoor salt-water swimming pool.

47c Great Torrington. Indoor heated swimming pool.

52c Yeovil. Swimming pool.

54d Hartland Quay Hotel: swimming pool that is open to the public.

55a Westward Ho! Heated swimming pool at the Kingsley Leisure Club.

55b Barnstaple. Open-air swimming pool.

55e Great Torrington. Indoor heated swimming pool.

59d Taunton. Many swimming pools.

60c B3153: Manor Farm Holidays, Manor Farm (tel. Wheathill 096 324 330). Organised holidays for all ages; includes covered swimming pool with swimming tuition; unaccompanied children over 9 years.

60f Yeovil. Swimming pool.

62a Lundy: Bristol Channel Divers, The Old Light (tel. Ware 0920 871151). Facilities for sub-aqua divers. *May to September.*

62e Ilfracombe. Heated indoor swimming pool (tel. 0271 64480); sub-aqua club.

62i Barnstaple. Open-air swimming pool.

63e Lynton. Tidal swimming pool on Blacklands Beach.

64f Minehead. Well-equipped modern swimming pool; children's bathing pool.

67i B3153: Manor Farm Holidays. See 60c.

68d Shepton Mallet. Swimming pool.

70g Weston-super-Mare: Seacrest Water Ski School, Sunny Leigh Hotel, 6 Park Place (tel. 0934 21687). Waterskiing holidays with tuition for beginners and towing for experienced skiiers. *March to April.* Two indoor heated swimming pools and an outdoor swimming pool with multi-stage 10 m diving platforms.

71 Bristol. 12 swimming pools and municipal baths, including Bristol South Swimming Baths, Dean Lane. (off Coronation Road); Broad Weir Baths, Newfoundland Road; Clifton Pool, off Queens Road; Jacob's Well Baths, Jacob's Well Road.

71a Portishead. Heated outdoor swimming pool.

72 Bath: Sport and Leisure Centre, North Parade Road. Varied facilities include a swimming pool.

Sailing and Boating

Sailing clubs and schools where temporary membership and/or other facilities are available to the short term visitor. Also: windsurfing, canoeing, rowing and power boating centres; and places where you can hire - for long or short term - canal boats, yachts, dinghies, motor boats and beach craft.

19f Penzance. Sailing in Mount's Bay is exceptionally good; facilities in the town are excellent for the holiday sailor.

20c Stithians's Reservoir. Sailing, windsurfing, rowing and canoeing. Permits in advance from: P. Upton, Anvil Cottage, Porkellis, Helston (sailing); M. Frampton, 16 Cathedral View, Kenwyn, Truro (rowing); and B. Smith, Cornwall Youth Office, Pendarves Road, Camborne (canoeing).

21b Mylor. Busy yacht harbour with offshore boat moorings; sailing, rowing and motor boats for hire.

21b Flushing. Good sailing centre with an annual regatta.

21b Falmouth. One of the most popular boating areas in the country; sailing school and clubs; powerboat racing; regattas in August.

21b St Mawes Sailing School (tel. 032 66 561). Courses in coastal sailing; no experience necessary, minimum age 18 years. *Mid-May to mid-October.* Also: Motor and rowing boats for hire.

21c Porthscatho. Sailing school with moorings for visitors.

21d Helford. Sailing school; boats for hire to explore the Helford River and Frenchmans Creek, made famous by the novel of the same name by Daphne du Maurier.

24h Tolverne. Rowing and motor boats for hire.

25c St Veep: John Sharp Sailing, Brockles Quay (tel. Lostwithiel 0208 872470). RYA certificate and holiday courses in dinghy and cruiser sailing; minimum age 10 years, 14 if unaccompanied. *Easter to October.*

25f Fowey. Fine sheltered anchorage in the harbour; very popular port for holiday yachts in the summer; boats for hire.

27a St Germans: Lt-Cdr Esmond Friend. The Causeway (tel. 050 33 429). Adventure cruises in the West Country and along the coast of Brittany; training for RYA yachtmaster certificate. For ages 17-30 years; some sailing experience necessary. *April to September.*

27b Plymouth: Mayflower Sailing Club. Dinghy sailing in The Sound and cruising in coastal waters. Unrestricted launching and good space for dinghy parking. Racing season from April to September.

Midway Marine Ltd, Weir Quay, River Tamar

Wind Speed

This is normally indicated by a numerical scale of force, known as the Beaufort Scale after Sir Francis Beaufort (1774-1837), the English admiral who invented it.

Beaufort Number	Wind Speed (mph)	Description of conditions on land and sea
0	0-1	**Calm** Smoke rises vertically.
1	1-3	**Light Air** Smoke drifts.
2	4-7	**Light Breeze** Can be felt on the face.
3	8-12	**Gentle Breeze** Moves leaves and small twigs. Small waves
4	13-18	**Moderate Breeze** Raises dust and waste paper; thin branches move. Waves 4-5ft; 'White horses' form.
5	19-24	**Fresh Breeze** Small trees sway. Waves 6-8ft.
6	25-31	**Strong Wind** Large branches move; wind is distinctly audible. Waves up to 12ft; crests foaming.
7	32-38	**High Wind** Large trees move; resistance to walking against the wind. Waves up to 16ft, breaking in gusts
8	39-46	**Gale** Breaks twigs off trees; difficult to walk against wind. Waves 20-25ft; sea 'boiling' in places.
9	47-54	**Severe Gale** Tears tiles off roofs; picks up relatively large objects. Waves up to 30ft; sea foaming everywhere; poor visibility in spray.
10	55-63	**Storm** Uproots trees; damages buildings. Waves up to 40ft; difficult to see through spray.
11	64-75	**Hurricane**
12	75 plus	**Hurricane**

Slipways

No details of individual slipways are given, but the location of all those with public access is accurately marked. Please note that in some cases permission may be needed and/or a small fee may have to be paid for access; also that launching times may be restricted by the tide. Check locally before using any slipway.

(tel. Birmingham 021 705 0992). Yacht charter—self-skippered or skippered—and instructional cruises; minimum age 8 years. *April to October.*

South Western Windsurfing, 6 Belmont Villas, Stoke (tel. 0752 57659). Windsurfing tuition (residential); minimum age 8 years. *All year.*

Tuition Afloat, Mayflower Marina, Richmond Walk (tel. 0752 52352). Courses in navigation and seamanship in 35 ft offshore sailing cruiser; minimum age 18 years. *April to October.*

Drake's Island Adventure Centre, c/o Mayflower Sports Centre, Central Park (tel. 0752 54112). Canoeing instruction; swimming needed; minimum age 12. *March to October.* ☆

27f Newton Ferrers. Sheltered fjord-like harbour is haven for many small yachts. Sailing school; rowing, motor and sailing boats for hire; regatta in July/August.

28f Courtlands Centre (tel. Loddiswell 054 855 227). Adventure holidays with tuition in canoeing, dinghy sailing and yacht coastal cruising. No

experience needed; minimum age 6 years, 9 if unaccompanied. *March to October.*

28i Salcombe. Popular area for dinghy sailing. Good launching and parking facilities. Racing season March to December.

Blue Water Sailing, Braemar, Herbert Road (tel. 054 884 2674). RYA courses and holidays; minimum age 12 years unaccompanied. *May to September.*

29b Dartmouth: The Royal Dart Yacht Club and Dartmouth Sailing Club, both on the river, have moorings for visiting yachts and dinghy parking; Royal Regatta in August; boats for hire.

29c Paignton: Harbour Sports, The Harbour (tel. 0803 550180). Windsurfing tuition and hire (including wet suit); minimum age 10 years. Boats for hire.

29c Goodrington Sands. Motor and pedal boats for hire; boating lake behind the beach.

29c Brixham. Two sailing schools and a sailing club; boats for hire.

30f Padstow. Canoes for hire. At Rock (opposite) is a sailing school; also motor, rowing and sailing boats for hire.

32e Siblyback Lake. Sailing, windsurfing, canoeing and rowing organised by the Recreational Centre; short term membership available from the Warden at the site.

34f Widecombe in the Moor: Dartmoor Expedition Centre (tel. 036 42 249). Adventure holidays which include sailing and canoeing on Dartmoor and the South Devon coast. Minimum unaccompanied age 11 years.

35f Coombe Cellars. Powerboat races.

35f Teignmouth. Boats and pedaloes for hire; regatta in August.

35f Maidencombe. Motor and pedal boats for hire.

35i Torquay. Sailing school and club; regattas and powerboat racing in summer; boats for hire.

35i Paignton. See 29c.

35i Goodrington Sands. Motor and pedal boats for hire; boating lake behind the beach.

37g Siblyback Lake. See 32e.

38c Meldon Reservoir: Meldon Sailing Club. Membership details from A. B. Clapham, The Knoll, Northlew, Okehampton.

40h Coombe Cellars. Powerboat races.

40i Teignmouth. Boats and pedaloes for hire; regatta in August.

40i Maidencombe. Motor and pedal boats for hire.

41b Sidmouth. Sailing Club.

41d Exmouth: Seaforth Sail Training, Seaforth Hotel, 45 Morton Road (tel. 039 52 3421). RYA sailing courses in cruising; tuition in Wayfarer and Enterprise dinghies. *April to October.*

42f Lyme Regis. Powerboat club, sailing club; regatta in August; boats for hire.

44e Weymouth. Sailing club; rowing boats and canoes for hire.

45c Lower Hamworthy: Rockley Point Sailing School, Rockley Sands (tel. Poole 020 13 77272). Residential courses in dinghy sailing and windsurfing; no experience necessary; unaccompanied children over 10 years. *March to October.*

Seascope Sailing School, 162 Lake Road (tel.

Poole 020 13 2442). Sailing and seamanship tuition; minimum age 14 years. *April to October.*

45c Poole: Poole School of Sailing and Power-boating, 43 Panorama Road, Sandbanks (tel. Canford Cliffs 0202 709231). Courses in all levels of dinghy sailing and windsurfing; unaccompanied children 9 years.

Poole Windsurfer Centre, 111 Commercial Road, Lower Parkstone (tel. Parkstone 0202 741744). Windsurfing tuition and hire; no experience needed; minimum age 10 years. *June to September.*

Parkstone Yacht Club. Races a variety of dinghies; will accept temporary members.

46e Bude. Rowing boats for hire to explore Bude Canal, which runs south for about 2 miles.

46f Tamar Lakes: Upper Tamar Lake Sailing Club. Sailing, canoeing and windsurfing; membership details from J. A. Spiers, 1 Queen Street, Bude. This club also controls sailing on Tamar Lake (lower).

54h Tamar Lakes. See 46f.

55b Instow Sailing Tuition Centre, The Quay (tel. 0271 860475). RYA dinghy courses, in all grades, on the Torridge and Taw estuaries. Minimum age 9 years, 12 if unaccompanied. *Easter to October.*

55e Bideford. Rowing and sailing boats for hire; regatta in September.

57c Wimbleball Reservoir: Wimbleball Sailing Club. Sailing, windsurfing, canoeing, and rowing. Membership details from D. K. Turner, Meadow Stream, Lower Bilbrook, Minehead.

58a Wimbleball Reservoir. See 57c.

58a Clatworthy Reservoir. Sailing is available.

61i Sturminster Newton. Canoeing on the River Stour.

62e Ilfracombe. Sailing boats for hire.

64f Minehead. Sailing club; boats for hire; regattas.

64i Wimbleball Reservoir. See 57c.

65g Clatworthy Reservoir. Sailing is available.

66b Burnham-on-Sea. Sailing in Bridgwater Bay; regatta in August.

67a Cheddar Reservoir. Dinghy sailing club; wind-surfing.

69d Shear Water: Shearwater Sailing Club. Members can sail on any of the lakes in the Longleat Estate,

70g Weston-super-Mare: Southwest Smallboat School, 28a Bedford Road (tel. 0934 27889). Small-boat sailing, seamanship and coastal navigation courses. Minimum age 5 years. *May to October.* Also Powerboat racing. *May to September.*

71h Chew Valley Lake. Popular lake for dinghy sailing.

72i Bradford-on-Avon. Sailing club holds a regatta in July.

73a Chippenham. Sailing and canoeing on the River Avon.

73g Melksham. Good canoeing on the River Avon.

Sail marks

These are some of the more popular types. Details of each class and its rules can be obtained from the local sailing clubs

A	Albacore	M	Mirror Dinghy
C	Cadet	18	National 18
D	Dragon		Osprey
E	Enterprise	R	Redwing
	Finn		Scimitar
	Fireball		Scorpion
	Flying Fifteen		Seabird
FB	Folkboat	S	Shearwater
	GP14	SII	Silhouette
GD	Graduate	S	Skipper
	Gull	T	Tempest
H	Heron	30	Thirty Square Metres
	Hornet	W	Wayfarer
	Kestrel	w	Westerly
	Merlin Rocket	DB	YW Dayboat

Fishing

Game, coarse and sea fishing available to the general public, either free or on purchase of a permit. The species of fish mentioned are those most frequently caught in the area marked. If in doubt about what bait or tackle to use, consult the local tackle shops or angling associations.

19c Clodgy Point to Porthmeor Sands. Shore: excellent bass, cod, flatfish and mackerel both from the beach and from rocks nearby.

19d Aire Point. Shore: good bass, as well as cod, flatfish, garfish, mackerel, tope and whiting. Popular fishing mark.

19e Drift Reservoir: 64 acres of brown trout and rainbow trout (fly only). Permits from Fishing Warden, 'Driftways', Drift (tel. Penzance 0736 3869) or from The Agent, Chyandour Estate Office, Penzance (tel. 0736 3021). *1 April to 12 October.*

19f Marazion. Wheel Grey Pool: 4 acre lake stocked with carp, bream, tench, roach, rudd and perch. Permits from Gilbert Sports, Helston; Bill Knott, Mount Haven; or Marazion Angling Club, 1 Trewartha Road, Prah Sands (tel. Germoe 073 676 3329).

19f Penzance. Shore: good bass from the harbour walls.
Offshore: shark and mackerel trips run all summer.

19f Newlyn Harbour. Shore: superb bass fishing from the 3 piers plus mackerel, wrasse, pouting, flatfish and many other species.

19h Porthcurno/Logan Rock. Shore: bass, cod, conger, mackerel, mullet, plaice, tope and whiting, amongst many species. ♏ ☆

19i Mousehole. Shore: excellent bass and flounder from the harbour wall.

20a River Hayle Estuary. Shore: light bottom fishing for bass and flatfish is very productive.

20a Goldsithney. Tindene Fishery Lakes: 3 pools (1 acre each) of carp, rudd, tench and trout—some of the biggest in Cornwall. Permits from G. J. Laity, Bostraze, Goldsithney (tel. Germoe 073 676 3329).

20c Stithians Reservoir: 274 acres of natural brown trout and stocked brook and rainbow trout. Permits from F. Hollis Tackle Shop, Goonlaze and Post Office, Carmenellis. *15 March to 12 October: dawn to dusk.*

20e Porthleven. Shore and offshore: superb variety of fishing from beach, rocks and boat for bass, blonde ray, coalfish, flatfish, dogfish, mackerel, mullet, pollack, thornback ray, turbot and wrasse. Worm bait available locally.

20e Loe Bar. Shore: bass, cod, flounder, mackerel, mullet, plaice, tope and wrasse. Very popular mark.

20f Constantine Brook: trout. *Free* fishing along entire river but permission must be sought from riparian owner (mainly farmers).

20i Mullion Cove. Shore: good float fishing and spinning for pollack, mackerel and garfish from the harbour wall.

21a Penryn River Estuary. Shore: good sport for flounder.
Penryn Harbour. Shore: excellent for flounder, bass and mullet. Best mark in the area.

21a Resrs.—College Reservoirs: 38 acres of trout and coarse, including carp, roach, tench and bream. Permits from ticket machine. *Coarse and rainbow trout all year; brown trout 15 March to 12 October; dawn to dusk.*

21a Argal Reservoir: 65 acres of brown and rainbow trout (fly only). Permits from ticket machine. Boats for hire. *1 April to 12 October: dawn to dusk.*

21b Falmouth. Offshore: shark fishing trips for blue, porbeagle, mako and thresher. *May to late September (best in June-July).*

21e Rosemullion Head to Nare Point. Offshore: excellent for bass, pollack and mackerel.

21g Coverack. Shore: good bass fishing from harbour and surrounding beaches. Other species: blonde ray, conger, dogfish, mullet, red bream, whiting. Worm bait available.

21h Coverack. Offshore: Whiting Ground Sand is good venue for turbot. Boats for hire at Coverack.

22i Clodgy Point. See 19c.

23c Perran Bay. Shore: surf casting for bass is very good all along the beach.

23g Upton Towans. Shore: excellent fishing for bass, cod, flatfish and mackerel.

23h Portreath. Shore: surf casting for bass, cod, flatfish and mackerel is the only fishing available along this hazardous shore.

24a Towan Head. Shore: excellent bass, flounder and mullet from the rocks.

24a Pentire—Gannel River Estuary. Shore: surf casting, mainly for bass, flounder and mullet.

24a Perran Beach. Shore: surf casting for bass is very good all along the beach.

24b Newquay. Shore: both quays in the harbour are good for bass, flounder and mullet.
Offshore: good yields of bass, black bream, cod, conger, dogfish, mackerel, monkfish, shark, tope, turbot and many other species. Worm bait and boats available locally.

24b Porth Reservoir: 40 acres of brown and rainbow trout, fly only. Permits from ticket machine. Boats for hire. *1 April to 12 October: dawn to dusk.*

24e Allan River: trout. Entire river is *free*, although permission must be obtained from riparian owner.

24i Tretheake Lake: 1 acre of bream, carp (mirror, common and crucian), roach and tench. Permits from A. Julyan, Tretheake Caravan/Camping Site, Veryan (tel. 087 250 213).

24i Fal River: moderate trout and sea trout. Mostly *free* but permission must be sought from riparian owner.

24i Trenestrall Lake: 2 acres of carp, roach and tench. Permits from W. Palmer, Trenestrall Farm, Philleigh (tel. Veryan 087 250 264).

25a Roche Lakes: perch, roach, carp, rudd, bream. Permits from Appleton and Cragg, Wadebridge; Central Sports, Newquay; Post Office, Roche.

25a Bugle—Sand Burrow Pond: coarse. Permits from tackle shops in Newquay, St Austell, Truro and Bodmin.

25b Penwithick—Carbis Moor Pool: coarse. Permits from Cossport's, 6 Victoria Place, St Austell (tel. 0726 2883).

25b St Blazey—Wheal Rashleigh Pond: coarse. Permits from tackle shops in Newquay, Truro, Bodmin and St Austell.

25c Fowey River: salmon, sea trout and brown trout. Permits from B. Gatehouse, F. G. Motors, Quay Street, and K. Cooper, 15 Queen Street, Lostwithiel; Bunts of Bodmin, Turret House, Bodmin (tel. 0208 2540); Cossports, 6 Victoria Place, St Austell. (tel. 0726 2883).

25d Trencreek Lakes: trout (fly only) and coarse. Permits from D. Borradaile, Trencreek Farm, Hewas Water (tel. Grampound Road 0726 882450).

25d Mevagissey. Shore: float fishing and spinning for pollack, mackerel, garfish and bass from harbour

wall; grey mullet on light tackle in early morning. Best sea-angling resort in West Country.
Offshore: blue and porbeagle shark caught from boats stationed in this shark fishing centre.

25e Carlyon Bay. Shore: good beach fishing for many species, including bass, flounder, sole, whiting, pollack, plaice and wrasse.

25e Par Sands. Shore: many species, including bass, flatfish, mullet, whiting, wrasse and mackerel.

25e St Austell Bay. Offshore: abundant variety of fish, including shark, thornback ray, skate, tope, turbot, gurnard, ling and coalfish. Boats for hire out of Fowey (25f).

25e Black Head. Shore: bass, conger, dab, flounder, garfish, pouting, sole, whiting and wrasse are among many species caught from rocks on this coastline.

25f Blackbottle Rock. Shore: many species caught from the rocks; popular mark.

25f Fowey. Offshore: centre for shark fishing as well as other types of boat fishing. Many boats for hire.

25g Dodman Point. Offshore: large variety of species, including angler fish, bass, black bream, conger, cod, haddock, ling, monkfish, shark, thornback ray, tope, turbot. Boats for hire out of Mevagissey (25d).

25h Portmellon. Shore: many species of fish (see 25e Black Head).

25h Gwineas Rock. Offshore: abundance of fish (as at 25g Dodman Point).

26b Watergate—West Looe River: trout and sea trout from Moorswater, Liskeard (32h) to Terrace Crossing in Looe. Permits from P. Gardner, Southgate Street, Launceston; W. S. Buckingham, 40 Fore Street, Liskeard.

26b Trenant Park—Looe River: trout and sea trout. Permit details as for West Looe (above).

26b Looe. Shore: bass, red and black bream, cod, conger, flatfish, mackerel, mullet, pollack, whiting and wrasse. Good marks at East Looe quay and all around the harbour.
Offshore: the centre of British shark fishing—mainly blue shark but also occasional mako, porbeagle and thresher—with numerous boats for hire.

26c Hessenford—Seaton River: brown trout and sea trout *(May and June).* Permits from tackle shops in Launceston, Callington and Liskeard or Post Office, Rilla Mill.

26d Polperro Brook: 6 miles of small trout. *Free.*

26e Portnadler Bay. Shore: popular mark for cod, bass, mackerel, mullet, flatfish, bream and many other species.

27a Port Eliot—Tiddy River: trout and sea trout. Entire river *free* but permission needed from riparian owner.

27b Plymouth. Shore: bass, conger, flounder, garfish, mullet, plaice, turbot and many other species from marks at West Hoe Pier, Bovisand Pier, the Barbican and much of tidal stretches of Rivers Tamar and Plym.

27c Plym Bridge—Plym River: 5 miles of salmon, trout and sea trout. Permits from Stafford's, 179 Union Street, Plymouth. *Monday to Saturday.*

27d Whitesand Bay. Shore: perfect surf casting beach for bass, flounder and plaice.

27e Plymouth Sound. Offshore: large variety of species, including flounder, bass, plaice, pollack, whiting and wrasse. Rag and lug locally available.

27e Penlee Point. Shore: large bass, cod dab, conger, pollack and turbot from good rocky marks at Penlee and west to Polhawn Cove. ☆

27f Great Mew Stone. Offshore: good bass, mackerel, pollack and wrasse close in to Mouthstone Point, while in deep water there are excellent conger, skate and shark.

27f Gara Point to Stoke Point (28d). Shore: good rocky marks for big bass, dab, conger, pollack, whiting, plaice and turbot.

27f Yealm River Estuary. Shore: fine sport for bass, flounder and mullet. Worm bait available locally.

28b Ivybridge— Erme River: sea trout and brown trout. Permits from B. S. Wilmot, Cleeve, Ivybridge (tel. 075 54 2534). Free to members of Anglers Co-operative Association.

28c South Brent— Avon River: 8 miles to Aveton Gifford (28f) of salmon (very few), sea trout (May to early July) and trout (March to September). Permits from tackle shops in the area; Anchor Hotel, South Brent; Avon Fishing Association.

28d Yealm River Estuary. See 27f.

28e Bigbury Bay. Offshore: mainly slow trolling for bass with some pollack near Burgh Island and close inshore.

28e Avon River Estuary: good bass, flatfish and mackerel from the sand flats and Bantham Rocks, Abundant lug at low tide.

28i Salcombe. Shore: excellent bass, large plaice, dabs and flounder from harbour and marks at Splat Cove, Lambury Point and Rickham Sands.

Offshore: good port for shark fishing trips which run all summer.

28i Mew Stone. Offshore: black and red bream, gurnard, cod, pollack, shark, pouting, turbot, wrasse, mackerel and monkfish are among many species found off this coast.

29a Harberton— Harbourne River: 1 mile of trout, sea trout and salmon (fly only). Permit from tackle shop in Totnes.

29b Dartmouth. Shore: good flounder in the estuary and dab, mullet, plaice, whiting and wrasse from the Embankment and the Castle.

Offshore: excellent base for fishing trips; many craft for hire.

29c Goodrington Sands. Shore: notable bass, conger, flatfish, mackerel and pollack. ⚠

29c Broad Sands/Saltern Cove. Shore: good mark with similar fishing to Goodrington (above).

29c Shoalstone Point. Offshore: good bass, conger, dogfish, flatfish, pouting, wrasse and mackerel.

29c Berry Head. Offshore: bass, conger, dogfish, flatfish, mackerel, pouting and wrasse from inshore.

29c Brixham. Shore: bass, mullet, pollack, wrasse and mackerel from Pier Head and Victoria Breakwater; prime marks at local beaches will also bring in cod, flounder, sole and whiting.

Offshore: superb deep sea and wreck fishing which bring in giant coalfish, conger, ling, shark, tope and turbot.

29e Blackpool. Shore: dab, mullet, plaice, whiting and wrasse. Popular mark.

29e Slapton Ley: 200 acres of freshwater, containing 'beautiful' rudd, pike, perch and eels, from boat only. Permits from Slapton Ley Field Centre,

Slapton (tel. Torcross 054 858 466). ♣ 🐦

Slapton Sands. Shore: superb beach for bass, plaice and mackerel.

29f Mew Stone. Offshore: abundance of species including bream, conger, ling, mackerel, monkfish, turbot, dogfish and whiting. Rag and lug readily available locally.

29g Prawle Point. Shore: good rock fishing for bass, dab, flounder, plaice, sole and wrasse.

29g Lannacombe Bay. Offshore: good deep sea fishing with black and red bream, ling, gurnard, shark, turbot and many more.

29h Beesands. Shore: bass, plaice and mackerel. Boats for fishing trips available for hire.

30f Padstow and Rock. Offshore: boats for hire for shark fishing as well as other types of deep sea fishing.

30g Towan Head. Shore: excellent bass, flounder and mullet from the rocks.

30h Mawgan Porth. Shore: bass, plaice and mackerel. Good surf casting beach; best results from first half-hour of flood tide.

30h Newquay. See 24b.

30h Porth Reservoir. See 24b.

31a Port Isaac. Offshore: good mackerel and shark fishing area. Boats for hire. 🛶

31c Crowdy Reservoir. 115 acres of brown, rainbow and brook trout; zoned spinning, bait and fly fishing. Permits from ticket machine. 15 March to 12 October: dawn to dusk. 🐦

31d Camel and Allan Rivers: 4 miles upstream from Wadebridge, offering salmon, sea trout and brown trout. Permits from A. E. Cave and Son, Polmoria Road, Wadebridge (tel. 020 881 2591). 1 April to 30 November.

31g Burlorne— Camel River: 12 miles upstream; salmon, sea trout, trout. Permits from A. Cowl, Camel Valley Cottage, Dunmere. 1 April to 30 December.

31i Fowey River: 2 miles of salmon and sea trout. Permits from Lanhydrock Angling Association, Lanhydrock Park (tel. Bodmin 0208 4281).

32b Tredidon Barton Lake: ¾ acres of tench and carp (mirror and crucian). Permits from Raddalls Sports Shop, Westgate Street, Launceston (tel. 0566 2716) or G. Jones (tel. Pipers Pool 056 686 288).

32c Rockwell— Ottery River: 1½ miles of trout (fly only). Permits from tackle shop in Launceston. 1 March to 30 September.

32c Dutson Water: tench, rudd, perch and carp. Permits from E. J. Broad, Lower Dutson Farm, Launceston (tel. 0566 2607).

32c Tetteridge Barton— Tamar River: 5 miles to Boyton (37b) of salmon, sea trout and trout. Permits from tackle shop, Launceston. 1 March to 14 October.

32c Launceston— Kensey River: 1½ miles of trout (fly only). Permits from tackle shop in Launceston. 1 March to 30 September.

32e Siblyback Reservoir: 140 acres of brown and rainbow trout, fly only. Boats for hire. Permits from ticket machine. 1 April to 12 October: dawn to dusk. 🐦 ✂ ⚠

32f Inny River: 2 miles of trout, sea trout and small run of salmon. Permits from tackle shops in Launceston, Callington and Liskeard. March to October.

33b Lewdown— Alder Quarry Pond: 4½ acres of coarse. Permits from R. Westlake, Alder Farm, Lewdown (tel. 056 683 241).

33b Lyd River: ½ mile of trout, sea trout and salmon. Permits from Forestry Commission, Southern House, Lydford. 16 March to 7 September.

33e Wilminstone Lake: trout, fly only. Punt available. Permits from tackle shop or owner, The Keep, Tavistock.

33e Broadwell— Tavy/Walkham Rivers: 3½ miles of salmon, trout, sea trout (fly only). Permits from Barkells, 15 Duke Street, Tavistock. March to October.

33f Walkham River: salmon, sea trout and trout (fly only). Permits from Barkells, 15 Duke Street, Tavistock.

33f Burrator Reservoir: 150 acres of zoned fly and spinning for brown, rainbow and brook trout. Boats for hire. Permits from ticket machine. 15 March to 30 September: sunrise to midnight.

33i Meavy— Meavy River: trout, sea trout and salmon (fly only). Permits from Barkells, 15 Duke Street, Tavistock.

34b Fernworthy Reservoir: 76 acres of stocked trout (fly only). Boats for hire. Permits from ticket machine. 1 April to 12 October: 0900 to dusk. ♣ 🐦

34d West Dart River: salmon, sea trout and trout. Permits from tackle shop, Newton Abbot; Forest Inn, Hexworthy; Post Offices at Princetown and Postbridge (34b). February to September.

34d Burrator Reservoir. See 33i.

34e East Dart River: trout and sea trout. Permits details as 34d West Dart River. 🐦

34e Walla Brook: salmon and trout; entire river (fly only). Permits details as 34d West Dart River.

34e Hexworthy— West Dart River: 1 mile of trout and salmon (fly only). Permits from Forest Inn, Hexworthy.

34e Swincombe River: 3 miles of trout and sea trout (fly only). Permits details as 34d West Dart River.

34f North Stock— Dart River: 6 miles down to Buckfastleigh (34i); salmon, sea trout, trout. Permits from D. M. Blake, 73 Fore Street, Totnes; Hodge Sports, 104 Queen Street, Newton Abbot; Sports Shop, 35/36 Fore Street, Buckfastleigh.

34h Avon Reservoir: 50 acres of zoned worm, spinning and fly for trout. SWWA rod licence only. 15 March to 12 October: dawn to dusk.

34i South Brent. See 28c.

35a Kennick Reservoir: 45 acres of brown and rainbow trout (fly only). Permits from ticket machine. 1 April to 25 December: dawn to dusk.

35a Tottiford Reservoir: 35 acres of trout, fly only. Permit from ticket machine. 1 April to 12 October: dawn to dusk.

35a Trenchford Reservoir: experimental brook trout fishery. Permits from ticket machine. 1 April to 12 October: dawn to dusk.

35e Stover Lake: coarse. Permits from local tackle shops or Newton Abbot Fishing Association, 1 Balmoral Close, Newton Abbot (tel. 0626 69360).

35e Preston Ponds (5 lakes): coarse. Permits from tackle shop, Kingsteignton or Newton Abbot Angling Association, 1 Balmoral Close, Newton Abbot (tel. 0626 69360).

35e Abbrook Pond: tench, roach and rudd. Permits from tackle shop, Kingsteignton or Newton Abbot Angling Association, 1 Balmoral Close, Newton Abbot (tel. 0626 69360).

35e Wolborough— Rackerhayes Ponds: coarse, including bream and carp. Permits from keeper on site or local tackle shops.

35f Teign River Estuary. Shore: good bass, cod, plaice, conger, mullet, pouting and wrasse; lug and rag above Sheldon Bridge.

Offshore: sheltered for small boats; the same species can be caught as from the shore.

35f Teignmouth. Shore: bass, cod, conger, flounder, mullet, plaice, pollack and wrasse from marks on the beach and sea wall.

Offshore: fishing boats for hire. Sea-angling festival in September.

35f Bundle Head. Offshore: prime mark for many species including bass, conger, flounder, mullet, plaice, pollack, pouting and wrasse. Slipways at Teignmouth.

35f Bell Rock. Shore: abundance of bass, flatfish, mullet, garfish, pollack and whiting.

35g Dart River: 6 miles upstream to Buckfastleigh (34i); salmon, sea trout and trout. Permits from tackle shop, Totnes. *Monday to Saturday.*

35i Hopes Nose. Shore: Bass, conger, dab, flounder, garfish, pouting, sole, plaice, turbot and whiting.

35i Torquay. Shore: bass, cod, conger, dab, flounder, plaice, sole, tope and turbot. Good marks at harbour piers and jetties.

    Offshore: fishing trips to good marks in Tor Bay.

35i Hollicombe. Shore: popular mark for bass, cod, conger, dogfish, general flatfish and wrasse.

35i Goodrington Sands. See 29c.

36f Crowdy Reservoir. See 31c.

36g Camel and Allan Rivers. See 31d.

37e Rockwell—Ottery River. See 32c.

37e Dutson Water. See 32c.

37f Tetteridge—Tamar River. See 32c.

37e Tredidon Barton Lake. See 32b.

37e Launceston—Kensey River. See 32c.

37g Siblyback Reservoir. See 32e.

37h Inny River. See 32f.

38c Meldon Reservoir: 54 acres of trout. No permit; only SWWA rod licences. *15 March to 30 September; dawn to dusk.*

38d Lewdown. See 33b.

38e Lyd River. See 33b.

38h Wilminstone. See 33e.

38h Broadwell. See 33e.

38h Walkham River. See 33f.

38i Burrator Reservoir. See 33f.

39a Taw River: 1½ miles of brown trout. Permits from Mr Hall, Davencourt, Sticklepath (tel. Okehampton 0837 325)

39b Chagford—Teign River: 12 miles of trout downstream to Dunsford (39c). Permits from Bowdens, Chagford; Anglers Rest, Fingle Bridge, Drewsteignton. *15 March to 30 September.*

39c Dunsford—Teign River: 12 miles upstream to Chagford (39b); trout, sea trout and salmon. Permits from Bowdens, Chagford; Anglers Rest, Fingle Bridge, Drewsteignton. *15 March to 30 September.*

39d Fernworthy Reservoir. See 34b.

39f Kennick Reservoir. See 35a.

39f Tottiford Reservoir. See 35a.

39f Trenchford Reservoir. See 35a.

39g West Dart River. See 34d.

39g East Dart River. See 34e.

39g Hexworthy—West Dart River. See 34e.

39g Swincombe River. See 34e.

39h Walla Brook. See 34e.

39h North Stock—Dart River. See 34f.

40a Dunsford. See 39c.

40b Exeter—Exe River: trout, salmon and coarse. Marks at Countess Wear, Salmon Pool Weir, Quay and Haven Banks, Exwich Mill. Permits from tackle shops in Exeter.

40c Exeter Canal: 4½ miles from Double Lock Hotel to Turf Hotel; coarse, including carp, pike and eels. Permits from tackle shops in Exeter or Bridge Cafe, Countess Wear. Good access.

40d Kennick Reservoir. See 35a.

40d Tottiford Reservoir. See 35a.

40d Trenchford Reservoir. See 35a.

40f Exe River Estuary: good dinghy fishing for bass and flatfish.

40g Stover Lake. See 35e.

40g Preston Ponds. See 45e.

40h Abbrook Pond. See 35e.

40h Wolborough. See 35e.

40i Teign River Estuary. See 35f.

40i Horse Cove. Offshore: main species caught are bass, cod, conger, dogfish, flatfish, mackerel and pollack.

40i Teignmouth. See 35f.

40i Bundle Head. See 35f.

40i Bell Rock. See 35f.

41b Sidmouth. Shore: feathering, spinning and bottom fishing from the beach for bass, mackerel, garfish, pollack, conger, dogfish and thornback rays.

    Offshore: fishing trips available to the many good marks in the area.

41d B3179—Squabmoor Reservoir: 4½ acres of rainbow trout (fly only) and coarse (June to March). Permits from Knowle Post Office and The Tackle Shop, 20 The Strand, Exmouth.

41d Exmouth. Shore: bass, flatfish, garfish, bream, mackerel, whiting and wrasse from marks at Exmouth Pier and Jetty, Bull Hill Bank and Shelley Gut. Lug and rag from Shelley Beach.

    Offshore: fishing boats for hire.

41d Orecombe to Sandy Bay. Shore: popular mark for bass, bream, wrasse, mullet, flatfish and whiting.

41e Catson Hill—Otter River: sea trout, brown trout for 1½ miles. No permit, but SWWA licence needed. *1 April to 30 September.*

42c Perry Street Pond: most coarse species. Permits from G. Bartlett, 20 Fore Street, Chard (51f).

42c Winsham—Axe River: brown trout. Permits from G. Bartlett, 20 Fore Street, Chard (51f).

42f Lyme Regis. Shore: night fishing off harbour wall for conger; spinning for bass, mackerel, garfish and pollack from shingle beaches.

    Offshore: fishing trips to various good deep water marks for angler fish, bass, bream, cod, gurnard, monkfish, shark, mackerel and pollack.

43d Seatown. Shore: shingle beach for bass, mackerel, garfish, pollack.

43d Eype Mouth. Shore: spinning for garfish, bass and mackerel.

43d Bridport—Nallers Farm Fishery: coarse. Permits from The Tackle Shop, West Bay Road, or at site.

43h Burton Bradstock. Shore: bass, conger, ray, flatfish, garfish, pollack and whiting. Worm bait available locally.

43h West Bexington. Shore: similar mark to Burton Bradstock (above).

43i Chesil Beach. Shore: ray, conger, bass, mackerel and garfish from steep-ridged shingle beach offering deep water close inshore. Biggest fish caught at night.

44d Chesil Beach. See 43i.

44d East Fleet. Salt-water lake which supports large numbers of bass, mullet and eels. Beware the large amount of seaweed.

44e Radipole Lake: game and coarse fishing. Permits from The Tackle Shop, 56 Park Street, Weymouth.

44e Weymouth Sands. Shore: bass, black bream, cod, conger, flatfish, garfish, mullet and whiting. Popular mark.

44e Weymouth. Shore: good marks at the Stone Pier and Town Pier for bass, cod, conger, flatfish, garfish and whiting.

    Offshore: fishing boats for hire; numerous good marks with an abundance of different species.

44f Ringstead Bay. Shore: bass, cod, conger, flounder, plaice, sole, mullet and whiting.

44h Bill of Portland. Shore: excellent rock fishing for bass, cod, conger, mullet and whiting.

45a Wool—Frome River: 1½ miles below and above Wool Bridge; sea trout and salmon. Permits from Woolbridge Manor Hotel, Wool. *1 March to 30 September.*

45b Wareham—Frome River: 2 miles from South Bridge to Poole Harbour; salmon and coarse. *Free,* but permission must be gained from riparian owner.

45c Poole. Shore: quays in the harbour fish well for mullet and plaice; Hamworthy Beach, Fishermans Dock and sea wall at sandbanks for bass, cod, dab, flounder, mullet, plaice, sole and whiting. Worm available locally.

    Offshore: good base for shark fishing; many boats for hire.

45d Durdle Door. Shore: good mark (shingle beach) for bass, flatfish, mullet, mackerel and whiting.

46d Sandy Mouth. Shore: superb surf casting for bass; other species include mackerel, flatfish, dogfish, silver eel, tope and wrasse.

46d Northcott Mouth. Shore: fine surf casting for bass. See Sandy Mouth (above) for other species.

46e Bude—Bude River Estuary: popular bass venue. Summerleaze Beach and Breakwater are also good for bass.

46f Upper Tamar Reservoir: 81 acres of brown and rainbow trout, fly only. Permits from ticket machine on site. Boats for hire (except Thursdays). *1 April to 12 October (winter rainbow trout until 24 December); dawn to dusk.*

46f Tamar Lake: 51 acres of trout (fly only) and coarse, including rudd, carp, dace and bream. Permits from ticket machine near the dam. *15 March to 12 October; 0900 to dusk.*

46f Broomhill—Tamar River: 6 miles of brown trout. Permits and map from Weys, Queen Street, Bude; C. & M. Tidball, Fore Street, Holsworthy; Village Stores, Whitstone.

46g Widemouth Sand. Shore: superb surf casting beach for bass.

46h Bude Canal: 2 miles from Bude to Rodsbridge; coarse. Permits from Bude Angling Association and tackle shop in Bude. *1 April to 31 May*

47c Darracott Moor Reservoir: 26 acres of trout (fly only) and coarse. Permits from ticket machine on site. *Coarse—16 June to 14 March; trout—15 March to 12 October; dawn to dusk.*

47c Great Torrington—Torridge River: 3½ miles of salmon, sea trout and trout. Permits from West of England School of Game Angling, Caynton House, Great Torrington (tel. 080 52 3256).

47d Woodford Bridge—Torridge River: 4 mile stretch with salmon, sea trout and trout (fly only). Permits from Woodford Bridge Hotel, Milton Damerel (tel. 040 926 252).

47f Sheepwash—Torridge River: 10 miles to Great Torrington (47c); salmon and trout. Permits from Half Moon Inn, Sheepwash.

48b Colleton—Taw River: 7½ miles south to Hawkridge; trout and salmon. Ghillie available. Permits from Fox and Hounds, Chulmleigh.

48d Stafford Barton—Stafford Moor Fishery: large trout (fly only). Permits from site office (tel. Dolton 080 54 360 for advance booking). *1 April to 12 October.*

48h Honeychurch—Taw River: 1 mile of brown trout. Permits from K. Dunn, The Barton, North Tawton (tel. 083 782 230). *25 March to 30 September.*

48h Okement River: brown trout. Permits from Mr Pennington, Hill Barton Farm, Okehampton (tel. 0837 454).

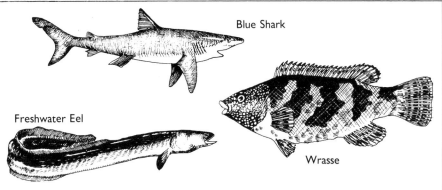

Blue Shark

Freshwater Eel

Wrasse

49a Dart Raffe Lake: 2 acres of brown and rainbow trout. Permits from G. Manning, Dart Raffe, Witheridge (tel. 088 481 557).

49b Batsworthy Fisheries: 1½ acres of rainbow trout. Permits from Mr Gardner, East Batsworthy, Rackenford (tel. 088 488 278).

49b Creacombe—West Backstone Lake: 2 acres of brown trout, fly only. Permits from Mr Thomas, West Backstone, Rackenford (tel. 088 488 251).

49c Nethercott—Bellbrook Valley Trout Fishery: 4 large ponds of brown and rainbow trout. Permits from J. Braithwaite, Bellbrook, Oakford (tel. 039 85 292). *1 April to 24 December.*

49i Thorverton—Exe River: 2 miles of brown trout. Permits from T. Mortimer, High Banks, Latchmore, Thorverton (tel. Silverton 039 286 241).

49i Stoke Canon—Culm River: ¼ mile above and below A396 road bridge; coarse. Permits from tackle shops in Exeter.
      Exe River: ½ mile of coarse between the railway bridges. Permits from tackle shops in Exeter.

50a Tiverton-Exe River: 2 miles of salmon and trout from Washfield to Head Weir. Permits from Hartnoll Country House Hotel, Tiverton.

50b Ford—Besley Lake: trout (average 2 lbs, fly only). Permits from Lower Besley Farm, Holcombe Rogus.

50b Sampford Peverell Ponds: carp, tench, bream, pike and roach. Permits from tackle shops in Exeter or Exeter & District Angling Association, 46 Hatherleigh Road, Exeter.

50b Uffculme—Culm River: 1½ miles of brown trout. Permits from T. L. Metters, The Old Parsonage Farmhouse, Uffculme.

50d Tiverton—Grand Western Canal: 10 miles from Tiverton to Burlescombe (50c); Permits from County Hall, Exeter (tel. 0392 77977) or local tackle shops.

50e Cullompton—Culm River: coarse for ¼ mile from road bridge. Permits from Exeter tackle shops.

50i Luton—Payhembury Trout Ponds: trout (fly only). Rowing boats and punts for hire. Permits from office at site. *1 May to 30 September.*

50i Weston—Otter River: brown trout, fly only. Permits from L. L. Stevenson, Otter Inn, Weston (100 yards of river) and C. P. May, Bridge House, Weston (600 yards).

51a Culm River: 4 miles of brown trout. Permits from Upper Culm Fishing Association, Palmers, Clayhidon or H. N. Saunders, The Bakery, Hemyock. *Monday to Saturday.*

51b Churchingford—Otterhead Lakes: trout (fly only). Permits from ticket office.

51d Odle Farm—Spurtham Fishery: 3 acres of rainbow trout (fly only). Permits from Harbour Court, 49a Harbour Road, Seaton (tel. 0297 21990).

51f Perry Street Pond. See 42c.

52b Pitway—Parrett River: 8 miles from Bow Bridge to Thorney Mill (60d); coarse. Permits from Half Moon Hotel, Stoke-sub-Hamdon.

52d Winsham. See 42c.

52f Sutton Bingham Reservoir: 5 miles of shoreline; trout (up to 4 lbs, fly only). Boat for hire. Permits from ticket office at site. *Monday to Saturday.*

53a Yeo River: 7½ miles from Sherborne to Yeovil (52c); trout and coarse. Permits from Hagas Fishing Centre, Silver Street, Yeovil.

53c Lydden River: 2½ miles to junction with the Stour (61f); trout (limited) and coarse. Permits from Meaders, Stalbridge.

54a Hartland Point. Shore and offshore: good porbeagle shark. ☆

54f Clovelly Bay. Shore: big bass, conger, pollack and pouting, particularly after dark. Good marks at harbour wall and local beaches.

54g Sandy Mouth. See 46d.

54h Upper Tamar Reservoir. See 46f.

54h Tamar Lake. See 46f.

55b Taw River Estuary: excellent mullet from the shore and boat. Permission must be obtained from riparian owner.

55b Appledore. Shore: bass, conger, flounder, garfish, mullet, plaice, pouting and wrasse. The quay is good for light float fishing, especially near high water.

55c Yeo River: sea trout and trout (fly only); 2 miles from Raleigh Weir. Permits from tackle shops in Barnstaple and Bideford. *Weekdays only.*

55c Barnstaple—Taw River: 2 miles of brown trout, salmon and sea trout. Permits from Barnstaple tackle shops. *Weekdays only.*
      Venn and Bestridge Ponds: most coarse species. Permits from tackle shops in Barnstaple. *Weekdays only.*

55d Jennets Reservoir: trout (fly only). Permits from Pethericks, High Street, Bideford. *15 March to 31 October.*

55e Bideford. Shore: bass, conger, flounder, garfish, mullet, plaice, pollack, pouting and wrasse. Good marks at the Quay and Iron Railway Bridge. Worm bait available locally.

55e Gammaton Reservoirs: trout (fly only). Permits from Pethericks, High Street, Bideford. *15 March to 31 October.*

55e Darracott Moor Reservoir. See 47c.

55e Great Torrington. See 47c.

55g Woodford Bridge. See 47d.

56a Yeo River. See 55c.

56a Swimbridge—Bestridge and Swimbridge Ponds: coarse. Permits from Barnstaple tackle shops.

56b High Bray—Bray River: 1 mile of trout (fly only). Permits from C. Hartnoll, Little Bray House, Brayford.

56b Brayley Barton—Bray River: trout, sea trout and salmon for 3 miles. Permits from Poltimore Arms Hotel, North Molton (tel. 059 84 338).

56d Umberleigh—Taw River: 3½ miles of salmon, sea trout and brown trout (fly only). Permits from Rising Sun Hotel, Umberleigh (not if hotel is fully booked). *March to September; weekdays only.*

56e Bray River: 2 miles of sea trout and trout. Permits from South Molton Angling Club, 40 Parklands, South Molton (tel. 076 95 2161) or The Gun and Sports Centre, 130 East Street, South Molton.

56f South Molton—Mole River: 1¼ miles of sea trout and brown trout. Permits from South Molton Angling Club, 40 Parklands, South Molton (tel. 076 95 2161) or Thompsons, 6 The Square, South Molton (tel. 076 95 2615).

56g Stafford Barton. See 48d.

56h Churchland. See Colleton 48b.

57b Winsford—Barle River: 3½ miles of salmon and trout (fly only). Permits from Tarr Steps Hotel, Winsford (tel. 064 385 293).

57b Dulverton-Exe and Barle Rivers: 5½ miles of trout and salmon. Ghillies available. Permits from Carnarvon Arms Hotel, Dulverton or from Lambs Hotel, Dulverton. *February to October.*

57c Wimbleball Reservoir: 374 acres of trout (fly only). Boats for hire. Permits from ticket machine at site. ✔

57c Haddeo River: 3½ miles of trout and salmon. Permits from Lamb Hotel, Dulverton.

57d Batsworthy Fisheries. See 49b.

57d Creacombe. See 49b.

57e Nethercott. See 49c.

57f Exebridge—Exe Valley Fisheries: 2 lakes containing large rainbow trout (up to 10 lbs). Permits from keeper on site or from riparian owner (tel. Dulverton 0398 23328). *4 April to 30 September: Monday to Saturday.*

57g Dart Raffe Lake. See 49a.

57i Tiverton. See 50a.

58a Wimbleball Reservoir. See 57c.

58b Clatworthy Reservoir: well stocked with trout; 5 miles of shoreline. Boats available for hire. Permits from ticket machine on site. *Monday to Saturday.*

58e Ford. See 50b.

58f Sandylands—Tone River: 2 miles west to Harpford Farm; trout, grayling, dace, roach and chubb. Permits from Wellington Angling Association. *15 April to 15 October.*

58g Manley. See 50d Tiverton—Grand Western Canal.

58g M5 junction 28. See 50e Cullompton.

58h Sampford Peverell Ponds. See 50b.

58h Uffculme. See 50b.

58i Culm River. See 51a.

59a Langford—Bridgwater and Taunton Canal: 5 miles from Taunton to the A361 bridge near Durston (59b); coarse. Permits from Bridge Sports or St Quentin Hotel, Taunton.

59b Charlton—Bridgwater and Taunton Canal: 7½ miles north to Bridgwater (66h); coarse. Permits from tackle shops in Bridgwater, Langport and Highbridge.

59b Tone River: 12 miles of trout and 5 miles of coarse. Permits from tackle shops in Taunton or St Quintin Hotel, Taunton.

59c Woodhill—West Sedge Moor: 1½ miles from Stathe to Pinkham; coarse. Permits from Bridge Sports, Taunton.

59d Taunton—Tone River: coarse; downstream to Atherley (the 300 yards from French Weir are *free*). Permits from Taunton tackle shops.

59g Churchingford. See 51b.

60a North Moor—Aller Moor Relief Channel: coarse. Permits for the entire drain from tackle shops in Bridgwater, Langport and Highbridge.

60a Langport—Parrett River: 6 miles of coarse between Oath and Thorney (60d). Permits from A W Rule, 8 Parrett Close, Langport.

60b Henley Corner — Eighteen Foot Rhyne: 1½ miles of coarse from Walton to Kings Sedgemoor Drain. Permits from Bridgwater and Langport tackle shops.

60d Isle River: ¾ mile of coarse. Permits from Newton Abbot Fishing Association, 1 Balmoral Close, Newton Abbot (tel. 0626 69360).

60d Pitway. See 52b.

60e Ilchester—Yeo River: 5 miles to the River Cam (south of Yeovilton); coarse. Permits from A. D. Coles, The Square, Ilchester.

60i Sutton Bingham Reservoir. See 52f.

61g Yeo River. See 53a.

61i Lydden River. See 53c.

61i Sturminster Newton—Stour River: 7 miles of coarse fishing. Permits from tackle shop or White Hart, Sturminster Newton.

62e Lee Bay. Shore: bass, conger, cod and flatfish. Best mark in a poor area for fishing.
Offshore: tidal conditions can be very dangerous for small boats. Fishing trips are available.

62e Ilfracombe. Shore: bass, cod, conger, flatfish, mullet, pollack and wrasse. Good marks at promenade and pier.
Offshore: boats available for hire. In addition to the above species dogfish, ray, shark and tope are to be caught. Annual fishing festival held in August.

62e Slade Reservoirs: 10 acres of trout (fly only) and coarse. Permits from ticket machine on site. *Daily: dawn to dusk.*

62f Combe Martin. Shore: bass, conger, cod and flatfish. Best to fish at high tide.
Offshore: fishing boats available for hire.

62h Taw River Estuary. See 55b.

62i Yeo River. See 55c.

62i Barnstaple. See 55c.

63a Heddons Mouth. Shore: good mark for bass, conger and flatfish. Access from Hunters Inn by footpath.

63b Lynmouth Bay. Shore: bass and flatfish from the beach. Bait scarce locally.

63d Wistlandpound Reservoir: 41 acres of stocked trout (fly only). Permits from ticket machine. *1 April to 12 October: dawn to dusk.*

63e East Lyn River: 3½ miles of salmon, sea trout and trout. Permits from J. Lyon & Co., Porlock. *1 February to 31 October.*

63f Brendon—East Lyn River: 1¾ miles of salmon, sea trout and trout. Permits from M. J. Lang, Idyll Cottage, Brendon, (tel. 059 87 314) or Mrs Stevens, Glebe House, Brendon.

63h High Bray. See 56b.

63i Simonsbath—Barle River: 6 miles of trout (fly only), from Pinkery Pond (63e) to Cow Castle (63i). Permits from Exmoor Forest Hotel, Simonsbath (tel. Exford 064 383 341). *15 March to 30 September.*

64b Porlock Bay. Offshore: angler fish, bass, bream, cod, conger, dogfish, garfish, mackerel, ray, tope and whiting.

64e Hurlstone Point. Shore: good casting for bass, cod, conger, dab, flounder, mullet, pouting, tope and wrasse.

64f Minehead. Shore: bottom or float fishing yields bass and grey mullet; shore casting is also productive for cod, conger, dab, mullet, pouting and wrasse. Popular marks at harbour, promenade and beach.

64h Winsford. See 57b.

64i Chargot Water: trout, fly only. Permits from C. Catley, Ponds Cottage, Chargot or Sir E. Malet, Chargot (weekly tickets only). *1 April to 30 September: Monday to Saturday.*

64i Wimbleball Reservoir. See 57c.

65d Blue Anchor Bay. Shore: bass, cod, dab, flounder, mullet, pouting, tope and wrasse.

65e Watchet. Shore: harbour wall yields good bass and grey mullet.

65e Black Rock—St Audries Bay. Shore: excellent for bass, cod, rays and conger. Best time is towards dusk on a flooding tide.

65f Kilve Beach. Shore: bass, cod, dab, flounder, mullet, sole and wrasse.

65g Clatworthy Reservoir. See 58b.

66b Burnham-on-Sea. Shore: flounder and bass from River Parrett Estuary.

66c Hamwood—Lox Yeo River: 1 mile of coarse fishing. Permits from tackle shops in Weston-super-Mare, Bristol and Bridgwater.

66c Loxton—Axe River: 16 miles from Lympsham Coal Wharf to Clewer (67a); coarse. Permits from tackle shops in Weston-super-Mare, Bristol and Bridgwater.

66c Compton Bishop—Yeo River: ½ mile from here to the confluence with the Axe at Crab Hole; coarse. Permits from Weston-super-Mare, Bristol, Clevedon, Highbridge and Bridgwater.

66d Combwich Ponds: coarse. Permits from tackle shops in Bridgwater, Langport and Highbridge.

66e Highbridge—Newtown Pond: coarse. Permits from P. Thyer, Church Street, Highbridge.

66e Brue River: 8 miles to Burtle (66f); coarse. Permits from P. Thyer, Church Street, Highbridge.

66e Pawlett—Parrett River: bass, cod, general flatfish and mullet can be caught from here down to the sea at Huntspill.

66f Huntspill River: 3½ miles from Gold Corner to Sloway Bridge; coarse, particularly roach and bream. Permits from tackle shops in Bridgwater, Langport and Highbridge.

66f Huntspill Moor—Cripps River: entire river; mainly bream and roach. Permits from Bridgwater, Langport and Highbridge.

66f River Bridge—Brue River: 8 miles to Highbridge (66e) to Burtle; coarse. Permits from P. Thyer, Church Street, Highbridge (open Sundays).

66g Ashford Reservoir: coarse. Permits from tackle shops in Bridgwater, Langport and Highbridge.

66g Hawkridge Reservoir: trout, fly only. Permits from ticket machine on site.

66h Durleigh Reservoir: popular trout fishery (fly only). Boats for hire. Permits from ticket machine at site.

66h Dunwear Ponds: 5 ponds with coarse fish. Permits from Bridgwater, Langport and Highbridge. Highbridge.

66i Kings Sedgemoor Drain: 7½ miles (entire drain) of coarse, mainly rudd. Permits from tackle shops at Bridgwater, Langport and Highbridge.

67a Cheddar Reservoir: excellent coarse fishery with the accent on roach and pike. Permits from ticket machine at site.

67a Clewer—Axe River: 16 miles of coarse fishing from here to Lympsham Coal Wharf (66c). Permits from tackle shops in Weston-super-Mare, Bristol and Bridgwater.

67d Tadham Moor—North Drain: coarse, mainly bream, rudd and perch. Permits from tackle shops in Bridgwater, Langport and Highbridge.

67d Stileway—Brue River: coarse, including chub, roach, bream, dace and pike, for 13 miles from Westhay to West Lydford (67i). Permits from Nicholls Sports, Street; Millers, Glastonbury.

67g Henley Corner. See 60b.

67h Brue River: 13 miles of coarse fishing—see 67d Stileway for permit details.

68f Tytherington—Frome River: 8 miles north to Rhode (68c); trout (fly only) and coarse, especially good roach. Permits from tackle shops in Frome.

68i Stourton—New Lakes: 5 privately owned lakes with trout (fly only) and coarse. Permits from site or riparian owner: A. E. Bealing, The House on the Lake, Stourton.

69c Erlestoke Lake: coarse. Permits from Badgerland, Lower Road, Erlestoke.

70c Portishead. Shore: cod, conger, dogfish, flatfish, thornback ray and whiting from the sandbanks.

70d Sand Point. Shore: bass, cod, flatfish, silver eel and whiting.

70f Ladye Bay. Shore: popular mark for cod, conger, flatfish, thornback ray and whiting.

70g Weston-super-Mare. Shore: bass, cod, dab, flounder, plaice, silver eel, sole and whiting. Marks at Black Rock, Old Pier and Knightstone harbour wall.
Offshore: conger, dogfish, mackerel and ray can be caught, in addition to those species above. Good marks in Weston Bay, mouth of Axe estuary and off Brean Down.
Hutton Pond: coarse. Permits from Weston-super-Mare tackle shops.

70g Brean Down. Shore: bass, cod, dab, flounder, plaice, silver eel, sole and whiting.

70h Loxton: See 66c Hamwood.

71b Eastfield—Henleaze Lake: coarse. Permits from ticket office. *May to end September.*

71 Bristol. Avon River: from Hanham Weir (71f) to the estuary; coarse. *Free.*
Biterwell Lake: excellent coarse, including carp, tench and pike. Permits available from lakeside.

71e Barrow Gurney Reservoirs: trout (average of 2 lbs, fly only). Boats for hire but must be booked in advance from Bristol Waterworks, Woodford Lodge, Chew Stoke (tel. Chew Magna 027 589 2339). Permits from ticket machine. *Mid-April to 15 October.*

71g Blagdon Lake: good-sized trout (fly only). Boats for hire (see 71e for details). Permits from ticket office or machine. *Mid-April to 15 October.*

71h Chew Valley Lake: extremely popular trout fishery (fly only). Boats available for hire (see 71e for details). Permits from ticket office or machine. *Mid-April to 15 October.*

71i Cameley Lakes: 2 lakes with trout averaging 2-2½ lbs (fly only). Permits from Hillcrest Farm, Temple Cloud. *1 April to 15 October.*

72c Castle Combe: Manor House Hotel (tel. 0249 782206). ½ mile of trout (fly only) in By Brook. Permits from the hotel. *1 April to 30 September.*

73b Rawlings Farm—Avon River: 3½ miles from Chippenham to Kellaways Road Bridge; coarse. Permits from tackle shops in Chippenham.

73g Semington—Kennet and Avon Canal: 15 miles east to Wilcot; coarse. Permits from Devizes tackle shops or Barge Inn, Seend.

73h Bulkington—Semington Brook: ¾ mile from Pineckley Bridge to sewage works; trout and coarse. Permits from local tackle shops.

Riding and Pony Trekking

Includes riding schools, pony trekking and hacking centres, pony and donkey rides on beaches, race courses (flat and National Hunt). Always telephone the school or hire centre in advance for booking information. The figure at the end of most entries denotes the number of horses or ponies for hire.

19c Halse Town Stables, Towednack Road (tel. St Ives 073 670 7160). Hacking; instruction. ✈

19f Lelant Down: Old Mill Stables (tel. Hayle 0736 753045). Hacking; instruction. ✯

19f Penzance: Rosehill Riding Establishment (tel. 0736 3264). Hacking; instruction. 13.

20a Lelant Down. See 19f.

20b Releath Riding Stables, Black Rock (tel. Praze 020 983 582).

20c Bolenowe Riding Stables (tel. Camborne 0209 713690).

20e Rinsey Riding Stables.

20e Sithney: Lonon Farm.

20f Treloskan Farm, Cury Cross Lanes.

20i Predannack Wollas: Manor Farm (tel. Mullion 0326 240298). Mrs. Wilkes, Hervan Lane, Predannack (tel. 0326 240555).

21a Carclew: South Carclew Riding, Mylor Downs (tel. Devoran 0872 864397).

21a Mabe Burnthouse: Nanturrian Riding School (tel. Penryn 0326 72394). Hacking.

21a Trevera Farm Stud and Riding Centre (tel. Constantine 032 64 629 or Penryn 0326 72394). Hacking; instruction. 14.

21b St Mawes: Nancorras Stables (tel. 032 66 391).

21d Gillan: Albia Riding Stables (tel. Manaccan 032 623 454).

21g Kennack Sands: Green Meadows Riding Stables, Kuggar (tel. The Lizard 0326 290661).

22b Hugh Town: Atlantic View Riding Stables, High Lanes (tel. Scillonia 0720 22684). Limit of 12 stones weight.

22i Halse Town. See 19c.

23f Perranporth: Polglaze Riding School, Liskey Hill (tel. 087 257 2303). Trekking; hacking; instruction. 11.

23f Chapel Coombe: Chapel Porth Riding Stables (tel. St Agnes 087 255 3291).

23f Goonbell Farm Riding School (tel. St Agnes 087 255 2063 or Truro 0872 560600). Hacking; instruction; jumping facilities.

23f Mingoose Riding Centre (tel. St Agnes 087 255 3185 day or Redruth 0209 216901 evening) Trekking; hacking; instruction. 12. *April to October.*

23f Blackwater: Chiverton Riding Centre (tel. Truro 0872 560471). Hacking; instruction. 14.

23h Reskudinnick: Strawberry Gardens Riding Stables (tel. Camborne 0209 713690).

23h Bolenowe. See 20b.

24a Crantock: The Stables, Sandy Close (tel. 0637 830394).

24a Holywell: Trevornick Farm (tel. Crantock 0637 830272).

24a Cubert: Hilbre Stables, Commons Road (tel. Crantock 0637 830402).

24b St Columb Minor: Trelawny Riding School, Rialton Barton.

24c Killaworgey: Killieworgie Mill Stables (tel. St Columb 0637 880570).

24e Hendra Farm House (tel. Perranporth 087 257 3563).

25b St Blazey: Woodlands Riding Stable (tel. Par 072 681 2963). Hacking; instruction. 14

25b Carclaze: Phernyssick Stables.

25c Lostwithiel: Tregontha Stables. Cedar Lodge Stables.

25d Lanjeth Riding School, The Green.

25d Sticker: Porth Hall Riding Centre (tel. St Austell 0726 4103). Hacking; instruction. 16.

25d St Austell Riding School, Sawles Road.

25f Fowey: Green Lane Riding Stables (tel. 072 683 3506 or 2344). Hacking; instruction. 10.

26b Duloe: Polpever Riding Stables.

26b Morval: Venton Vanes Riding Centre.

26c B3247, south of Hessenford: Seaton Valley Riding Stables, Keverill Mill (tel. Hessenford 050 35 574). Trekking; hacking; instruction. 13. *May to October.*

26e Porthallow, north east of village: Tencreek Riding Stables, Polperro Road (tel. Looe 050 36 2991).

27f Wembury: Wembury Bay Farm Riding Stables, Churchwood Estate (tel. Plymouth 0752 862676).

28a Cornwood: Bridge Farm Riding Centre (tel. 075 537 274).

28a Hemerdon: Ploughlands Riding Centre (tel. Plymouth 0752 338006).

28b Wrangaton: Cheston Riding Centre (tel. South Brent 036 47 3266). Trekking; hacking; instruction. 17.

28b Bittaford: Beacons Riding School (tel. Ivybridge 075 54 2260). Hacking; instruction. 35.

28c South Brent: Lower Downstow Stables (tel. 036 47 3340). Little Aish Stables (tel. 036 47 3177).

28c Colmer: California Riding Stables (tel. Gara Bridge 054 882 346).

28d Dunstone: The Devon Shire Horse Farm Centre (tel. Plymouth 0752 880268). Shire horses, farm carts, children's farm animals, adventure playground. *Daily from 1000.* 🐎

28d Membland: Newton Ferrers Riding and Leisure Centre, Pool Mill Farm (tel. Plymouth 0752 872837). Hacking; instruction. 17.

28f Courtlands: Field Study and Outdoor Pursuits Centre (tel. Loddiswell 054 855 227). Pony trekking is among many activities arranged here. ✈ ✗ ⚓

28f Kingsbridge: Croft Farm School of Riding, north of town (tel. 0548 2221).

28f High House Farm: Felgywn Stud Riding School, Bowcombe Creek (tel. Kingsbridge 0548 2814). Hacking; instruction; jumping. 13.

29b Galmpton: Manor Farm Riding Stables (tel. Churston 0803 843338). Hacking; instruction. 20.

29c Paignton: Primley Riding Centre, Waterleat Road.

29d East Allington: Nutcombe Farm (tel. 054 852 369).

30f Portreath Farm: Polzeath Riding Stables (tel. Trebetherick 020 886 3364). Trekking; basic instruction.

30f Padstow: Dennis Farm, Dennis Cove, south of town.

30f Trevorgus: Tressalyn Farm (tel. Padstow 0841 520454).

30h Gluvian: Merlin Farm Riding Centre (tel. St Mawgan 063 74 236). Hacking. 20. *May to September.*

30h Tregurrian Stables, Seawynds Farm.

30h St Columb Minor. See 24b.

31a Port Isaac: Homer Park Farm'otel Riding Stables (tel. 020 888 250). Trekking; hacking. 14.

31c Davidstow: Tall Trees Riding Centre, (tel. Otterham Station 084 06 249). Hacking; instruction. 25.
    Treworra Pony Camps, south of town on Tremail road (tel. 084 06 220). Hacking. 30. *May to September.*

31d Wadebridge: Wadebridge Riding Stables, Trevanson Street.
    Lower Croan Stables.

31d Egloshayle: Clapper House Stables, A389 Bodmin road.

31f St Breward: Hallagenna Riding Stables. Coombe Mill Stables.

31f Bradford: Moss Farm Riding Centre (tel. Bodmin 0208 850628). Competent riders aged over 18 only.

31h St Lawrence Riding School and Stud Farm (tel. Lanivet 020 883 223). Hacking; instruction. 18.

31h Lanivet: Newgate Farm.

32b Laneast Stables and Trekking Centre (tel. Pipers Pool 056 686 401). Trekking; instruction.

32c Launceston: Riding Stables, St Leonards, Polson.

32e North Hill: Nine Tor Riding Centre (tel. Coads Green 056 682 232). Trekking. *Easter; Whitsun to end September.*

32e Upton Cross: Eldon Stables. Lower Tokenbury Farm, south of village (tel. Rilla Mill 0579 62747).

32g St Neot: Northwood Trekking Centre (tel. Dobwalls 0579 20683).
    Menaridden Riding (tel. 057 98 355).

32h Common Moor: Little Barton Riding Centre (tel. Liskeard 0579 42444). Trekking; hacking. 28.

32h Liskeard: Ninestones Farm and Stables (tel. Dobwalls 0579 20455). Trekking; hacking; jumping. 27.

33a Kelly: Yeomans Riding School.

33b West Blackdown: Trescot Stables (tel. Mary Tavy 082 281 683).

33c Lydford: Manor Farm Riding Centre (tel. 082 282271). Trekking; hacking; unaccompanied children.

33c Gibbet Hill: Penwill Stables, Cholwell Farm (tel. Mary Tavy 082 281 526). Instruction; unaccompanied children over age 9.

33f Petertavy: Moorland Riding Stables Will Farm (tel. Mary Tavy 082 281 293).
    Horndon Stables, Rock View (tel. 082 281 564).

33f Dousland: Yennadon Riding Stables (tel. Yelverton 082 285 2061).

33g St Dominick: Trehill Farm (tel. 0579 410).

33g Hatt: Bush Farm (tel. Saltash 075 55 2148).

33h Buckland Monachorum: Fairtown Farm (tel. Yelverton 082 285 3495).

33i Yelverton: Crossways Stables, Axtown Lane (tel. 082 285 3025). Trekking; hacking; instruction. 17.
    Moorland Links Riding School (tel. 082 285 3540).

33i Cadover Bridge: Trowlesworthy Farm Riding Stables.

34c Moretonhampstead: Boathill Farm Equitation Centre (tel 064 74 283).

34c North Bovey: Relko Riding Holidays, Old Yarde Farm, west of village (tel. Moretonhampstead 064 74 423). Trekking. *April to September.*

34e Sherberton: Great Sherberton Pony Stud (tel. Poundsgate 036 43 276).

34e Hexworthy: Forest Inn.

34f Widecombe in the Moor: Dartmoor Expeddition Centre, Rowden (tel. 036 42 249). Full board holidays with dormitory accommodation: various riding courses arranged. Unaccompanied children over 11 accepted. ⏼ ▲
    Shilstone Rocks Dartmoor Stud (tel. 036 42 281). Trekking; unaccompanied children.
    Chittleford Farm, south of town (tel. 036 42 281).
    Blackslade Farm Riding and Trekking Centre (tel. 036 42 304).

34f Poundsgate: East Shallaford Farm (tel. 036 43 273).
    Foxworthy Stables (tel. 036 43 210).
    Drywell Farm (tel. 036 43 349).

34f Littlecombe Stables (tel. Poundsgate 036 43 260). Trekking; hacking; instruction. 10.

34g Cadover Bridge. See 33i.

34g Cornwood. See 28a.

34i Buckfastleigh: Hawson Stables (tel. 036 44 2267).

34i South Brent. See 28c.

35a Haytor: Haytor Vale Riding School (tel. 036 46 348). Hacking; instruction. 15.
    Pinchaford House Riding Centre, south of village (tel. 036 46 251). Trekking; instruction.

35b Race Course: Devon and Exeter National Hunt course (tel. Exeter 0392 832599).

35b Chudleigh: The Rock Stables.

35d Ilsington: Smallacombe Farm Stables (tel. Haytor 036 46 265).

35d Rora Farm: stables (tel. Bickington 062 682 255).

35d Bickington: Sigford House.

35d Caton Cross: The Glen (stables).

35e Race Co.: Newton Abbot National Hunt Racecourse (tel. 0626 3235). ⛻

35f Maidencombe Park Riding Centre, Teignmouth Road (tel. Torquay 0803 34913). Hacking; instruction. 14.

35g Blackler: Blackler Barton Riding Stables (tel. Staverton 080 426 236). Hacking; instruction; unaccompanied children; riding for disabled. 45.

35g Little Hempston: Coombe Park (tel. Totnes 0803 863473).

35h Marldon: Torbay Chalet Riding Stables, Churscombe Road (tel. Paignton 0803 552380).

35h Cockington: Lanscombe Farm.

35h Paignton. See 29c.

35i Barton Cross: The Croft (stables).

36b Tredole: Farmhouse, stables.

36d Portgaverne. See 31a (Port Isaac).

36f Davidstow. See 31c.

36g Egoshayle. See 31d.

36h St Breward. See 31f.

36h Bradford. See 31f.

37d Laneast. See 32b.

37e Launceston. See 32c.

37f Kelly: Yeomans Riding School.

37g North Hill. See 32e.

37h Upton Cross. See 32e.

38b Bridestowe: Leawood Equitation Centre, Diggaport House (tel. 083 786 271). Instruction.

38e Lydford. See 33c.

38e West Blackdown. See 33b.

38e Gibbet Hill. See 33c.

38h Petertavy. See 33f.

38h Dousland. See 33f.

39a Belstone: Skaigh Stables (tel. Sticklepath 083 784 429). Trekking; unaccompanied children.
    Dartmoor Riding Centre (tel. 083 784 461).

39a Sticklepath: Crownest Farm (tel. 083 784 240). Trekking. 8.

39b Chagford: Buda Farm. Stinhall (tel. 064 73 3337).

39c Coombe Court Farm, north of Moretonhampstead (tel. Moretonhampstead 064 74 377). Trekking.

39e North Bovey. See 34c.

39f Moretonhampstead. See 34c.

39f Haytor. See 35a.

39g Sherberton: See 34e.

39g Hexworthy: Forest Inn.

39h Widecombe-in-the-Moor. See 34f.

39h Poundsgate. See 34f.

39h Littlecombe. See 34f.

39i Ilsington: Smallacombe Farm Stables.

39i Rora Farm. See 35d.

39i Bickington: Sigford House.

39i Caton Cross: The Glen (stables).

40b Exeter: Hilltop Riding School, Pennsylvania Road (tel. 0392 51370 or 70218). Hacking; basic instruction. 15.

40b Kennford: Splatford Paddocks.

40c Ebford: Exeter and District Riding School, The Sheiling (tel. Topsham 039 287 3472). Hacking; instruction. 17.

40e Race Course. See 35b.

40e Chudleigh: The Rock Stables.

40g Rora Farm. See 35d.

40g Bickington: Sigford House.

40h Race Co. See 35e.

40h Maidencombe. See 35f.

41d Exmouth: Pine Hollow Riding Stables, Upper Hillham Road, Marley (tel. 039 52 72873).

43a Broadwindsor: Colcombe Stables (tel. 030 86 360). Hacking; instruction. 20.

43d Morcombelake: Grand View Riding Stables, Ship Lane (tel. Chideock 029 789 581).

44e Sutton Poyntz: The Stables (tel. Preston 0305 833027).

44e Weymouth: Lanehouse Equitation Centre, Overbury Close (tel. 030 57 74103 or 72720).

44f Osmington Mills: East Farm Stables (tel. Preston 0305 833578-stables or 833240 — house). Hacking; basic instruction. 12.

44h Balaclava Bay, Portland: HMS Osprey Saddle Club, The Verne (tel. 0305 820311 ext 2454).

45b Wareham: Doddings Riding and Trekking Centre (tel. Bere Regis 092 97 240). Trekking; Hacking. 10.

45f Harmans Cross: Tabbits Hill Riding School (tel. Corfe Castle 092 93 466). Trekking. 20.

46b Gooseham Barton Riding Stables (tel. Morwenstow 028 883 204). Hacking. 15. *March to November.*

46e Bude: Maer Lane Riding Stables.
    Efford Farm Riding Stables (tel. 0288 4244).

46e Red Post: The Paddock (tel Bridgerule 028 881 256).

47a Bucks Cross: Kingsland Riding Stables, Woolsery (tel. Clovelly 023 73 378). Call at Post Office for instructions on how to find the stables. Basic instruction.

47a Parkham: Pierces Farm Riding School (tel. Horns Cross 023 75 219). Hacking; basic instruction. 8.

47c Taddiport Riding Stables, Buckingham House.

47d Thornbury: Green Horse Equitation Centre (tel. Milton Damerel 040 926 237).

47h Halwill Junction: Breybury Stables, on minor road to east of junction (tel. Beaworthy 040 922 259).

47i Highampton: South Trew Farm Stables, A3072 east of village (tel. Black Torrington 040 923 277). 27.

48c Chulmleigh: Bold Try Stables (tel. 076 98 485). Hacking; instruction.

48e Winkleigh: Wagon Wheels Stables. Hacking; instruction.

48f Lapford Riding Centre, South View.

48i Bow: Pennines Riding Stable.

48i Spreyton Equestrian Centre.

49c Templeton: Mount Pleasant Farm.

49c Calverleigh: Rose & Crown Riding Centre.

50b Burlescombe Riding Centre.

50c Culmstock: Benshayne Farm.

50h Higher Willyards Farm (tel. Whimple 0404 822423). Hacking; instruction. 15.

51a Clayhidon: Heazel Farm Equestrian Centre.

51b Curland Equestrian Enterprises, Crosses Farm Stud (tel. Buckland St Mary 046 034 234). Hacking; instruction. 10.

51g Farway: Sallicombe Riding Centre (tel. 040 487 249). Hacking; instruction. 12.

52a Seavington St Mary: West Street Farm (tel. South Petherton 0460 40984).

52c Chilthorne Domer: Newhills Farm.

52c Yeovil: Greggs Riding School, West Coker Road (tel. 0935 23894). Basic instruction. 10.
    Stone Lane Riding Stables (tel. 0935 6649).

52e Crewkerne: The Chestnuts, Lyme Road (tel. 0460 74228).

52e North Perrott: Perrott Hill School, west of village (tel. Crewkerne 0460 73391).

52e Misterton: Hill View Riding Stables (tel. Crewkerne 0460 72731).

52g Morcombelake. See 43d.

52h Broadwindsor. See 43a.

53b Sherborne: The Cedars, Long Street (tel. 093 581 2532).
    Leigh Equestrian Centre, The Abbey Close (tel. Holnest 096 321 469).

53d Closworth: Princes Place (tel. Yetminster 0935 268). Hacking; instruction. 16.

53h Cerne Abbas: Wessex Equestrian Centre, Piddle Lane (tel. 030 03 500).

54f Bucks Cross. See 47a.

54f Parkham. See 47a.

54g Gooseham Barton. See 46b.

55a Westward Ho! Riding Centre, Venton Farm (tel. Bideford 023 72 4244).

55b Appledore: Evans Stables, Golf Links Road. Tuition; hunting.

55b Horwood East Barton Farm, east of village (tel. Newton Tracy 027 185 222).

55c Penhill Riding Stables, Penhill House (tel. Barnstaple 0271 73868).

55c Tawstock: Northgate Riding School, Peacehaven, Harepie Lane (tel. Newton Tracy 027 185 330). Hacking; basic instruction. 10.

56b Filleigh: Rapscott School of Equitation (tel. 059 86 247) Instruction. 10.

56g Winkleigh. See 48e.

56h Chulmleigh. See 48c.

56i Lapford Riding Centre, South View.

57b Knaplock Riding Stables (tel. Winsford 064 385 271).

57d Knowstone: Crooked Oak Riding Holidays, East Crosside, west of village (tel. Anstey Mills 039 84 206).

57h Templeton: Mount Pleasant Farm.

57i Calverleigh: Rose & Crown Riding Centre.

58b Langley Marsh: Deepleigh Farmhouse Hotel Riding Stables (tel. Wiveliscombe 0984 23379).

58c Milverton: Coach House Stables (tel. 082 340 356).

58e Burlescombe Riding Centre.

58f Bradford: Mill House Equestrian Centre and Riding School (tel. 082 346 322).

58f Nyehead Stables (tel. Wellington 082 347 2139).

58h Culmstock: Benshayne Farm.

58i Clayhidon: Heazel Farm Equestrian Centre.

59b West Monkton: Walford Riding and Livery Stables, south east of village (tel. 0823 412267).
Brean Riding School (tel. 0823 412777).

59b Creech St Michael: Husk Farm Riding Stables (tel. Henlade 0823 442791).

59d Taunton: Obridge Riding Stables, A361 Obridge Road (tel. 0823 5659).

59d Orchard Portman: Taunton National Hunt Racecourse (tel. 0823 75575).

59e Lillesdon: Oakhill Farm Riding Stables (tel. Hatch Beauchamp 0926 480781).

60b Midney Farm Riding and Livery Centre (tel. Somerton 0458 73240).

60b South Hill: Southfield Stables.

60c West Lydford: Manor Farm Holidays, B3153 (tel. Wheathill 096 324 330). Riding, archery and squash arranged. ✒

60f Chilthorne Domer: Newhills Farm.

60f Yeovil. See 52c.

60g Crewkerne. See 52e.

60h Misterton. See 52e.

60h North Perrott. See 52e.

60i Closworth. See 53d.

61b Charlton Musgrove: Wincanton National Hunt Racecourse (tel. 0963 2344).

61c Penselwood: Long Lane Farm Riding Establishment (tel. Bourton 074 784 283).
Beech Equestrian Centre (tel. Bourton 074 784 697). Hacking; instruction. 10.

61d Sherborne. See 53b.

61f Rodgrove House Farm (tel. Templecombe 096 37 374).

62d Woolacombe: South Street Riding Stables (tel. 027 187 332).

62e Mortehoe: Warcombe Farm Riding Stables (tel. Woolacombe 027 187 501).

62e Ilfracombe: Elmfield, Torrs Park, west of town (tel. 0271 63377).

62f East Stowford Barton Riding Stables.

62f Combe Martin: riding on the beach.

62g Putsborough: riding on the beach.

62h Penhill. See 55c.

63d Lower Dean Farm (tel. Parracombe 059 83 215).

63f Brendon Manor Farm (tel. 059 87 246).

63f Oare: Doone Valley Riding Stables, Oaremead and Parsonage Farms (tel. Brendon 059 87 234 or 278). Trekking; hacking. 37. *April to November.*

63g Tidicombe Farm Riding Stables (tel. Shirwell 027 182 300).

63i Simonsbath: The Gallon House (tel. Exford 064 383 283). Hacking. 10.

64d Oare. See 63f.

64e Porlockford: Porlock Vale Equitation Centre (tel. Porlock 0643 862338). Instruction. 31.

64e West Luccombe: Burrowhays Farm (tel. Porlock 0643 862463).

64e Horner Farm Stables (tel. Porlock 0643 862456).

64e Huntscott House Stables (tel. Timberscombe 064 384 272).

64f Minehead: The Exmoor and Metropole Stables, 1 North Road (tel. 0643 2779).

64f Higher Ellicombe Stables (tel. Minehead 0643 3009).

64f Knowle Riding Centre (tel. Timberscombe 064 384 342). Trekking; hacking; instruction. 45.

64g Higher Blackland Riding Stable (tel. Exford 064 383 252). Hacking; instruction. 15. *April to October.*

64g Withypool: Winaway Stud (tel. Exford 064 383 338).

64h Wheddon Cross: North Wheddon Farm (tel. Timberscombe 064 383 224). Hacking; instruction. 20. *April to October.*

64h Knaplock. See 57b.

65f Kilve: Quantock Riding Centre, Beech Hanger Farm (tel. Holford 027 874 374). Trekking; hacking.

65f Holford: The Lodge Stables (tel. 027 874 332).

65f Nether Stowey: Scotts Riding Stables (tel. 0278 732422).

65g Leigh Barton: Hook Hill Farm (tel. Washford 098 44 752).

65i Adscombe Riding Stables (tel. Nether Stowey 0278 732737).

66b Berrow: Rose Tree Farm (tel. Burnham-on-Sea 0278 783055).

66g Enmore: Blaxhold Farm Riding School (tel. Spaxton 027 867 314). Hacking; instruction. 18.

67a Cross: Circle D Riding Centre (tel. Axbridge 0934 732577). Trekking; hacking. 16.

67a Tynings Farm Riding Centre (tel. Cheddar 0934 742501).

67b Lodge Hill Farm (tel. Priddy 074 987 387).

67b Wookey Hole: Ebborlands Farm Riding Centre (tel. Wells 0749 72550). Hacking; instruction.

67c Hinton Blewitt: Waytonbury Equestrian Centre, Greenway House.

67d Westhay: Homeway House (tel. Meare Heath 045 86 269).

67e Lower Burcott Riding School (tel. Wells 0749 73145). Basic instruction. 14.

67g Ashcott: Millslade Farm Stud, Station Road (tel. 045 821 278). Basic instruction.

67i West Lydford. See 60c.

68d East Compton House (tel. Shepton Mallet 0749 2075). By appointment only.

68f Witham Friary: Grazemoor Farm (tel. Upton Noble 074 985 204).

68g Alhampton: Millcroft House Riding School (tel. Ditcheat 074 986 300). Hacking; basic instruction.

68g Wyke Champflower: Manor Farm (tel. Bruton 074 981 3253).

68h Charlton Musgrove: Wincanton National Hunt Racecourse (tel. 0963 2344).

68i Penselwood. See 61c.

69a Westbury: Westacre Stables. Wellhead Drive (tel. 0373 823161).

69f Codford St Mary: White Horse Riding and Trekking Centre (tel. 098 55 395).

69i Wylye: Bathampton House, A36 (tel. 098 56 281).

70g Weston-super-Mare: Worlebury Riding School, 14 Worlebury Hill Road (tel. 0934 31446). Hacking; instruction. 28.
J. Vowles Treks, 33 Sandford Road (tel. 0934 22395). Trekking.
Pony, donkey and carriage rides on the beach and seafront.

70h Norton Court Stables (tel. Weston-super-Mare 0934 23007).

70i Hewish: Villa Farm Riding School (tel. Yatton 0934 838814). Hacking; basic instruction. 14.

70i Sandford: The Mendip Equestrian Centre, Lyncombe Lodge Farm (tel. Churchill 0934 852335). Trekking; hacking; instruction. 30.

70i Shipham: Hollow Rocks Riding Establishment, Lippiatt Lane (tel. Winscombe 093 484 3706).
Bracken Hill Riding School (tel. 093 484 3354).

71a Clapton-in-Gordano: Gordano Valley Riding Stables, Moor Lane (tel. Portishead 0272 843473). Hacking; instruction.

71b Compton Greenfield: Northcote Riding School.

71b A359: Haberfield School of Equitation (tel. Pill 027 581 2020). Hacking; instruction. 8.

71c North Woods: Leyland Court Riding School (tel. Winterbourne 0454 773163).

71d Backwell: Southfield Farm Riding School (tel. Flax Bourton 027 583 3807). Hacking; instruction.

71f Willsbridge: Abbots Lea School of Riding, Court Farm Road (tel. Bitton 027 588 3125). Hacking; basic instruction. 14.

72d Willsbridge. See 71f.

71f Compton Dando: Mill House Stables.

71g Tynings Farm. See 67a.

71h Hinton Blewitt. See 67c.

71i Hunstrete: The Saw Mills.

72a Lyde Green: White Cat Stables (tel. Bristol 0272 564370). Hacking; basic instruction. 20.

72a Westerleigh: Brices Farm.

72b Dyrham Park Stables (tel. Abson 027 582 2500). Hacking; basic instruction. 24. 🐗 ✳ 🎴 🎏

72d Willsbridge. See 71f

72d Compton Dando: Mill House Stables.

72e Lansdown: Bath Flat Racecourse (tel. Bath 0225 24609).
Blathwayt Riding Stables.

72e Upper Weston: Montpellier Riding Centre, Weston Farm Lane (tel. Bath 0225 23665). Hacking; basic instruction. 21. *April to December.*

72g Hunstrete: The Saw Mills.

72h Monkton Combe: Stables in Summer Lane.

72h Midford Valley Riding Stables.

72i Widbrook: Southview Pony Stud (tel. Bradford-on-Avon 022 16 3361).
Widbrook Farm Riding Stables (tel. 022 16 2297).

73d Lacock: The Old Coaching House Centre (tel. 024 973 338). Hacking; instruction. 14.

73f Heddington: Hampsley Hollow Riding Centre (tel. Bromham 038 085 333). Hacking; instruction. 60.

Skiing Climbing

Rock climbing, severe hill walks and orienteering; artificial ski slopes; also activity centres offering courses and/or tuition in either sport. (See page 14 for information about safety in the hills).

19b Wicca Pool: Rock Climbing. Fine pinnacle; also short walls and scrambles.

19b Porthmoina: Rock Climbing. Fine cliff faces, including some mechanical routes. At Rosemergy, to the south, are further cliffs offering several stiff routes and some scrambles.

19e Carn Galver: Rock Climbing. The Count House at Carn Galver tin mine is now the headquarters of the Climbing Club of Great Britain, who have developed several excellent routes in the immediate area.

19g Gamper Bay: Rock Climbing. The cliffs west of Sennen Cove offer several popular routes up to 70 ft long, often used as a commando training area.

19g Gwennap Head: Rock Climbing. The sea cliffs below the CG station offer spectacular routes, including a 200 ft crag which is the finest in Penwith, with buttress and traverses for most grades of climber. The 'Chair Ladder' route is famous, and the cliffs are often used by the Royal Marines for training. Beware of heavy sea swells at the cliff base.

22h Wicca Pool: Rock Climbing. Fine pinnacles; also short walls and scrambles.

33f Vixen Tor: Rock Climbing. Several routes on this and the surrounding granite summits, most requiring previous experience.

33i Dewerstone Rock: Rock Climbing. Despite its wooded location, this moutain-sized granite crag offers climbs of all standards, including the 'Devil's Rock' wall. Used for commando training

34f Widecombe in the Moor: Dartmoor Expedition Centre, Rowden (tel. 036 42 249). Full board holidays with dormitory accommodation: caving, climbing, hiking, orienteering and mountain leader courses. Unaccompanied children over 11. ⚐ ∪

34f Haytor Rocks: Rock Climbing. Some two dozen routes up to 100 ft long, all near the summit; also some climbing on a smaller rock 100 yards south west.

35f Shaldon: Skiing. Outdoor artificial slope at The Ness; toboggans also allowed.

35i Torquay: Skiing. Open air plastic ski slope.

38i Vixen Tor. See 33f.

39f Haytor Rocks. See 34f.

39h Widecombe in the Moor. See 34f.

40b Exeter: Skiing. Exeter and District Ski Club (tel. 0392 74303) have a 60 yd artificial slope at the Clifton Hill Sports Centre. Practice and instruction, equipment can be supplied. *1 October to 31 March: daily (telephone for times). April to September: Tuesdays and Thursdays 1900-2100.*

40i Shaldon: Skiing. Outdoor artificial slope at The Ness; toboggans also allowed.

67a Cheddar Cliffs: Rock Climbing. Several long routes; easier climbs on the north west walls.

71b Bristol: Rock Climbing. The Avon Gorge downstream of Clifton Suspension Bridge offers limestone crags with many routes between 30 ft and 200 ft long; many locations are for experts only, and none are for novices, as the rock is crumbling.

Skiing, Bryant Outdoor Centre, Colston Street (tel. 0272 23166) has a 15 yd indoor dry slope and offers tuition for adults and children. *November to February: Monday to Saturday.*

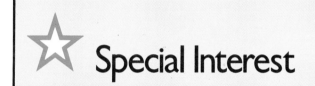

Special Interest

A potpourri of lighthouses, military training areas, caves, model villages, natural oddities and many other fascinations which simply could not be listed under any other heading.

19c St Ives: Lifeboat Station. Founded in 1840, its boats have saved over 650 lives since. *Daily in summer.*

19d Pendeen Watch: Lighthouse and fog station, visible for 20 miles. *Monday to Saturday: 1300 to dusk (not in fog). Free.*

19g Land's End: the most westerly point in Britain; hotel and 'First & Last' house; 6 lighthouses can be seen, including Longships (1½ miles west) and the 135 ft high Wolf Rock (7½ miles south). Land's End Hole, a 150 ft long cave running under the headland, can be visited with a guide.

19g Porthcurno: Minack Theatre. Open air amphitheatre carved from the cliffs in 1932, with seating for 600. It is still used for Shakespearian and modern plays each summer. *Performances June to early September.*

19h Logan Rock. A granite stone weighing 60 tons which used to rock at the touch of a finger; it was removed by sailors in 1824 and although later replaced, has never rocked as well since.

20a Lelant: Model Village (tel. Hayle 0736 752676). Miniature Cornish fishing village, largely modelled on real buildings. Also an exhibition of smuggling and ship wrecking; displays of tin mining and Cornish folklore; art gallery and water gardens; junior commando course. *Easter to end October: daily 1000-1700 (2200 in summer).*

20f Helston: Blue Anchor Beer. Specially brewed only in the Blue Anchor, a tiny 15th century thatched pub which also has a 17th century skittle alley, still in use. *Usual licensing hours.*

20f Goonhilly Downs: Earth Satellite Station. Two huge reflectors which receive and boost signals from satellites orbiting 22,300 miles above. It was opened in 1962 when it received the first TV

signals from Telstar I. *Viewing area open daily; station visits by appointment.*

20i Lizard Point: Lighthouse. (tel. 032 629 231). Standing at the most southerly point in Britain, this is the largest lighthouse in Cornwall open to the public. Built in 1752, it was modernised in 1903 and has a single lamp producing 5¼ million candlepower. *Monday to Saturday. 1300 to dusk (not in fog). Free.*

21b St Anthony Head: Lighthouse (tel. Portscatho 087 258 213). *Monday to Saturday 1300 to dusk (not in fog). Free.*

21d Durgan: Glendurgan Maze. Built in 1833 of laurel bushes. *March to end October: Mondays, Wednesdays and Fridays 1030-1630.* ✿

21d Porth Navas: Oyster Farm, run by the Duchy of Cornwall. The oyster beds, on either side of the creek, are marked with wooden stakes.

22b Piper's Hole: a giant cave, 80 ft long, with a freshwater lake. Narrow entrance is hard to find. *Not at high tide.*

22d Bishop Rock: the last inhabited part of Britain, with its remote lighthouse protecting one of the busiest transatlantic shipping lanes. Boat cruises from Hugh Town, St Mary's.

22e St Mary's: Telegraph Hill. At 160 ft this is the highest point in the Scilly Isles, from which all the other islands, plus 5 lighthouses can be seen.

22i St Ives. See 19c.

23f St Agnes: Model Village. Miniature scenes of Cornish domestic and industrial life on a 10 acre site with a children's Fairyland (Piskies, goblins, etc), model railway and other attractions. *March to November daily.* ☛

25d Mevagissey: Model Railway (tel. 072 684 2457). Superb indoor exhibition of British, European and American models running in realistically detailed layouts; also models of a China Clay pit and an Alpine ski resort. *End May to end September: daily 1100-1700 (2100 in summer). Rest of year: Sundays only 1400-1700.*

26d Polperro: Model Village (tel. 0503 72378). Miniature version of Polperro itself; also animated models depicting Cornish legends; garden containing exotic plants. *Mid March to October: daily 1030-1830 (2130 in season).*

27b Drake's Island: Youth Adventure Centre (tel. Plymouth 0752 54112). Six acre island with remains of Henry VIII fort and prison buildings, now used for residential courses to teach outdoor skills and build character. Unaccompanied children aged 12 to 18 accepted. Guided tours of the island. Boats from Mayflower Steps, off Madeira Road. *May to September: Sunday to Friday.*

27b Plymouth: Royal Navy Dockyards, Davenport. Established by William III in 1691 and now home base for many modern warships. *Guided tours April to September weekdays (not bank holidays).*

Viewing Gallery, Civic Centre. The view from the rooftop of this modern skyscraper is unparalleled, stretching from Dartmoor to the north to the Eddystone Lighthouse 14 miles to the south. ☛

27f Wembury Point: HMS Cambridge. The Royal Navy Gunnery School, from which guns often fire at air-towed targets. *Firing when red flags fly.*

28d River Yealm: Kitley Caves (tel. Yealmpton 075 531 202). Caverns discovered during the 19th century and now floodlit; also old lime kilns. *Easter, then late May to end September: daily 1000-1700.* ☕

28e Burgh Island: 'Walking' Ferry. A high platform whose four legs each stand on a caterpillar track, which run under the water. *High tide only.*

29c Brixham: *Golden Hind* replica, The Harbour. Copy of Sir Francis Drake's famous ship, built to the original dimensions. Contains interesting Elizabethan relics. *Daily.*

29c Berry Head: Lighthouse. The highest, lowest and smallest in Britain: it stands 200 ft above sea level, but is only 6 ft tall. It was built in 1906 and can be seen for 40 miles.

29h Start Point: Lighthouse (tel. Torcross 054 858 225). *Monday to Saturday 1300 to dusk (not in fog). Free.*

30e Trevose Head: Lighthouse. Built in the 19th century, it can be seen 25 miles out to sea. Access via a toll road. *Monday to Saturday 1300 to dusk (not in fog). Free.*

30e Porthcothan: Smugglers' Tunnel. Impressive underground passage, over 1000 yards long, where illicit booty was stored.

30h Bedruthan Steps. Huge granite rocks said to have been stepping stones for the giant Bedruthan. Some have odd shapes—Queen Bess Rock is supposed to resemble Elizabeth I in profile. National Trust information centre and shop at nearby Cernewas Iron Mine. 🐾

32d Dozmary Pool. The legendary resting place of King Arthur's magic sword Excalibur, thrown into the supposedly bottomless pool by Sir Bedivere.

34d Princetown: Dartmoor Prison. The site was chosen for its bleakness in 1806, when the gaol was built to house prisoners taken in the Napoleonic wars. It became disused after 1815, when the wars ended, but was reopened in 1850 to alleviate overcrowding at other English prisons. Its basic design consists of 5 blocks radiating from a central point like the spokes of a wheel. The town, which did not exist before the prison was completed, is now a tourist centre.

34i Buckfast Abbey Farm. Run by the Benedictine monks of the Abbey, who also keep bees and produce stained glass, pottery and other products. ◪ ✝

35b Belvidere Tower. Triangular memorial to General Lawrence Stringer, the 'Father of the Indian Army'. Spiral staircase with 98 steps to the top, from where the views are magnificent. *Summer PM only.*

35b Cudleigh Rock. Limestone outcrop containing prehistoric caves, the subject of local legend. In summer, children carry candles to guide visitors through the 'Pixie's Cave'.

35i Babbacombe: The Model Village, Hampton Avenue (tel. Torquay 0803 38669). Miniature village set in 4 acres of miniature landscaped gardens; over 400 models, including a farm, churches and a floodlit football pitch; 400 yards of model railway. *Easter to October: daily 0900-2200. November to March: daily 0900-1700.*

35i Kents Cavern, Ipsham Road, Wellswood. One of the oldest known dwelling places of humans in Britain, it was occupied at least 100,000 years ago. Sights include well floodlit stalagmites and stalactites, a sabretooth tiger skull and other prehistoric relics. *Daily.*

36a Rocky Valley: Maze. The oldest in Britain, its pattern was carved on the rocks before 1500BC.

36b Boscastle Harbour. The only natural shelter on 40 miles of stormy coast; boats must turn through two right angles to enter the port, which is protected by a hollow slate breakwater built in 1584.

36i Dozmary Pool. See 32d.

38i Princetown: Dartmoor Prison. See 34d.

40b Exeter: Underground Passages, Princesshay (tel. 0392 56724). Aqueducts, some carved through solid rock, built to carry water to the city early in the 13th century. Guided tours last 20 minutes. *Tuesday to Saturday 1000-1630.*

Matthew the Miller Clock, St Mary Steps Church, New Bridge Street. Matthew and his two sons emerge whenever this 17th century clock strikes.

40e Belvidere Tower. See 35b.

40e Chudleigh Rock. See 35b.

41b Sidmouth: Jacob's Ladder, Connaught Gardens. Lookout tower offering superb sea views.

41b The Norman Lockyer Astronomical Observatory, west of Salcombe Regis. Founded in 1912 by the man who discovered helium. *Occasional open days.*

44d Westham: Chipperfield's Amusement Park. The largest in Dorset, it includes all the usual attractions, including a miniature railway and a big wheel.

44e Lodmoor: Model Village.

44h Portland Harbour: Royal Navy Base. Tours of the dockyards and of a warship. *May to August: weekends.*

44h Bill of Portland: Lighthouse (tel. Portland 0305 3195). *Monday to Saturday 1300 to dusk (not in fog). Free.*

45f Corfe Castle: Model Village. Miniature version of Corfe Castle village, but with the castle in original condition. *Easter to October: daily.*

46e Cleave: Dish Aerials. Used by the Ministry of Defence to track communications satellites. *Not open.*

54a Hartland Point: Lighthouse (tel. 023 74 328). *Monday to Saturday: 1300 to dusk (not in fog). Free.*

54g Cleave: Dish Aerials. See 46e.

56f South Molton: Quince Honey Farm, North Road (tel. 076 95 2401). Comb and liquid honey; beeswax candles, cosmetics and polish; observation hive. *Weekdays 0800-2000; weekends 0800-1800.*

59c Curry Rivel: Burton Pynsent Monument. This 140 ft Doric column was erected in 1765, designed by Capability Brown. Although it contains a spiral staircase, it was bricked up after a cow climbed to the top and fell off.

60a Langport: Dolphin Hotel (tel. 0458 250200). This fishing inn is one of many pubs in the village to feature a traditional wooden skittle alley, the playing of which requires considerable skill. *Usual licensing hours.*

62e Ilfracombe: Dinosaur Exhibition, The Artisan, Northfield Road (tel. 0271 62107). Indoor display of life-size models in realistic setting, including Tyrannosaurus Rex, Stegosaurus and others; also crafts, paintings and local fashions. *Easter to end September: daily 1000-1730.*

International Model Village, Torrs Walks. Wide range of miniature displays. *Daily from 0930.*

62e Bull Point: Lighthouse. *Monday to Saturday 1300 to dusk (not in fog). Free.*

62f Watermouth Castle (tel. Ilfracombe 0271 63879). Family entertainment centre, including model railway, mechanical music collection, cider making and dairy equipment, dungeons, etc. *Whitsun to end September: weekdays 1030-1700; Sundays 1400-1700. October: limited opening.* 🐾 🎪 🛶 ✧

63b Lynton: Exmoor Brass Rubbing Centre, The Smugglers Den, Queen Street (tel. 059 85 2529).

Guidance for novices; diploma for experts. *Easter to end October: Monday to Saturday 1000-1300, 1400-1730; Sundays PM.*

63c Foreland Point: Lighthouse (tel. Brendon 059 87 226). *Monday to Saturday 1300 to dusk (not in fog). Free.*

63f Malmsmead: "Lorna Doone" Village. Unspoilt group of farmhouses which was the setting for R D Blackmore's famous novel. Two miles south is the 'secret' Doone Valley, nowadays visited by thousands.

64d Malmsmead. See 63f (above).

64f Minehead: Model Town and Pleasure Gardens, The Sea Front. Miniature "Little England" with cathedral, fire station, docks, a 3½ inch gauge model railway, many working models and even a cricket game. One the same two acre site are a 10¼ inch gauge miniature railway, mini golf and other attractions. *Summer: daily 0900-2200.*

64f Holiday Camp: Butlin's Amusement Park. Miniature railway, monorail, boating, swimming, etc., all free once a general admission charge has been paid.

65e Kilve: Royal Navy Fighters. Military training area where low-flying jets can be seen attacking targets with rockets.

66d Holford: 'Mud Horses'. Wooden framed devices used by local fishermen to empty their shrimp nets far out on the mud flats, where they must move quicky to beat the incoming tide. *April to December: daily at low tide.*

67a Cheddar Caves (tel. 0934 742343). Fascinating series of large caverns, with three main chambers containing pools, 250,000-year-old stalactites and stalagmites and limestone formations; also the site where the skeleton of a man who lived 12,000 years ago was found; Jacob's Ladder, Waterfall Grotto, Swiss Village, King Solomon's Temple and other attractions. *Easter to October: daily 1000-1730.* 🐾 ◪ ▨

67b Wookey Hole Caves (tel. 0749 72243). Giant limestone caverns carved by water. Of the six caves open to the public (many others are underwater), one measures 135 ft across and 12 ft high, with 280,000 tons of rock pushing on the roof—engineers say that this structure is theoretically impossible! The caves were inhabited by man from Iron Age to Roman times and many relics can be seen in Wells Museum. Great Cave contains the 'Witch of Wookey'—a giant stalagmite. Underwater lake, tunnels and bridges high over the River Axe. Also Titania's Palace, a model stately home with scale works of art. *April to September: daily 1000-1800. Rest of year: daily 1000-1630.* 🐾 ◪ 🚂 ♨

68d Oakhill Manor: World of Models (tel. 0749 840210). Superb collection of transport models; travel from car park by ¾ mile miniature steam railway. Many other attractions in 45 acre estate. *Easter to early November: daily 1200-1800.* 🐾 ✿ 🏚

68e Cranmore Tower. Italianate 'folly' built in 1862 and now a prominent landmark.

68i Alfred's Tower. This 160 ft triangular 'folly' was built in 1772 to commemorate King Alfred's victory over the Danes on this spot in 879AD.

69d Longleat House (tel. Maiden Bradley 098 53 551). Many attractions include a collection of 19th century dolls' houses and the world's largest maze, a 3-dimensional puzzler with bridges, and underpasses added to the usual hedges. *Easter to end September: daily 1000-1800. Rest of year: daily 1000-1600.* 🐾 ✿ 🏚 🐘 🚂

70g Weston-Super-Mare: 'Little Britain' Model Village, adjoining Winter Gardens. Miniature market town with castle, manor, wind and water mills, church, farm, school, shops and cottages. *Summer: daily 1000 to dusk. Winter: Tuesday to Thursday and weekends.*

Model Railway. Impressive layout housed in the Cove Pavilion.

71a Battery Point: Lighthouse. Good views of passing freighters. *Monday to Saturday 1300 to dusk (not in fog). Free.* The 45 ft high tide here at Spring Equinox is the second highest in the world.

71 Bristol: Camera Obscura, Clifton Observatory, off Clifton Down. Darkened chamber into which a lens projects a panoramic view of the city.

SS Great Britain, Floating Harbour (tel. 0272 20680). The first propellor-driven iron ship built for transatlantic passenger routes, she was designed by Isambard Kingdom Brunel and launched in 1844;

at 3618 tons and 322 ft long, she was also the world's largest ship. A troubled career ended in 1866 when she ran aground in the Falkland Islands, but her hulk was rescued in 1970 and towed home to Bristol to public acclaim. She is now undergoing lengthy restoration in dry dock. *Daily 1000-1700 (1800 in summer).*

Cabot Tower, Brandon Hill, off Jacob's Wells Road. 105 ft monument erected in 1897 to mark the 400th anniversary of the discovery of Newfoundland. Fine views from a gallery at the

top. *Daily 0900 to dusk.*

71g Burrington Combe. Limestone gorge with 250 ft cliffs containing many caves, some of which have produced human bones dating from 10,000BC.

72e Lansdown Park: Beckford's Tower (tel. Bath 0225 858106). Built to neo-classical design in 1827. Small museum on first floor; fine views from Belvedere, reached via 156 steps. *Early April to late October: weekends and Bank Holiday Mondays 1400-1700.*

Aviation Motor Sport

Aviation entries include flying clubs, aircraft museums, popular gliding and hang gliding venues. Motor sport information includes permanent and temporary race tracks (for cars, karts and bikes); hill climb and sprint courses; stock car and speedway stadia.

20f Cornwall Aero Park,Culdrose Manor,south of Helston (tel. 032 65 3404 or 4549). Edwardian flying machines from the TV Series "Wings" and "Flambards"; replica SE5A World War I fighter; Wings & Wheels exhibition with street scenes, rooms and motor vehicles of 1900-1956; operate the controls of a Shackleton bomber, a hovercraft, a helicopter and Concorde; display about Goonhilly space tracking station; video games; children's amusements; free aerogolf; shops. *Easter to early November: daily 1000-1700 (1800 July-August).*

23f Trevellas: Cornish Gliding Club. Tuition available, including holiday courses (details tel. Helston 032 65 62294)

25d Trevellas. See 23f (above).

30h Downhill: Motor Sport. Sprint races run on St Eval Airfield by Newquay Automobile Club Ltd (Secretary tel. Fraddon 0726 860545). *Occasional Sundays in summer.*

31d Whitecross: Motor Sport. Sprint races on the showground site organised by Camel Vale Motor Club Ltd (Secretary tel. Truro 0872 76958).

35e Newton Abbot Race Course: Motor Cycle Trail Park. Owned by the famous stunt rider, Dave Taylor, it has 3 trails: one for novices, including children on mini bikes; one intermediate; and a ½ mile main trail. Machines for hire.

35h Blagdon: Torbay Aircraft Museum (tel. Paignton 0803 553540). About 20 machines on display, all dating from 1924-54 and including Spitfire, Messerschmitt 109, a replica Hurricane, Westland Whirlwind, Meteor, Dragonfly, Provost and others; exhibition of "The Red Baron and Fighter Aces of World War I'; many items under cover. *Daily 1000-1600 (1800 in summer).*

35i Oddicombe: Motor Sport. Hill climb track 750 yds long, used for meetings organised by Torbay Motor Club Ltd (Secretary tel. 0803 37787). *Two Sundays per year, usually in March and October.*

40b Exeter: Stock Car Racing. Regular meetings at a stadium in the town.

Speedway. Regular meetings at a stadium in the town.

40c Exeter Airport: Flying Club (tel. 0392 67653). Offers a range of tuition services, including Private Pilot's Licence course; also radio and ground instruction.

40h Newton Abbot. See 35e.

41c Wiscombe Park: Motor Sport. Hill climb course 1000 yds long used for several meetings, including national championship events. Local organisers: Bristol Motor Cycle & Light Car Club (Secretary tel. 0272 560908). *Three weekends per year, usually in April, May and September.*

42d Wiscombe Park. See 41c (above).

44e Weymouth: Motor Sport. Speedway and motor cycle scrambles organised regularly at stadium in town.

45c Poole: Speedway. Regular meetings organised in the town's greyhound stadium.

50f Dunkeswell Airfield: International Skydiving Centre (tel. Luppit 040 489 350). Two-day training courses in all aspects of parachute jumping; minimum age 16; some equipment and a health certificate needed.

Dunkeswell Aero Club (tel. 040 489 643 or 648). Range of tuition offered, including Private Pilot's Licence, radio and night flying instruction. Link trainer.

Kart Track. Permanent race circuit used for regular meetings organised by Dunkeswell Kart Racing Club Ltd (Secretary tel. Crediton 036 32 3839). *March to November: usually last Sunday of each month (national meeting in September).*

50g Exeter Airport. See 40c.

52d Cricket House: Motor Sport. Short hill climb used for occasional meetings organised by Taunton Motoring Club Ltd (Secretary tel. 0823 86527). Two

weekends per year, usually April-October.

58i Dunkeswell Airfield. See 50f.

59i Cricket House. See 52d.

60f Yeovilton Airfield: Fleet Air Arm Museum (tel. Ilchester 0935 840551 ext 521). Two preserved Concordes, including the UK prototype, plus the largest collection of historic military aircraft under one roof in Europe; more than 40 naval aircraft include Swordfish, Sea Fury, Walrus, Vampire, Firefly, Buccaneer, helicopters, etc. Fleet Air Arm flying can be watched on weekdays; gliding at weekends. *Monday to Saturday 1000-1730; Sundays 1230-1730.*

60g Cricket House. See 52d.

67a Stadium: Cheddar Stock Car Racing track. Details of meetings posted locally.

70g Weston-Super-Mare: Sand Racing organised on the beach by Weston-Super-Mare Motor Club Ltd (Secretary tel. Bristol 0272 832088). *One meeting, usually last Sunday in April.*

Sprint Track, Sea Front at South Beach: British championship event organised by Burnham-on-Sea Motor Club Ltd (Competition Secretary tel. 0278 786817). *Usually 1st Saturday in October.*

71 Bristol: Parascending. Flying on the end of a 300 ft rope above the Mendip Hills. Courses arranged by Skysales Ltd (tel. 0272 422956) and based at the Avon Gorge Hotel. Ballooning also available. Minimum age 12; no experience needed. *April to November: weekends.*

71g Stadium: Cheddar Stock Car Racing track. Details of meetings posted locally.

72c Castle Combe Motor Racing Circuit (tel. 0249 782205; on race days 782395). Permanent track 1.84 miles long. *April to August: 5 or 6 weekends.*

72f Colerne Airfield: Motor Sport. Used for sprint meetings organised by Bristol Motor Cycle & Light Car Club Ltd (Secretary tel. 0272 560908). *National championship meeting in July.*

Golf Courses

The location of all known courses is shown accurately, along with the relevant number of holes at each course. Because membership qualifications, tournament dates and rules vary so much, however, no details are given here.

Application to use any course should be made at the club house in person, or ask the nearest Tourist Information Office (see page 122) for details.

Towns with Extensive Facilities

In order to qualify for this symbol, a town must offer a combination of good commercial facilities (shopping, accommodation, etc.) *and* a range of all-weather facilities. These may not be available out of season, and you should first check with the relevant Tourist Information Office (see page 122).

19c St Ives: The Guildhall, Street-an-Pol (tel. 0736 796297).

19f Penzance: Alverton Street (tel. 0736 2341 or 2207).

21b Falmouth: Town Hall, The Moor (tel. 0326 312300).

22e Hugh Town: Town Hall (tel. Scillonia 0720 22536).

22i St Ives. See 19c.

23h Camborne: Council Offices (tel. 0209 712941).

23f Perranporth: Betty Pitman's Agency (tel. 087 257 3601).

24b Newquay: Cliff Road (tel. 063 73 4558, 2119, 2716, 2822 or 5211).

24d Perranporth. See 23f.

24h Truro: Municipal Buildings Boscawen Street (tel. 0872 74555).

25f Fowey: Toyne Carter, Albert Quay (tel. 072 683 3320).

26b Looe: *The Guildhall, Fore Street (tel. 050 36 2072).

27b Plymouth: Civic Centre (tel. 0752 264851); 12 The Barbican (tel. 0752 23806); also at *Ferry Terminal, Millbay Docks.

28f Kingsbridge: *The Quay (tel. 0548 3195).

28i Salcombe: Market Street (tel 054 884 2736).

29a Totnes: *The Plains (tel. 0803 863168).

29b Dartmouth: 8, The Quay (tel. 080 43 2281). Includes National Trust information.

29c Paignton: Festival Hall, Esplanade Road (tel. 0803 558383).

29c Brixham: *Brixham Theatre. New Road (tel. 080 45 2861). (Winter tel. Paignton 0803 558383).

30f Padstow: Council Offices, Station Road (tel. 0841 532296).

30h Newquay. See 24b.

31d Wadebridge: Town Hall (tel. 020 881 2643).

31h Lanhydrock: National Trust Cornwall Information Office (tel. Bodmin 0208 4281).

34b Postbridge: *Dartmoor National Park centre (tel. Exeter 0392 77977).

34d Two Bridges: *Dartmoor National Park centre in caravan at Two Bridges Hotel (tel. Princetown 082 289 253).

34f New Bridge: *Dartmoor National Park centre (tel. Exeter 0392 77977).

35a Bovey Tracey: *Lower Car Park (tel. 0626 832047).

35c Dawlish: *The Lawn (tel. 0626 863589). (Winter tel. Teignmouth 062 67 6271).

35d Haytor: *Dartmoor National Park centre (tel. Exeter 0392 77977).

35e Newton Abbot: 8 Sherborne Road (tel. 0626 67494).

35f Teignmouth: The Den (tel. 062 67 6271).

35g Totnes. See 29a.

35h Paignton. See 29c.

35i Torquay: Vaughan Parade (tel. 0803 27428).

36b Boscastle: Old Blacksmith's Forge, Boscastle Harbour. April to end September daily 1000-1800.

39d Postbridge. See 34b.

39g Two Bridges. See 34d.

39h New Bridge. See 34f.

40b Exeter: Civic Centre, Dix's Field (tel. 0392 72434).

40c M5 Motorway Service Area (tel. Exeter 0392 37581).

40d Bovey Tracey. See 35a.

40f Dawlish. See 35c.

40g Newton Abbot. See 35e.

40i Teignmouth. See 35f.

41b Sidmouth: *The Esplanade (tel. 039 55 6441).

41d Budleigh Salterton: *Rolle Street Car Park (tel. 039 45 5275). (Winter tel. Sidmouth 039 55 6551).

41d Exmouth: *Alexandra Terrace (tel. 039 52 3744). (Winter tel. 039 52 4356).

42d Seaton: *The Esplanade (tel. 0297 21660). (Winter tel. 0297 21345).

42f Lyme Regis: The Guildhall, Bridge Street (tel. 029 74 2138).

43d Bridport: *local information only (tel. 0308 2301).

44b Dorchester: Antelope Hotel Yard, South Street (tel. 0305 67992).

44e Weymouth: Department of Leisure Activities, 12 The Esplanade (tel. 030 57 72444); *The Esplanade (tel. 0305 785747); also at Ferry Terminal.

45c Poole: Civic Centre (tel. 020 13 5151).

46e Bude: *Bencoolen Road (tel. 0288 4240).

47c Great Torrington: Town Hall, High Street.

50c Wellington: Bowermans Travel Agency Ltd., 6 South Street (tel. 082 347 2716).

50g Killerton House: National Trust Devon Information Office (tel. Hele 039 288 691).

51a Taunton Deane M5 Service Area: (tel. 0823 77601).

51f Chard: Taylors Travel, Fore Street (tel. 046 06 4414 or 4415).

52c Yeovil: Johnson Hall, Hendford (tel. 0935 22884).

55c Barnstaple: Civic Centre (tel. 0271 72511 ext 203).

55e Bideford: *The Quay (tel. 023 72 77676). (Winter tel. 023 72 6711).

55e Great Torrington. See 47c.

56f South Molton: Town Hall (tel. 076 95 2501).

57b Dulverton: Exmoor House. Exmoor National Park information (tel. 0398 23665).

58f Wellington. See 50c.

59d Taunton: The Library, Corporation Street (tel. 0823 84077 or 74785).

59d Taunton Deane M5. See 51a.

59i Chard. See 51f.

60f Yeovil. See 52c.

61b Wincanton: The Library, 7 Carrington Way (tel. 0963 32173).

62d Woolacombe: *Hall '70, Beach Road (tel. 027 187 553).

62e Ilfracombe: The Promenade (tel. 0271 63001). Includes National Trust information.

62f Combe Martin: 'Mimosa' (tel. 027 188 3333); *caravan at The Beach Car Park (tel. 027 188 3319).

62g Croyde: Parminter (tel. 0271 890363). Includes information for Croyde Bay, Braunton, Georgeham, Heanton and Saunton.

62i Barnstaple. See 55c.

63e Lynton & Lynmouth: Lee Road, Lynton (tel. 059 85 2225). National Trust centre and shop: Watersmeet House, Lynmouth (tel. 059 85 2509). Exmoor National Park centre: Lyn & Exmoor Museum, Market Street.

63f County Gate: *Exmoor National Park centre, on A39 (tel. Brendon 059 87 321).

64d County Gate. See 63f.

64e Porlock: Doverhay (tel. 0643 862427).

64f Minehead: Market House, The Parade (tel. 0643 2624). Exmoor National Park Centre at same address (tel. 0643 2984).

66b Burnham-on-Sea: Berrow Road (tel. 0278 782377 ext. 43/44, or 787852).

66c Brent Knoll: *M5 Picnic Area.

67a Cheddar: The Library, Union Street (tel. 0934 742769).

67e Wells: *Town Hall, Market Place (tel. 0749 72552).

67e Glastonbury: *7 Northload Street (tel. 0458 32954).

68i Stourton: National Trust Wessex Information Office (tel. Bourton 074 784 560).

69g Mere: The Square (tel. 0747 860341).

70f Clevedon: local information only (tel. 02723208).

70g Weston-super-Mare: Beach Lawns (tel. 0934 26838).

71 Bristol: Colston House, Colston Street (tel. 0272 293891).

71a Gordano M5 Service Area (tel. Pill 027 571 3382).

72e Bath: Abbey Churchyard (tel. 0225 62831). (Accommodation enquiries tel. 0225 60521).

73a Chippenham: Emery Lane (tel. 0249 55864).

Index

Abbreviations

B.	Bay	Mtns.	Mountains
C.	Cape	Pen.	Peninsula
Hd.	Head	Pt.	Point
I.	Island	R.	River
Is.	Islands	Res.	Reservoir
L.	Lake, Loch	Sd., sd.	Sound
Mt.	Mountain	St.	Saint

KEY TO MAP SECTION

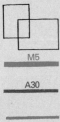

1:100 000
MAP COVERAGE

— M5 — Motorway

— A30 — Through Route

——— County Boundary

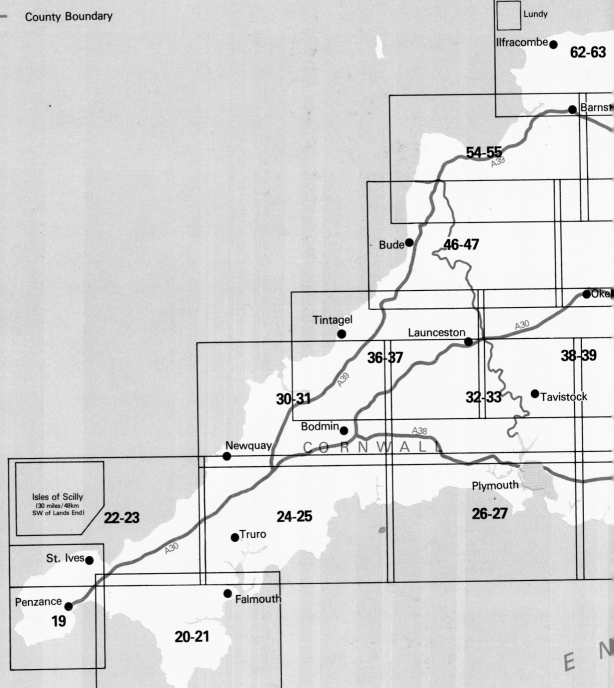

Br

Lundy

Ilfracombe ● **62-63**

Barnst

54-55
A39

Bude ● **46-47**

Oke

Tintagel ● Launceston ● A30 **38-39**

36-37

A39 Tavistock

30-31 **32-33**

Bodmin ● A38

Newquay ● C O R N W A L L

Plymouth

Isles of Scilly
(30 miles / 48km
SW of Lands End) **22-23** **24-25** **26-27**

Truro ●

St. Ives ●

Penzance ● Falmouth ●

19 **20-21**

E N